To dear Sybil, with much
Jean -

And also inscribed for
dear Sybil with much love
from *[signature]*

A-SITTING ON A GATE

Also by Ben Travers

Novels
The Collection Today
A Cuckoo in the Nest
The Dippers
Mischief
Rookery Nook

Plays
Banana Ridge
The Bed before Yesterday
A Bit of a Test
Chastity my Brother
Corker's End
A Cuckoo in the Nest
A Cup of Kindness
The Dippers
Dirty Work
Five Plays
Mischief
A Night Like This
Nun's Veiling
Outrageous Fortune
Plunder
Rookery Nook
She Follows Me About
Spotted Dick
Thark
Turkey Time
Wild Horses

Autobiography
Vale of Laughter

A-sitting on a gate

AUTOBIOGRAPHY

BEN TRAVERS

W. H. ALLEN · LONDON
A Howard & Wyndham Company
1978

Printed and bound in Great Britain by
Butler & Tanner Ltd, Frome and London
for the Publishers, W. H. Allen & Co. Ltd,
44 Hill Street, London W1X 8LB

ISBN 0 491 0 2275 1

I'll tell thee everything I can:
    There's little to relate.
I saw an aged, aged man,
    A-sitting on a gate.
"Who are you, aged man?" I said.
    "And how is it you live?"
And his answer trickled through my head
    Like water through a sieve.

Through the Looking-Glass
LEWIS CARROLL

CONTENTS

ILLUSTRATIONS

1

There is something very odd about me.

I will not describe myself as unique because everybody is unique. There is only one of each of us and quite enough too in many cases. And what makes me so odd is not my appearance or my character, though these may call for some comment. But has anybody ever had an experience which can be compared to the present situation in which I find myself? At a smooth guess, no.

As I write these words I am exactly ninety and a half years old. The past eighteen months surrounding my ninetieth birthday have been spent in a whirlpool of unprecedented activity, by far the busiest, most exciting, most rewarding of my professional life. I was plunged into the whirlpool at the end of September 1975 and I am still being whirled around in the midst of it. I can't think of anybody else that has ever happened to, can you?

You will leave people of my ilk on one side for a start and search for likely specimens from among the great past masters of the Arts. Verdi didn't quite reach ninety. Titian lived to be ninety-nine and Shaw ninety-four. But neither they nor any of the minor contributors can have spent the most gruelling eighteen months of their careers at my stage of senility.

In fact I can't believe that this has ever happened to anybody in any walk of life. Some of the venerable characters of the Old Testament might appear to be contenders but the ancients' methods of reckoning time must be open to conjecture. No doubt Noah was kept pretty busy during the eighteen months before the flood, but according to the Scriptures he was six hundred years old at the time. We are further informed that he took only his wife, his three sons and his sons' wives into the Ark and that all his grandchildren (Cush and Phut and the rest of them) were born post-Ararat. All this goes to indicate such a frightful muddle in the records of early Biblical scribes, to say nothing of the incredibly virile (and enviable) physical abilities of Shem, Ham and Japhet, that I must ignore lore and legend in my search for a rival and stick to recorded fact. There may have been someone else whose ninetieth and ninety-first years were

1

incomparably the most frantically strenuous period of his whole existence, but who was he?

The whirlpool must be the terminus, way down at the far end of my life's long river. I have set myself the task of going back to the source and letting my poor old memory make the best job it can of sailing once more along the course of that river, now placid, now pretty choppy, to this, its bubbling end. By the time I complete this second voyage it will be the end indeed. I only hope I will find myself still careering around in the whirlpool and waving my farewell from the vortex. Kind heaven, that would be a truly happy ending to a happy life.

Autobiographers of my period tended to begin with their progenitors. They indulged in speculative estimates of notable ancestors and proceeded to deal in some detail with parents and grandparents. The volumes were illustrated with reproductions of tintypes of fathers and grandfathers, their faces obscured by jungle and their legs by corrugations, and of mothers and grandmothers with their overworked bosoms encased in the final satin and decorated with a long-service locket. The text dealing with these worthy people has often been as ponderous as the grandmothers' bosoms themselves. My own family history, though it goes back a long way, of which I am duly proud, may fortunately be dealt with pretty briefly.

There is no record of the rank or duties allotted to young Travers in the army of William of Normandy; but he was important enough to get his name included among those of the Conqueror's henchmen on the Roll of Battle Abbey. All that is certain about him is that he survived Hastings and that he then decided or was commanded to remain and settle in this country. And I am very glad that he did or was.

His progeny, so far as a study of my family tree can determine, seem to have conformed to a decent, unspectacular and modestly patrician standard throughout the subsequent centuries. None of them, until my great-grandfather appeared on the scene, achieved eminence in any field. One of them appears to have had the ambition to do so, but he was executed for high treason and his successors evidently decided to revert to the doldrums of unadventurous propriety. Shakespeare, in *Henry IV, Part 2*, named one of his characters Travers, but found no more exalted job for him than that of retainer to the Earl of Northumberland; so it would seem that whoever the Travers was that Shakespeare knew, he must have suggested to the poet's mind a somewhat unpretentious type of individual.

For the past eight generations the eldest son of the eldest son of my branch of the family has been christened Benjamin. The fourth of these Benjamins was my great-grandfather. He had an exceedingly successful career and eventually became Sergeant-Surgeon to Queen Victoria and President of the Royal College of Surgeons, where a copy of his bust still stands at the foot of the main staircase (my son possesses the original). He never had occasion to knife the old Queen and she expressed her gratitude for this escape by offering him a baronetcy which he refused. He made a fortune but spent it all on equipage; which appears wasteful, but, after all, it was the only means of getting about in London so he can't be blamed for wanting to do it in good style. His son, my grandfather, was also a surgeon. He was the author of a handbook (ghastly both in style and content) in which he discussed the alternative benefits of giving your patient a hearty straightforward bleeding or calling in the leeches. There must have been considerably greater reluctance to consult one's medical adviser a century ago.

The boyhoods of autobiographers will also be found to contain some literary plague-spots. I have tried to edit mine as scrupulously as I can but I will have to dwell on it for a while because anyone who spent his whole childhood and prep-school days in the reign of Victoria was bound to become branded for life with certain in-eradicable influences. Some few of these were beneficial, one any-how. From my earliest years Christianity was revealed to me in such a simple and gentle way at home (Highland Road, Bromley, Kent) that it withstood and survived the frightening and almost brutal manner with which it was drilled into me at school.

During the whole of her reign and for a good many years later, Queen Victoria exercised authority over the principles and conduct of a child's upbringing. The parents themselves had been brought up on the bigoted, puritanical and austere lines associated with this allegedly pious old dame. In my home, though I was taught to be good and in the happiest possible way, I was kept in pretty strict order. But I was never for a moment allowed to be frightened. At my prep school I was never allowed to be anything else.

I set eyes on Queen Victoria only once, on the day of her Diamond Jubilee. She was seated in her open coach outside St Paul's. It seemed a trifle inconsiderate that she should be shielding herself from general view with a white parasol. But in such awe was she held that even the respectful pigeons resisted the temptation to anoint the parasol.

During my five years at the Abbey School, Beckenham, I won the school prize for what was comprehensively termed 'Scripture'. But however well I knew by heart the Catechism and the Litany and most of the term-time collects and epistles and gospels, the one subject I learned to know even better and was taught to know was Fear.

I suffered from the start by being uncommonly short for a boy of eight or nine. I was in fact tiny. My mother was too; barely five

3

feet tall; and I took after her. On my first afternoon at the Abbey School all the other boys gathered round me in the playground and hooted with laughter. About five years later, when I was taken to Charterhouse to sit for my entrance exam by the second master of the Abbey, 'Pickle' Ellis (himself no Goliath), I remember taking anxious stock of the candidates from other prep schools to see whether by some heaven-sent boon any one of them was nearly as small as I. None was. They towered above me; many of them a good deal taller than Pickle Ellis. Throughout my whole time at Charterhouse I still remained the smallest boy there. I put on several saving inches when I was eighteen and nineteen and although I have always been a short man I have been spared the tribulation of going through life as the midget I was when young. Indeed by the time I had finished growing I had the satisfaction of being above the average male height in some countries such as Japan and Wales. And in my old age I have long ceased to worry about my size. But, my goodness, all through my boyhood how bitterly conscious I was of my littleness, and in those cruel schooldays how seldom was I given the chance to forget it.

So there I stood in the Abbey playground – an exhibit, a perpetual standing joke to the whole school, including the masters. From the first moment I felt myself in the grip of a sudden, unfamiliar, unexpected, crushing timidity. It never left me; it never quite has. But in the early stages the timidity settled down within me in the form of an instinctive moral cowardice.

One example of this cowardice remains vividly in my memories of eighty years ago. It was when I straightened myself up and faced Mr Gulliver to listen to the tirade which invariably followed the beating. On this occasion it was brief and pithy: 'You'll finish on the gallers,' said Mr Gulliver.

He put the stick back into his desk and slammed down the lid. I call it a stick but it was a strange implement like an outsized paper-knife, tapering to a thin flat end for the mere slapping-down of minor offences but with a great round thick end for the punishment of real wickedness. I had just had the thick end.

Mr Gulliver having delivered his awful Dickensian prophecy on my untidy blond head I crept back to my humble place in the form. I sniffed back my tears as I went, in order to show the rest of the form that these were a propitiatory sop to Mr Gulliver and not in any way to be attributed to the pain of the beating.

Mr Gulliver was the most formidable of the Abbey staff. I wonder how old he really was at the time and really how large. He wore a red waistcoat with brass buttons spread at its base to embrace his ample paunch. He sported the moustache luxuriant and he had the habit of twirling it with both hands with the sweeping action of one

4

swimming. His rapid, slightly provincial voice was thunderous. His breath would whistle through his great hairy nostrils like a steam exhaust. His eyes were swords.

To me he was a worthy representative of the God of Wrath, whom our infant minds were so incessantly impelled to observe and fear. It was sheer cowardice that had brought me that beating. For what had been my crime?

This – we did sums. When we had done what always seemed a grievously large number of these sums, Mr Gulliver read out the answers and we had to put R or W against each sum as it came along. On this occasion Mr Gulliver read out the answers too quickly for my convenience and, getting a bit muddled and behindhand, quite by mistake, I marked one sum R instead of W. I recall as if it happened yesterday the agony of the moment when Mr Gulliver discovered that fallacious R. His face came slowly down into mine. His green eyes pierced me with accusation. The huge moustache bristled down upon me and the huge nostrils whistled condemnation. It was utterly helpless to try to explain – I would only be confessing that I was a liar as well as a cheat. But terror drove me, I suppose, to the extreme limit of cowardice. I shrank back from that awful Kitchener moustache and my quivering lips blurted out the pitiable false admission, 'Oh, s–s–sir, the temptation was too great'.

If I have lingered in some detail over this unhappy episode, it is because it is difficult if not impossible to eradicate the convictions and habits and instincts which are engraven upon you or driven into you in the early stages of life. I have always suffered from a lack of self-assurance which, if you come to analyse it, is all part and parcel of my boyhood's moral cowardice. I am always too ready to agree with what anybody else says, particularly if the anybody is a woman. It's no good anyone trying to argue with me – I give way at once. In any case arguing gets you nowhere. I once listened to a long and heated argument between two railway porters, which concluded thus: First porter: 'Go on; I don't want any more to do with you.' Second porter: 'No more don't I with you bloody well neither.'

My play-writing has always been a very wobbly affair; every play I have ever had produced, and several that I haven't, have been rewritten and scrapped and revised and cut over and over. (Even my letters have to be written two or three times because I so often make a balls of what I want to say the way I want to.) I accept modification, even downright rejection, of my work (though I've seldom had to) because I like to let the director or whoever he is think he knows more about the job than I do. In short I suppose I am very weak-willed as the lasting result of my Abbey School training. But I am glad to be. It means my being on pleasant relationships with other people and that other people are very kind and indulgent to me, especially now that I'm so old.

So in the long run I bear no ill-will to Mr Gulliver (well, I could scarcely blame him, could I?). I only wish that I could have met him again later on to tell him so but, so I have heard, he was borne fairly early to the tomb, escorted thither by his confidential and constant associates, Messrs Haig and Haig. His ruler was only one specimen of the queer instruments selected by schoolmasters of those days for smiting or searing the bottoms of little boys. The headmaster of the Abbey, the Rev. H. E. Hill, kept the birch in reserve and meted out most of his corporal punishment with a fives-bat, a solid wooden utensil about an inch thick and between a ping-pong bat and a tennis racquet in size. His Reverence broke one on me in the course of a flogging, but he carried on with a duplicate. The bruise on my poor little buttocks lasted for about ten days. The unceasing panic of doing something I might get fives-batted for was all part of the cowardice but not the principal cause of it. The major abiding menace was that Old God of Wrath, of whom Mr Hill and Mr Gulliver were the disciples here on earth.

I would never have had any resentment that my young boyhood was saturated with religion if that religion had not been almost entirely based on fear. Even in my home special emphasis was placed on the Old Testament as a guide to infant morality and on the drastic judgments of the Almighty on some of the refractory characters in Hebrew lore. *Line upon Line*, a children's book of the period (I believe it is still in circulation), had a place in every self-respecting nursery. It related some of the Old Testament incidents in the form of a series of cautionary verses and certainly pulled no punches in emphasising what the God of Wrath kept in store for the unruly. I can still remember a typical extract:

> When children in their wicked play
>   Mocked old Elisha so
> And bade the prophet go his way –
>   'Go up, thou baldhead, go –'
> God quickly stopped their wicked sport
>   And sent two raging bears,
> Who tore them limb from limb apart,
>   'Mid blood and groans and tears.

But my mother, though observant of the Victorian ethos, was, as I have said, full of kindness and understanding. (She also had the endearing habit of dissolving into tears when she laughed. I have always loved people who do this.) No, it was the Abbey School which was the favourite haunt of the God of Wrath. There He was perpetually depicted as a stern and somewhat irritable Almighty, fairly itch-

6

ing to administer vengeance. The effect of this on my timorous mind was shown by my regular and secret observance of kneeling every night at my bedside in my little cubicle and repeating the word 'perhaps' a great many times: 'perhaps, perhaps, perhaps' – catching my breath in my haste. This was done in order to make negative the number of lies I had told during the course of the day and thus to ward off the impending punishment from God, who with any luck was too busy chastising the sins of even worse boys, to have caught up with me.

If my boyhood years were subjected to this incessant primitive state of funk it was bound to have a lasting effect on my character. And the funk was only nursed by the tedium and drudgery of the Abbey Sundays. My Sunday schedule seems almost incredible now. The boys had to don their Eton collars and top hats and in them to march to both morning and evening services at the local parish church. We had to learn by heart the collect and either the epistle or gospel appointed for the particular Sunday and to be able to repeat them to the headmaster on the following morning. The fives-bat hovered in waiting for anyone who was uncertain of his lines. But that was by no means all. Immediately after we had dragged our melancholy boots back from morning church, the headmaster recapitulated the sermon, giving us notes on the same and during the afternoon each boy had to write out his own version of the invariably dreary discourse. There was also, of course, the weekly obligation of writing a letter to one's parents. ('My dear Father and Mother. I hope you are quite well. Thank you very much for the butterscotch.') We had to put in a walk too, in crocodile formation, superintended by some unfortunate junior master. How the devil we got it all in the God of Wrath alone knows.

But both at home and at school religion's most important job was to suppress and intimidate a boy's natural sexual awareness and development. For him to reveal the mildest, vaguest inquisitiveness about what his elders referred to in hushed asides as the facts of life was sin, sin, mortal sin. At the Abbey the first minor hint of it was seized upon and reported to the Rev. Mr Hill (birch, in this case) by vigilant masturbating assistant masters. Not until the last evening of my prep-school days, when I was just fourteen, was the staggering secret of copulation broken to me by the same, more reverend than ever, Mr Hill. He began by referring to 'that funny little thing between your legs' and asking me whether I had noticed any odd expansions of it lately. As a matter of fact for some time past my funny little thing had been cocking up its head in a pert and puzzling manner and on my admitting this, Mr Hill told me it would stick up to an even greater extent later on; all grown-up men's do; and he added in a tone of contemptuous disdain 'sometimes some stuff comes out of it'.

He then proceeded to fill my horrified ears with a guarded disclosure of how I and others had come to be. He concluded with a stern warning that the exercise involved was permitted by God solely for the purpose of procreation in the marriage bed and that any misuse of my new-found friend would land me in serious trouble both on earth and in the hereafter. I was soon to find out that he was quite right so far as the 'on earth' side of it went. At Charterhouse, if a boy was caught indulging in self-abuse (perhaps beneath his desk, so urgent were the claims of puberty) he was flogged. If a master caught him obliging another boy (which do they call it, hetero-abuse or homo-abuse nowadays?) he was expelled. Even at that stage these penalties were enacted basically in the interests of the Almighty. Throughout the whole of my boyhood sex was sin.

As for girls of the upper class (the classes were distinct in those days) they were safeguarded in complete and blissful ignorance of Nature's ghastly secrets ('Hush, dear, don't speak of anything like that down here; Mabel's in the next room'); very often they had to find out for themselves on their wedding-night. A female cousin of mine on the eve of her marriage at the age of thirty (thirty, I repeat) stole to the side of my, by then, married sister in whispering agitation. 'Oh, Muriel, do tell me something about what happens. I don't know the first thing about it, except that it's something to do with that little button thing in the middle of one's stomach.'

It was all very puzzling at first; it rather repelled and grieved me to think that Mum and Dad should get up to this mundane and awkward-sounding business and that God should not only allow but decree them to. Anyhow, observance of His Will must be their first consideration – I felt sure my mother never did it on Sundays. Oh, what an intolerable, self-righteous little prig a Victorian upbringing tended to make one.

Needless to say that at Charterhouse, where bawdry was the main topic of out-of-school (and often in-school) conversations, I soon became enlightened about it all. And although I duly became as smutty as the rest, this meant that I was always at grievous odds with my conscience.

The chastity of my home, the preposterous bigotries of the Abbey haunted me for years ahead. Whatever my losing battles with my conscience at Charterhouse, once free from Charterhouse I put up a stern resistance. ('From fornication and all other deadly sin ... Good Lord, deliver us.' B. Travers, first prize for his flawless repetition of the Litany.) I was twenty years old before, randy beyond endurance, I treated myself to my first sight of a completely naked female. I was in Singapore at the time and she was a three-dollar Japanese whore. I stood gazing and frothing at the mouth – I did not achieve or even attempt intercourse. Even so I remember bowing my head in my homeward-bound rickshaw at the thought of how pitiably saddened my dear mother would have been had she known. Nevertheless I very soon flung resistance to the winds. I encountered a more enticing Jap a week or so later (the first was bandy-legged and under-breasted) and enjoyed my first full wallop. Thereafter, though my conscience still kept yelling accusations, I could only feebly compromise with it. Sex was still sin but sin was so damned irresistible.

Only old people like myself have experienced the two extremes in the sex conditions of this country – all this Victorian false-modesty and the permissible, indeed subsidised indulgence of today. Whereas I was fourteen before the Reverend Mr Hill divulged his startling information about what my funny little thing was for, children nowadays get to know all about it by the time they leave the kindergarten. It is only reasonable and natural that boys and girls should feel the urge to exercise their funny things in mutual enjoyment at a reasonably early stage. This, of course, is apt to lead to a lot of domestic problems and bother and grunting old grandfathers are often heard to say, 'Well, what do you expect? This is the ultimate result of the damned puritanical, hypocritical way we were brought up. It's the full-circuit reaction to all that psalm-smiting cock.' True enough, but this wholesale moral contrast is only a particle of the changes which have taken place over the past seventy years. When I was about twenty the internal combustion engine, the car, a few years later the aeroplane, came into being. Speed was discovered.

Speed. Hurry. Suddenly everyone caught the infection and recognised the importance of speed. Urgency became a prime consideration in all walks of life and old Father Time began to publish his annual book of records. The First World War was, of course, a great and essential incentive – we had to beat them to it. Of recent years we have never had to reckon much with change of speed but only with the speed of change. No wonder that the teenagers of today have become caught up in it. But it is funny to think how damaging it was to a Victorian young lady's character for her to be accused of being 'fast'.

As an illustration of the speed of general development, what about this? My mother died in 1908 – no longer a young woman; she was in her fifties. She never saw an aeroplane or a motion picture of any sort or sat in a car. I, her son, one generation later, watched men on the moon on television (and that was some years ago now). And yet progression has often left poor old progress lagging a long way behind. One need only cite modern architecture and building methods and materials in comparison with the not-so-distant past; or, to take an example much nearer my own regard, there has never been anything in the theatre world to compare with the lavish

9

magnificence of the Drury Lane, Augustus Harris, days of the pantomimes featuring the historic Dan Leno and Herbert Campbell.
(Leno was the precursor of the Chaplin little-man-up-against-it type
of comedian; Campbell, massive and stentorian.) A great speciality
of every pantomime was the end-of-Act-one transformation scene,
a long and amazing sequence of scene-shifting and lighting, with
Madame Grigolati and her troupe of airborne fairies gliding from
wing to wing above. I was taken to these pantomimes year after year
from the time I was seven or eight. For, along with the goody-goody
stuff, I enjoyed a great deal of fun in my home life. My mother was
very fond of the theatre and, bless her soul, of taking us on what
were known as children's outings.

Many of these were to the Crystal Palace which was only a short
journey from Bromley on the London, Chatham and Dover Railway
(or was it the South Eastern?). The Crystal Palace was a vast glass
Victorian paradise, fed by long corridors containing cautiously fig-
leaved statuary, crestfallen palm-trees, portentous echoes and a
curious pervading smell suggestive of consecrated urinals. On one
of our visits I saw Blondin. He performed his regular routine – halting
halfway along his wire to cook his habitual omelette on a miniature
stove and staging an impending fall from his roof-top perch to bring
a gasp from the audience. No doubt there have been, since his time,
many more spectacular performers on the wire, such as the man who
rides a bicycle along it with another gentleman upside down, head-
to-head on him as he pedals along; but I am glad I saw Blondin.
He was one of the great protagonists who in their day (and mine)
predominated in their respective lines of business in this country.
Tradition, and perhaps in some cases Madame Tussaud's, still
honour them for having established unprecedented standards, prodi-
giously surpassed since, but standards which initiated supremacy in
their respective lines of business. Tom Webster, the cartoonist, who
was my exact contemporary, used to call them 'the daddies' – Henry
Irving (the theatre), W. G. Grace (cricket), Harry Vardon (golf,
with Braid and Taylor breathing down his neck), Captain Webb
(swimming), John Roberts (billiards), Sandow (physical strength),
Cinquevalli (juggling), Houdini (escapism), Dr Crippen (murder) –
it was the age of the outstanding individual. Incidentally, Captain
Webb has been immortalised (I would like to think) in John Betjeman's 'A Shropshire Lad', a title borrowed from Housman, which still
remains my favourite Betjeman poem, and that's saying something.

About this time W. G. Grace, having forsaken Gloucestershire,
ran a side which he termed London County, whose headquarters
was the Crystal Palace, and here I saw the old man make a century.
Ranji was his partner during his innings and he made a century too.
Grace's innings had a special feature which justifies my recalling it,

for it confirmed the legend that he so enjoyed batting that he insisted on going on batting. When he had made about twenty he was caught at short leg by a Surrey pro named Brockwell, who threw the ball up delightedly. But W. G. indicated a bump-ball and turned on Brockwell, flourishing his bat as though to fell him, and the umpires, when appealed to, merely looked on, awestruck and mute.

Later in my boyhood's fervid cricket-watching days I saw W. G. playing in the same match as Jack Hobbs, which happened only twice. This was Hobbs' first appearance in first-class cricket. But most memorable of all my youthful cricket-gloating experiences was when I watched what is still quoted as the classic Test Match innings of all time, G. L. Jessop's 104 against Australia at the Oval in 1902. A special and, I think, hitherto unrecorded feature of this famous occasion was the astonishing enthusiasm of the ringside spectators. It was the time of boater straw hats and, when Jessop reached his century, many staid and frugal citizens were so carried away that they sent their boaters sailing like boomerangs into outer space.

My inherent weakness of nature, as illustrated by my encounter with Mr Gulliver and inspired by my littleness and cowardice and the wrath of God and all the rest of it, has been accompanied throughout my life by a lesser but egregious shortcoming. This was first exposed when I was still at the Abbey School stage. My mother took me, during the holidays, to stay at a small hotel at Martin Mill, near St Margaret's Bay. I had had flu or something and she thought I wanted a short rest-cure. It was not the summer season and we were the only hotel visitors except for a mysterious Italian and one or two of his associates. He was engaged in some fantastic attempts to communicate with another stooge who was stationed in the South Foreland lightship. So I can claim to have witnessed the earliest experiments by Marconi in wireless telegraphy. Marconi was very kind to me and only too ready to try to explain to me what it was all about. Most boys would have revelled in the novelty and fascination of the thing. I had been born without the right sort of intelligence to appreciate or candidly to bother about it. I found the eager Italian gentleman rather a well-disposed bore.

And all through my life I have remained devoid of interest in any sort or kind of applied science or practical mechanics. I once, late in life, learned how to deal with a fuse, but I immediately forgot what one does and now if a fuse occurs I have to telephone for the man. I can't even change a light-bulb without qualms of suspense and strange contortions of countenance. I am incapable of undertaking elementary household repairs, such as altering whatever it is that regulates the temperature of a fridge or that thermostat thing which heats up the water in the cupboard tank. The inner workings of such things as cars, lawn-mowers and ball-cocks in lavatory cisterns are

11

beyond my ken. I once tried to remove something which was stopping up the pipe of the kitchen sink, and flooded the whole ground floor of my cottage. Any attempt on my part to do any sort of repair work to a clock, a TV or radio set, a gramophone (I beg your pardon, record-player) or a camera inevitably results in complete wreckage. Before the days of ball-points nobody ever invented a fountain-pen which did not saturate my fingers with ink. Cigarette-lighters jib at the very sight of me. In the 1914–18 war I achieved and deserved a reputation as a pilot of aeroplanes and after the war I was awarded the Air Force Cross for my services; but I was never able to grasp more than the barest rudiments of the principle of the internal combustion engine. And as for topedoes—

Let me hastily add that I have always been glad to be like this. It has meant that those associated with me have never looked to me to mend things and would much rather I didn't try to. It has also meant the casual but welcome association with a large number of the men. And I don't think that this flaw in my make-up can be traced to my upbringing, as my lack of self-assertion can. It is simply that Nature never intended me to be one of those individuals who do clever things beneath the floorboards of rooms or the bonnets of cars.

I left Charterhouse by mutual consent. This was not surprising because, although I never got into any real disgrace, I distinguished myself at nothing. I didn't even get into the Upper School. I find it embarrassing to make an honest report on my few years at Charterhouse; the fact that I was there at all has resulted in bringing me so many great friends and the school has recently offered me the greatest compliment that could possibly be paid to this very Old Boy, which is to build a school theatre bearing my name. But at the turn of this century the whole way in which the place was run and many of the general conditions were simply shocking. I was in one of the smaller and rather disregarded houses, where the housemaster never saw us except for a brief session for evening prayers and didn't bother to memorise our names. The food, left in the hands of the villainous profiteer known as the butler, was often too rank for even a schoolboy to stomach. The junior boys had to change for games in what was known as the boot-hole which stank of boot-polish and where you had to shed your underclothes on to a floor half an inch thick with dust. Any form of indisposition meant throwing yourself on the ill-termed mercies of the matron, a blowzy old bitch with a cat called Missoof. (I remember Missoof being imprisoned in a playbox for a week by some revengeful funster.) The matron's invariable remedy was to make you drink gregory powder and to scrape the remnants, clinging to the glass, off with a spoon to ensure your being sick. The head-monitor was allowed to beat the smaller boys with single-sticks, which was justifiable enough, but some head-monitors were over-zealous in finding reasons for ther delightful privilege; more-over the victims suffered the added indignity of having to go and collect the single-sticks from Grindell, the drill-sergeant.

My littleness nearly accounted for me on one occasion during my first summer at Charterhouse. Baden-Powell, the school's and indeed nation's hero of the day, came to visit us on his return to England from the historic relief of Mafeking. The monitors towed his open victoria from Godalming station to the school itself to be greeted by a surging mass awaiting it there. I was squashed flat to the ground and only managed to scramble to my feet just in time to avoid a juggernaut extinction from the victoria. A painful and shaming moment, but I was the only person to be at all concerned.

But I had just one memorable stroke of luck at the very outset. The first form-master I was under was Leonard Huxley, father of Aldous and Julian, a kindly and sympathetic man in contrast to some of the fearsome old rogues in charge of other lower-school forms. Un-fortunately I got on so well with Huxley that I was promoted after one term with him and fell among thieves. But I have never lost my grateful memories of Leonard Huxley, a saint among school-masters. My subsequent school reports were invariably shocking; thought I did avoid being branded for good in the manner of one of my form-mates – 'The boy who plays the cad in chapel stands no chance in after life.'

One form-mate, almost as insignificant as myself and almost as small (he must have doubled in size in his later boyhood), was des-tined to become one of the outstanding figures in the 1939–45 war, 'Pug' Ismay. The nickname 'Pug' was given to him at school – I'm not at all sure I wasn't its originator. It had nothing to do with pug-nacity, as some people think. It was because, at any rate in those days, his features were so like those of a pug-dog.

All in all, I had a rooted objection to being a Carthusian. But I am very glad and a bit braggart about being an Old Carthusian, one of a race which, generation after generation, produces notable individuals in all vocations, often improbable ones. Above all, any boy who goes to Charterhouse becomes endowed with the most pre-cious possession that heaven can bestow – he becomes possessed of a sense of humour.

My parents were faced with a problem about what to do with me when I left school, as I was still too young to be regarded as having finished my so-called education. Someone – my mother I think – sug-gested that it might be a good idea for me to be sent to Dresden for six months to learn German. I don't think it was ever established why the idea was a good one but it was forthwith adopted and not long afterwards I was being seasick in a Hook of Holland steamboat.

13

But why Dresden? Because Dresden was where my elder and only sister had just been finished. This period of history was the peak-hour of the Continental finishing school for the daughters of British respectability. These establishments catered for ten or twelve of them at a time in an environment of impeccable maidenly refinement. They were escorted in huddled parties to the more innocuous productions at the opera house. Second-hand native professors supervised and extolled their excruciating exercises at the music-stand and the easel.

My sister, having finished being finished in Dresden, was now back home and had reached the stage of being courted by the local curate and accompanying him on the piano while he sang 'Down the Vale' in the drawing-room after dinner. So it was easy to get a recommendation about suitable accommodation for me in Dresden. And what could be more suitable than the domicile of Mr Virgin and his three sisters, the Misses Virgin, whose name was a recommendation in itself. Poor middle-aged ladies, Nature had in their case decreed that they were intended to live up to it whether they wanted to or not. But I think they preferred to.

I remember forming this estimate of the Misses Virgin at that time because by now my mind was constantly occupied by the normal and delightful seventeen-year-old allurements of sex. Mr Hill's funny little thing had become much less little and a great deal funnier. Any idea of engaging it on active service was to be sternly repressed for years ahead – it had to content itself with home-guard exercises. But finding myself in the midst of scores of adolescent English girls who were in the course of being finished, my yearnings began to take a more serious turn. I was a regular visitor to Miss Gilderdale's (my sister was an old Gilderdalian) and though I knew full well that, owing to my size, I was the pet subject of her girls' dormitory giggles, I fell desperately in love with the prettiest and least abashed giggler of the Gilderdale coterie. I only mention this episode because it serves to show how greatly my lack of self-confidence went on being brought home by my lack of inches. Somewhere or other there exists a pathetic faded snapshot of myself standing beside my inamorata in the snow (her expression still wearing a discouraging snigger) and raising myself on my toes in a vain effort to match her height.

But anyhow I began to feel independent for the first time. Mr Virgin did not bother me overmuch. All I remember of him is that he was a hearty character and one of those suck-back-your-breath-between-your-teeth people (eeee-oooo). Also that he used to rope me in to sing glees with his three sisters in the evenings (the word glee can seldom have been worse applied). My German tutor, Herr Fiedler, proved of greater value. His personal appeal was limited. He had a memorable and repellent smell which was all his own, luckily for everybody else. But he taught me a smattering of German which was to prove of use to me later on, for it gave utterance to Putz, the German stepfather in *Rookery Nook*.

It seems that in the whole course of my education there were only two brief periods which I can reckon as having been beneficial, associated with two instructors as unlike each other as you could imagine – the genial Leonard Huxley, the humourless and odoriferous Herr Fiedler. But despite my having been treated with contempt by my other Charterhouse masters I was not the little dismissible, unteachable fool they rejected. In fact I was no fool at all. If I tell you that of all my contemporaries both at the Abbey and at Charterhouse I have become the most celebrated in this country (except of course for Pug Ismay) it is not in boast. It is the result of my having, from my early boyhood, been obsessed with my love for the theatre. It was my one abiding predominating enthusiasm and if I was destined to become a successful playwright years and years later it was due to the enthusiasm being so abiding and dominating, wasn't it? In the early stages my ambition was, of course, to be an actor, as is the case with many boys and all girls. I knew it would be frowned upon at home, but we will come to that shortly. Meanwhile, throughout my boyhood I kept the ambition to myself and fostered it just as one of Saki's little boys fosters a forbidden pet animal and fondles it in wanton delicious secrecy. And the ambition got a splendid boost during my stay in Dresden.

Dresden, being in those days a treasure-house of the Arts, it was considered to be all part of the finishing of Miss Gilderdale's girls and others of their kidney that they should be accompanied to the various picture galleries and museums and (as I have said) to the opera. The same licence was granted to me by Mr Virgin, whenever I could escape the glee-singing, but I was permitted far greater freedom than the girls and was allowed to go on my own. So I lingered in the galleries and doffed my little bowler hat in the special sanctuary allotted to the Sistine Madonna. This was duty. But the opera house was far from duty; it was sheer pleasure.

Apart from Bayreuth, Dresden was the leading opera house in all Germany specially dedicated to Wagner, who was rightly regarded as the nation's opera composer sacrosanct and incomparable. And although I managed to wangle my way to patronise a good many operas which seemed to promise a somewhat lighter form of entertainment, one of the Misses Virgins (Kate, I think) always took care that I should be guided to a Wagner night. I am afraid that my musical ear, hitherto familiar chiefly with the melodies of Lionel Monckton and Leslie Stuart, was rather slow to appreciate *The Ring*. My favourite was *Tannhäuser*, which did after all contain three or four extracts which registered themselves with me as smash-hit

15

numbers. But on all occasions I assured the Misses Virgin that I was immensely edified. I, in my riper years, have become genuinely appreciative of Wagner. The secret is never to let your attention stray from the orchestra. This is particularly essential during some of the recitatives. If a character enters and takes his stance supporting himself on his spear or staff you are in for a pretty long and tough session. But listen to the orchestra and all will be well.

But if my moments of genuine relish of opera were few and, in the case of Wagner, far between, I took delight from the first in the opera house itself. It was that atmosphere which is only to be found in the great opera houses of the world and transcended any theatres I had seen or dreamed of. It seemed to me that, just as a cathedral stands in aloof superiority to a parish church, so this edifice stood in comparison to my London theatres (Drury Lane perhaps excepted). The vast setting, the lighting, the plush opulence of the auditorium and foyer, here was the world of my dreams in grandiose form – Theatre in excelsis.

The German audiences were impressive too, deadly solemn, hushed, reverential. If Wagner was their god, their cleanliness was often a pretty poor second to their godliness, though Herr Fiedler always preserved his own special brand of smell. But their understanding of and devotion to the music was positively awe-inspiring. When I allowed myself a chuckle at Beckmesser's inept attempt to sing the *Preislied* I was glared at by my neighbours as if I had let out a loud fart in church. Nor was there ever the slightest comment about a feature which gave me, in this my first taste of opera, a good deal of secret amusement, namely the physical appearance and shape of some of the principals. So long as they could sing (and sing they could) no-one worried about their figures, often mercilessly exposed by the costume designers. I was to discover later that this is the case in opera generally, especially as applied to tenors and to the diaphragms of sopranos.

Being such a raw hand at opera-going I failed to grasp the fact that the performers devoted the whole of their attention to the vociferous side of the job and that acting came second and in many cases nowhere. I regarded their acting with scorn and not without self-encouragement. I even indulged in demonstrations to myself of how much better some of the limited periods of actual drama in the Wagnerian operas might be performed. In my small bedroom at Mr Virgin's I would lie on the floor, a Tannhäuser with his head cushioned on the stomach of Venus and springing suddenly into conscious reality of his thraldom, aroused by his disturbing dream of church bells. I would whisper his opening lines, '*Zu viel, zu viel – O dass ich nun erwächte.*' I was jolly good, I told myself. Anyhow, a damn sight better than Von Bary or Scheidemantel.

I was quickly humbled and enlightened by two immense slices of luck. Sarah Bernhardt was making a tour of Germany and put in a week in Dresden, playing *La Tosca*. Also on tour, a few weeks later, came Lucien Guitry (father of the even more popularised Sacha). I saw him in *Les Affaires sont les Affaires*, which was one of his big hits of his latter years. (Beerbohm Tree tried his hand at it in London and had one of his major flops.) Guitry's character was a plutocrat to whom Business was indeed Business. His great scene was when he was just concluding a rich deal with two financial rivals. A manservant enters with an urgent written message. This tells him that his son, with whom he has just parted after a violent quarrel, has killed himself in a car crash (this was in the very early days of cars). Guitry informed the other two of what had happened; then bottled himself up and made them sign their contract and depart. He then, alone on the stage, re-read the message, crumpled it in his hand and burst into a flood of tears. None of your stage weeping and head-holding. He stood and blubbered loudly, with the tears streaming down his face, like a child in sudden pain. The audience remained absolutely silent and spellbound. I still remember it as the bravest and most moving bit of acting I have ever seen.

And Bernhardt? James Agate always refused to listen to anybody who tried to tell him that any other living actress was comparable to Sarah Bernhardt. I am glad to have Agate's authority to assure me about her, because when I saw her that night in Dresden I was only an impressionable seventeen-year-old. But she was still more or less in her prime – she rather marred her great fame later on when she insisted on carrying on acting with only one leg, and in sleeping in her coffin and in other elderly eccentricities and became almost a pathetic joke. And to be honest I have a clear recollection of only one scene in *La Tosca*, the great scene where Scarpia imposes his will on her by forcing her to listen to her lover, Caravadossi, being tortured. Bernhardt in that scene lives vividly in my memory seventy-odd years later. I have always thought and still think that I saw then, in one of her greatest moments, the greatest actress of my lifetime.

By that time I had already seen a few of the English members of the profession who were considered to rank among its leading lights – John Hare, the Kendals, Charles Hawtrey (still a young man) and Marie Tempest, but she too was in her youthful, musical comedy days. I had been hoisted up to sit on the rail running round the back of Daly's Theatre pit to get a clear view of her performance in *The Geisha*. All these had fired my enthusiasm for the stage and set me dreaming of the distant future when I would be a grown-up man doing what they were doing. I had seen one boy of my age (two or three years younger than I in fact) at it already – the Buttons in *Sherlock Holmes* with William Gillette – and he was jolly good and I envied him greatly. His name was Charles Chaplin. No doubt he would go on from there and get other parts and do quite well, but what a bit of luck for him to have been allowed to start so young.

The supreme brilliance of Bernhardt and Lucien Guitry may have fanned the glimmerings of a sense of proportion and told me that it was time I stopped being so childish and cocky. Perhaps my bedroom Tannhäuser, though still superior to that of the opera tenors, was not really all that hot. But nothing could rob me of that boyish, buoyant, ballyhoo dedication to Theatre. Seventy-odd years have passed since then and nothing ever has.

2

Heredity is like the wind that bloweth where it listeth. Not only do we all look like one or other of our parents or both, but also, to a far less general systemised degree, heredity is held responsible for what is right about us and, opportunely, for what is wrong. My father was a most conscientious and generous parent but he was impulsive by nature and given to expressing himself in strange unpremeditated figures of speech. I have inherited this impulsiveness, especially in old age, though it has never got me anywhere and I quickly stifle it or have it stifled for me. My loving and beloved mother's first consideration in life was religion and propriety. Thanks to her I have always had Christian belief as my first consideration too (though of latter years it has become rather singular and informal) but I'm afraid the propriety went west a long time ago. Heredity had nothing to do with my early and ever ripening yearning for the theatre, unless it was that my mother's pleasure in going to see a show now and then blossomed out in me to a prodigious extent.

I'm sure my parents never dreamed of fostering this yearning. It was simply a matter of giving my sister and myself a good time. Before my Dresden days we had been taken, as I have said, to see quite a number of the leading performers of the day during my school holidays; following the primary delights of the Drury Lane pantos and their poor relation *Bluebeard* at the Crystal Palace (book of the words sixpence; and I knew it by heart within a week). In the Christmas holidays of 1897 I was treated to my first straight play, *One Summer's Day*, at the Comedy Theatre. Charles Hawtrey played the lead and opposite him in the ingénue part, Eva Moore. The little boy who sat nail-biting in an intensity of admiration and delight at that matinée was to have his own first play produced by that same Charles Hawtrey a quarter of a century later. Half a century later that same Eva Moore played the part of an old lady in one of my films. This was the first and only time I met her and it gave her a pleasant surprise to be reminded of her first leading part. She was married to H. V. Esmond who was the author of *One Summer's Day*, and she was Laurence Olivier's first mother-in-law. So he knew her a good deal better than I did and liked her a great deal less.

I realise that the stage notabilities of the early days of this century may be of little interest to most people nowadays, except to the devoted historians of the profession like my friend, J. C. Trewin, but each one of them in turn rekindled my already brightly-burning enthusiasm. My as yet distant adventures were to owe so much to the influence of those old masters and mistresses (how apt a term in several cases) that loyalty demands mention of a few of them. I saw the Kendals in *The Elder Miss Blossom*. Mrs Kendal was, apart from Ellen Terry, the most prominent star actress of her day, gracious in the eyes of the public and, according to legend, the hell of a martinet with her company. Mr Kendal was the perfect example of the leading lady's submissive and mediocre helpmeet. In theatrical jargon he 'carried the band-parts'; he was what playgoers, including my father, were apt to term 'a stick'. John Hare, eventually knighted, was the foremost comedy actor of his generation. I saw him first in *School*, a T. W. Robertson comedy long forgotten, and later in *A Pair of Spectacles*, the most popular stand-by farce-comedy of Hare's whole career.

The revival of *Sherlock Holmes* not long ago proved its value as a good melodrama of those days. I saw the original show when I was fourteen with William Gillette as Holmes. I have always remembered the high spot in that production just as I have always remembered Bernhardt and Guitry, though in Gillette's case there was, I fear, a touch of the ludicrous. It was when Holmes, surrounded by Moriarty's evil gang in the Stepney Gas Chamber, plunges the place into darkness, through which gleams one pin-point of light upstage. 'Follow him by his cigar', cries one of the thugs. Another thug manages somehow to light up the place again and Holmes stands by the open doorway. Gillette surveyed the mob with leisurely imperturbability – 'Gentlemen, I left my cigar on the windowsill. Good evening' and exit. The baffled thugs remained stricken in their respective attitudes of bafflement. One of them I recall, nearly overbalanced. They could easily have sprung upon Holmes and collared him while Gillette positively dallied to emphasise his scorn and superiority. He didn't even save a quota of time by saying, 'Gentlemen'. 'Gentle men,' said Gillette. Splendid old melodrama. Of course at the time I didn't give a thought to its absurdity. I sat and revelled in the enchantment it brought me; the ineradicable enchantment. Others who helped to stimulate it to a minor degree were George Alexander and Cyril Maude. Up to my Dresden time I had not seen Tree or Wyndham; they were to come later. I never saw Henry Irving on the stage. My parents had paid him a visit before I was born and for some reason avoided him thereafter. How sad for me.

I saw him off-stage though, when I was still only about nine or ten. We were spending the summer holidays somewhere at the seaside and Irving was on tour in the neighbourhood. One morning my mother called us excitedly to the first-floor window of our lodging-house, 'Children, come here, quickly, quickly.' There, down the road outside came Henry Irving and Ellen Terry on a placid drive in an open victoria. Ellen Terry looked up at us as we flapped our paws in homage through the open window. She called the victoria to a halt, descended and sailed up the short flight of stairs to our room. She shook hands with us and kissed my infant brother (the only grudge I ever had against him). 'I can never resist children,' she told my mother. Irving remained in the victoria below in long-suffering detachment.

When I look back to those early-century days I keep reminding myself that I was at the impressionable age but the theatre-going public was at an impressionable age too. The stage-play was not, as it has now become, a representation of life; it was a dramatisation of life. Nobody would have paid sixpence at the box-office to have seen a mere representation of life. People wanted to be elevated from the humdrum daily routine by the colourful excitements of exaggeration. The profession too was a race apart. The stage-door remained the portal of a great mystery. From it emerged shadowy figures belonging to the mystery; mysterious themselves in the gaslight as the waiting hansom jingled them away into the further mystery of their private lives – great ghosts and minor ghosts. Having chosen to devote themselves to an existence larger than life they deliberately and habitually became larger than life themselves.

Without wishing to dwell too long on that theatre of three generations ago, I feel bound to recall one of its predominant personalities. The real reason why *One Summer's Day* was chosen for my first straight-play outing was that one of its support parts was allotted to Mr Henry Kemble. We had encountered him on a summer holiday at St Margaret's Bay where he used to go bathing every morning, taking with him a large barrel open at either end. He would exchange a few patronising 'oho's' with us children and I felt spellbound awe at being in actual contact with a prominent actor. He was a short, pot-bellied man, rather the shape of his own bathing-barrel. His name is still honoured by some of the older members of the Garrick Club, where some of his pronouncements became handed down through the years. Indeed, I hesitate to repeat his famous riposte to the tax-collector, so often has it been quoted: 'There, sir, is your tribute money; but you must tell the Berkshire widow that she cannot rely upon me as a permanent source of income.' Perhaps the most trenchant of Mr Kemble's utterances was unloosed when on one occasion he entered the Garrick in a state of assumed agitation. 'I have just passed Os-car Wilde in the street. And the cheeks of my ane-oos cloosed with an angry snap.'

The ooold ac-tor tradition died hard. Among those who preserved it beyond the Kemble generation was Lyn Harding, one of Beer-bohm Tree's regular henchmen. I sat opposite him one day at the Garrick while he ordered his luncheon with slight gesticulations of his right hand as he studied the menu. 'A portion of the best end of lamba. Rooost pootatooes.' But by then the flood-gates were open; the whole spate of modern actors streamed in and with the lamented departure of Donald Wolfit the old tradition passed away.

I was quite prepared for the response I was going to get when, home again from Dresden, I first ventured to mumble my aspira-tions. My mother's gentle, compassionate smile could not disguise her uncompromising denial. My father came more to the point with a memorable exclamation of dissent: 'Stage? Good Lord. To be an actor – just think of it. And marry a ballet girl who kicks up her legs——'

I couldn't blame my parents. My father was simply giving his own rather graphic expression to the average family man's estimate of stage life. In 1904 the stage was not only, as now, a hazardous pro-fession; there were social and moral objections too. It is true that Henry Irving had transformed that profession into one which a member of the genteel class could adopt if allowed to: Hawtreys and Maudes and Vanbrughs had already paved the way. But in the view of the respectable Caterham resident (we had advanced to Caterham by this time) the theatre world was rife with moral snares and pitfalls (as indeed it was; when wasn't it?).

So it became pretty clear what lay in store for me; I was to be sent to the City. Being sent to the City was then the inevitable lot of a youth who didn't have the aptitude to do any good for himself by being sent anywhere else. Patronising neighbours, the fathers of de-testable sixth-form sons destined to be shining lights in some pro-fession, would smooth their whiskers at me and say to my father, 'You'll be sending him to the City no doubt?' And my father, some-what nettled, would reply, 'Well, good lord, what do you suppose? He's a Travers. There's a place waiting for him in the old firm.'

The old firm was Messrs Joseph Travers and Sons Ltd. Founded in the year 1666, the date of the Great Fire of London, it was about the oldest business in the City of London, where at 119 Cannon Street my great-great-great-great-grandfather's brother had set himself up as a wholesale grocer. The only use I had had for the place up to this point, was to have been taken on to the roof as a small boy to watch the Diamond Jubilee procession and a Lord Mayor's Show, at which a waiting crowd of loafers amused themselves by kicking about the bustle which some lady had inadvertently let fall from her person. The concern was now a large limited company and my father had worked his way up into becoming the junior member of its board of directors. I viewed the prospect of working my own way up with dismal foreboding. I didn't think I would like it or be any good at it. I was to be proved only too right on both counts.

If you went into business it was with the hope of establishing yourself eventually as 'someone in the City', the accepted term for the plodder whose diligence and ability were finally awarded by elevating him to the £500-a-year City gent, nob or boss type of landed mandarin. I don't suppose that my father thought that I was ever likely to achieve this distinction as he had, but his generosity to me never wavered. At this stage it showed itself by giving me as stimulating an experience as can ever have fallen to the lot of a boy of seventeen, at any rate in those days.

The firm had branches and agents all over the world. My father was selected by the board to be the director who had to go to Singapore and sack the manager. He was then to proceed on a visit to various other countries in connection with the business. 'All right then: I'll tell you what – I'll take you along with me.'

What a splendid father to have. And if his naïvety and his peculiar choice of expression in giving vent to his impulsive feelings have left him a figure of fun in my memories of him, this surely is a sign of my affection. I think I must have caused him many moments of embarrassment in the course of our round tour. At seventeen I was the wrong age, height and gender for the sociabilities of ocean liners. Talk about my father's naïvety – I remember spotting the leading Australian belle of the passenger-list engaged with the ship's doctor (Dr Lothario) in some secretive moonlight leaning-over-the-rails dalliance and butting in to tell them some feeble old joke I had just remembered about a horse. I did, however, receive some encouragement from a charitable forty-year-old lady passenger, who invited me to visit her in her cabin, whither I stole, gnashing my teeth with excitement; but she turned out to be one of those, 'ho-ho, you funny boy' parties and I got nowhere until her husband arrived on the scene. Then I did pretty quickly.

Many of the episodes and impressions of that round-the-world journey abide in my memory but are of little interest to anybody else. In the course of the itinerary – Marseilles, Port Said (eagerly awaited by some of the male passengers, being at that time the fountain-head of filthy pictures), Colombo, Singapore, Hong Kong, Shanghai, Japan, Vancouver, Toronto, Montreal, New York and home – I saw many of the great cities and centres of the world as they were seventy years ago. New York was the New York of O. Henry's *Four Million*. The Flatiron Building was the showpiece of the city, its tallest building, the doyen of skyscrapers. Today it is, I suppose, respectfully preserved as a sort of venerated dwarf.

Canadian cities of the plain such as Banff and Medicine Hat were rows of shacks with small boys throwing baseballs at each other beside the track of the Canadian Pacific Railway as our train steamed by. My recollections of Tokyo are dim: I remember only watching a regiment of Japanese soldiers being marched off to give battle in the Russo-Japanese War; all of them about five feet in height and looking very determined.

Two minor episodes always seem to stick in my memory above all others, I don't know why. In Shanghai a guide escorted us to what was known as the Native City, in which the least privileged of the Shanghai community swarmed and stank in their thousands. The guide was keen to show us over its gaol, but we were politely told that the regulations forbade visitors that day because a popular criminal was due to be executed on the following morning. We were, however, invited to come along at the appointed hour and to see his head sawn off. I daresay that in some respects conditions in Shanghai remain much as they were seventy years ago.

I wonder whether the same remark applies to New York. The second episode I cherish is when we paid a visit to Coney Island. We drifted into a side-show which featured a troupe of well-worn females performing a song-and-dance act. An elderly pimp sidled up to my father and asked him whether he would care to satisfy his yearning for any one of the artistes. My father's reply was to leap up and make a headlong dash for the exit. 'Come on, quick. Good God, let's get out of this hole.'

One morning, a few weeks later, I found myself seated in gloomy reality in a stopping train on the London, Brighton and South Coast Railway, being sent to the City.

However repellent are my recollections of my inactivities in the fields of commerce I couldn't fail to be proud of the old firm's premises as they were then. (They are still dignified by being occupied by the City of London Library.) What was the spacious ground-floor sale-room must still be graced by the ghosts of silk-hatted, snuff-blown old brokers from Mincing Lane and of prosperous, whiskered retail grocers poking their critical noses into samples of dried fruit and spices. The sale-room covered a large area but it was all quite quiet; there was merely a continuous murmur such as you may hear in a cathedral regularly patronised by sightseers; and just as any sudden noise brings a jerk to the enshrined senses of a pious cathedral visitor so in the sanctuary of that vast sale-room one's ears might occasionally be assailed by the justifiable sibilations of some enraptured tea-taster.

Timid and averse as I was to participate, I must say that the old place remained a serene example of the long-lost composure and courtesy of commerce.

The habit of growing hair on all or on various sections of the face which is so popular among the young men of today (one hears of bearded sixth-formers in some cases) found no favour in my young days. Indeed we were quickly reprimanded by our seniors if they considered that we were in need of a hair-cut. But while many of the seniors themselves, my father for one, remained faithful to the moustache others stuck to the beards of their early manhood. Beards, beards decorated the board-room of Messrs Joseph Travers and Sons Ltd. Mr J. Innes Rogers, the Chairman, had the beard of one of those patriarchs who figure in Victorian engravings depicting some of the more dramatic incidents of the Old Testament. Mr J. Lindsay Travers had been brought up in Australia and had brought a good deal of the bush back with him. Mr Wilkinson had one of those wire beards. Mr Stapleforth was not actually chin-bearded but cherished whiskers which sprouted diagonally from his cheeks, as from those of an impassioned cat.

The Board, steeped in tradition as it was to the very inkpots, showed in my case a reformed sense of democratic duty. For on my joining the firm I was cast for the meanest beginner's job to be found. 'Let him start at the bottom and work his way up: an excellent principle.'

I worked my way not up but rather along. I had to proceed on foot every morning along various City streets into the mud-splashed recesses of the Borough of Whitechapel, carrying documents to warehouses. At these warehouses, some extremely vulgar and abrupt gentry did something to the documents, and handed them back to me to return to the place whence I came. This process was known as tea-clearing. I had no more idea what it was all about than I have now and vice versa. But it seems that I didn't do it very well. I was conscientious enough. I never dallied. I often ran. But after about six months of it I was relieved of my tea-clearing duties. What really happened I was never told but my imagination has always pictured the scene at the board meeting at which the decision about my immediate future was discussed and settled.

'Travers,' said the Chairman ominously to my father. 'This son of yours. Mullins has failed to furnish me with any very glowing reports of his tea-clearing.'

Mr Wilkinson spread his hands. 'If a lad cannot tea-clear what can he do?' he asked rhetorically.

'Why, what does Mullins say about the boy, Chairman?' inquired my father.

'Nay, nay,' replied the latter reprovingly. 'Heaven – if I may venture to mention Heaven in the board-room – forbid that I should stoop to so undignified a procedure as to pump Mullins. But the fact remains——'

A critical silence followed. Then Mr Stapleforth ventured a comment, shaking his head throughout it. 'I shrink with horror from the thought that the name of Travers should become dishonoured in our midst. Even,' he added, 'in tea-clearing circles.'

'Especially,' put in Mr Wilkinson briskly, 'in tea-clearing circles.'

'Nay, stay,' exclaimed the Chairman excitedly. 'I believe I have conceived a solution.'

He grasped both arms of his chair and swung his heavy stomach watch-chain in the direction of the Secretary.

'Which, pray,' he demanded, ' is the Colonial branch of this firm which is situated farthest from these headquarters?'

The Secretary dithered. 'Well, sir – if I may venture – on the spur of the moment, sir, I should presume Singapore. But if I may be allowed to verify my——'

'Singapore – that'll do,' cried the Chairman triumphantly. He expelled a breath of satisfaction so vigorous that it whirled his whole beard into a can-can of triumph. 'Singapore, eh? So be it – Singapore.'

At that period in the history of the Colonial Empire Singapore was regarded as an appropriate grave for the superior type of white man. Thither even an occasional woman went forth from England, to face the dual ordeal of marriage and the Malayan climate, with a smile of courageous determination in the manner of one taking leave of home to go and minister to a leper colony. Male candidates for jobs in Singapore had to possess two essential qualities. To be a gentleman was a recognised attribute in those days; so they had to be gentlemanly and they had to be healthy. For though, of course, nobody could be expected to remain healthy for long in that death-trap it was felt that he could at least remain a gentleman.

They were sent out for a primary spell of five years. Their directors at home, few of whom had ever been farther east than the Norfolk Broads, always gave them a few parting words of semi-jocular advice and encouragement but shook hands with them in a very final sort of way, as they bade them goodbye and wished them jolly good luck.

On his arrival in Singapore the novice received further and more practical advice from his local boss. There were three cardinal don'ts. Never venture out of doors in the daytime, even if it were to cross the road to the post office, without wearing your topee. Never fail to take some sort of violent physical exercise in the brief interval between office hours and sundown. Never (here the local boss's voice deepened an octave in intensity) never have any sort of social intercourse, however refined, with a young woman suspected of being Eurasian. The contemplation of any unrefined form of intercourse with an Eurasian girl never even arose. There was a universal theory that every Eurasian girl's sole ambition was to exercise some Delilah-like allurement over the young Englishman with the intention of beguiling him into marriage.

One eminent old merchant steered clear of the climatic death-trap long enough to retire home with a large fortune. His son succeeded him in the Singapore business. The son married an Eurasian girl. He was not only sacked from his job; his father never saw him or spoke to him again. I knew a young fellow, an assistant in the Singapore branch of a prominent firm, who was suspected of having a mild love affair with an Eurasian. Cabled messages flashed between his local manager and the head office and he was homeward bound on a liner within the week. Today marriages between Europeans and Chinese girls are quite common events. Such a marriage was unheard of then; never the twain were known to meet at the altar. But even if they had, it wouldn't have been looked upon as so disastrous as a meeting between the one and the one-half.

I was unfortunate in my boss – a pallid, contumelious young Lerpudian with gold-rimmed glasses and a settled manner of sneering self-sufficiently. He studiously disdained everybody else in his office and as studiously ignored any society outside it. He had discovered and married an elderly arty Englishwoman who had been a medical missionary and had written a play in blank verse called *The Travail of his Soul*. This excursion on her part into the realms of my own true and lasting interests brought me a certain preliminary respect for the lady, deplorable as, on examination, *The Travail of his Soul* proved to be. But the husband was not long in forming his own opinion of the latest specimen that had been foisted upon him by the London headquarters. And finding my very presence an offence he consigned me to Malacca. 'You may as well do nothing in Malacca as in Singapore,' he remarked coldly.

No doubt he was justified. I was ignorant of the first rudiments of business and although in the Singapore office I was only given the simplest jobs on hand I always made the most sickening hash of them. I remember having to start a new ledger recording the shipments of pineapples. It doesn't sound very difficult, but by the time I had completed the first page of the ledger the whole thing was in such a ghastly mess that I decided to tear the page out and start all over again. Apparently it was a dire offence to mutilate a ledger in this way, as I dare say those who enjoy a knowledge of commercial ethics will agree; but to me it seemed to be a reasonable enough measure in the interests of neat and practicable ledger-keeping.

One member of the staff of the Singapore offices shuffles again noisily up the wooden stairs in his wooden shoes at the smallest prompting of memory. Mr Hood Seck was an old Chinese employed by the firm to collect the sums of money falling due from the various local retailers. My morning greeting to him and his reply never varied:

'Good morning, Mr Hood Seck. How are you this morning?'

'I am very sick.'

'Oh dear. What's the matter with you?'

'Womit. And parting minutely.'

I never discovered what were the exact implications of this distressing and persistent form of malady. But they did not prevent Mr Hood Seck from appropriating a large proportion of the money he was paid by the retailers and hoodwinking the firm's book-keeper in the process. Needless to add that, owing I suppose to some temporary shortage of staff, I was in charge of the books at the time. And when eventually I cottoned on to Mr Hood Seck's little game and visited his private house with a policeman, some obscure agency had already tipped him the ominous wink and the expedient pill conveyed him to his ancestors just as retribution hammered at his door.

I remember Montero too. Montero was the office-boy and his written application for a day's leave of absence may be quoted as a good example of typical Eurasian Malapropism: 'Sir. I write to ask please leave from today's office business in order to get a nurse for my mother who is expecting a burst.'

Out of office hours I had a wonderful time. I revelled in the intense humidity of the climate. My salary of two hundred pounds sterling a year just about covered the cost of my keep and membership of the Cricket and Swimming Clubs and inevitable extras, chits for drinks, clothing, other necessities, in that order. Most visitors to Singapore during the past twenty or thirty years will be familiar with the Sea View Hotel (now, I believe, extinct) with its exotic lounge separating two raucous ballrooms. It opened in my time as a superior shanty in a grove of coconut palm trees. I was one of the original occupants of one of its four bedrooms. It had a combined bar-and-billiard-room and a stout Eurasian manager named de Sousa who cheated left-handed at snooker.

It was an hour's journey by rickshaw to and from the office where I allegedly worked but my rickshaw coolie, O Chye Lah, made light of it; I would have backed him against any other coolie on the road. The rickshaw was the only means of getting about except for the gharry drawn by a Malay pony (beyond my means). When I left Singapore in 1910 there were as yet only four motor vehicles in the whole island and two of these were fire-engines.

It was in Singapore that my first show as co-author and performer saw the light. This was a topical revue, *Ramsamy the Amorous*, acted and sung on the spacious verandah of a residential bungalow and patronised by invitation by practically the whole of the British community. I played the part of my own, by now celebrated, rickshaw coolie, O Chye Lah. I had to buy a pair of the floppy blue shorts invariably worn by rickshaw coolies, but these were, of course, far too clean to pass muster. So for three days before the production I left them in a friend's hen-run and they emerged in perfect condition for the job. I felt myself to be a worthy rival to that legendary actor who conscientiously blacked himself all over to play Othello.

I have already referred to my first, rather half-hearted response to the rampant yearnings of sex. This and my subsequent whole-hearted responses necessitated visits to the Malay Street quarter, the red-light district authorised by the Governor and subjected to sup-posedly regular medical inspection. Here, in a prevailing and memorable stench, hundreds of gaudily painted Japanese prostitutes swarmed in the verandahs of their wooden houses and screamed, against the uproar from adjacent shooting-galleries, their unvarying falsetto appeal 'Come inside, come inside, come inside.' There were a few elderly sullen German trollops to be found on the fringe of this parish and not far away a comparatively respectable and ex-cessively dull dance-hall known as the Tingle-Tangle, patronised chiefly and only very briefly by disillusioned merchant-seamen on their muttering way to Malay Street. Some time after I left, some misguided wife of a Governor persuaded him to eradicate Malay Street, with the result that in Singapore, as in London and many other cities, prostitution has been driven to conduct its functions and to spread its contaminations underground.

And now, briefly, Malacca. My Singapore boss was justified in anticipating that I would do nothing in Malacca for that is precisely what, for most of my time there, I did. Malacca was then, as in some respects it still remains, the capital of Lotus-land. Our Singapore branch acted as agents for the General Electric Company and I was bidden to try to persuade Malacca to favour the revolutionary offer to provide its township with electric light and power. The Resident received my suggestion like Shylock with a patient shrug. The Muni-cipality in general decided that it couldn't be expected to put up with any new-fangled nonsense of that sort. I cheerfully resigned myself to my lotus-eating, apart from making an occasional bad debt with a Chinese grocer.

Then, suddenly, a delightful discovery came my way. Among the small buildings tucked away on the dreamy sea-front was a small public library. In this I was surprised to find a complete uniform set of the plays of A. W. Pinero. What an amazing stroke of luck. I was Ben Gunn lighting on the treasure of Captain Flint.

They were not merely plays to read. They were guide-books to the technique of stagecraft. I studied them as such, counting and noting the number of speeches in any given scene. I discovered for myself the real secret of Pinero's mastery and success, the observance, in every line and every episode, of the value of climax.

My ambition underwent a switch. My genius as an actor must be sacrificed. I'd be a playwright.

Twenty-odd years later I was elected a member of the Dramatists' Club, when Pinero was still its president. I told him of my experience and of how much I'd learnt from him and all that. I asked him which of his plays was his own favourite. He put his face close to mine, as deaf people do when speaking confidentially. 'My boy,' he said, 'my favourite is the one that made the most money.'

My mother died very suddenly in 1908, a great shock to me. This meant that my father would have to be living on his own for most of the time, for my younger brother was still at school and my sister had duly married that curate and was getting down to a prolonged spell of incessant breeding. So I thought I'd better go home and keep the old man company. The manager of the Singapore branch seconded my proposal with an unprecedented show of goodwill.

I went back to 119 Cannon Street for another two or three years of futility and discontent. They put me into dried fruit. This was literally true; I spent my time with my hands plunging aimlessly into sample cases of currants and my shoes scuffling in a blend of sawdust and scattered sultanas. To escape the monotony I served a lengthy term in a dried-fruit broker's office and meandered around carrying packets of dried-fruit samples under each arm. This was worse than ever. I never sold any of the stuff, except once late in the evening to a friendly merchant who was drunk at the time. I used to give a good many of the samples to policemen on point duty. The policemen became the only people in the City who had any use for me.

My ambition to write plays or anything else did not get much encouragement during those boring City years. I can't remember having concocted any compositions and if I did they did not long survive. My first effort, a short narrative about a cat, which I had written in Malacca and had optimistically sent home for publication, hadn't brought me much encouragement. My mother had sent it to her friend, Stanley Weyman, the fashionable historical novelist of the period (*Under the Red Robe*, etc.) for his opinion. At one time Weyman had wanted to marry my mother but had wanted too long or too late. His advice to me was curt and expressive, 'The story, the story, the story'; which prompted my father to console me by disclosing that Stanley Weyman was 'a pedantic ass'.

There was one bright spot in the course of every weary week of those dried-fruit days. At one o'clock on Saturdays the City shut up shop and, except in the cricket season, I dashed off to the West End to get a good seat in the pit (two shillings and sixpence) at a matinée. The theatre was still governed by the sort of feudal system of my childhood days. Certain actor-managers had staked a claim to certain theatres and stayed there for years on end; Beerbohm Tree at His Majesty's; Cyril Maude at the Haymarket; George Alexander at the St James's; Arthur Bourchier at the Garrick; Oscar Asche at the Adelphi; Seymour Hicks at the Vaudeville. Less permanently but generally to be found somewhere or other were Lewis Waller, Fred Terry, H. B. Irving and Charles Hawtrey.

H. B. Irving had a personality and style which appealed to me above all others. (Dennis Eadie and Charles V. France were still support players up to that time, indeed, the latter was never anything else though supreme in his line.)

H. B. Irving and his brother Laurence, who in his short career gave one astonishing and renowned performance in a play called *Typhoon*, always had to endure disparaging comparisons with their father – reasonably enough I dare say. H.B.'s somewhat bizarre personality and methods might be derided nowadays, but he was my favourite figure in those romantic larger-than-life days of the drama. In impassioned moments his voice would rise and seem to lose itself in a sort of vibrant ecstasy; and in his more sinister parts his characteristic movements and the deliberate menace in the timing of his lines and looks were, to me at any rate, enthralling. He was not the most popular of actors with the general public but he was the man for me. I saw the classic Hamlet of Forbes Robertson and found it statuesque and machine-made in comparison to the vital Hamlet of H.B. Perhaps I was prejudiced in favour of my stage hero; but I still think I was a good judge.

My original stage hero, Charles Hawtrey, was generally to be seen at one theatre or another and had many successes, on which, as I afterwards learnt, the bookmakers were the first to congratulate him. He and Seymour Hicks both used a comedy technique which sounds very old-fashioned now but was effective and strangely convincing then. They took the audience quite openly into their confidence, as though the stalls contained their own, often rather guilty, consciences. They were a great contrast – Hicks full of ebullience and flummery; Hawtrey, portly, quiet and whimsical, whispering some awful self-confession to the front, with grave eyes slowly pursuing his line of thought. He held all the gifts of comedy in the palm of his hand and manipulated them gracefully and fondly like a master conjurer.

It was dating from this period that the technique of another leading actor, Gerald du Maurier, began to exert that influence which was to revolutionise acting. I don't think he did this intentionally;

it was simply that he possessed the ability and intuition to embody a character and to speak his lines so naturally that he stood out as a familiar human being in the midst of actors. Hawtrey before him had been endowed with a similar gift but Hawtrey allowed himself to exaggerate (delightfully) at times; du Maurier never did. His contemporaries often said 'Oh, he doesn't have to bother; he's only got to come on and be himself', but the fact is that he took an immense amount of trouble, aided by a very keen sense of humour, in making the most of his individual talent.

His methods caught on; for a long time in stage comedies youthful aspirants strolled on in a painfully studied ease of manner, tapping the end of a cigarette on its case before flicking it into their mouths. They only served to prove what a genius du Maurier really was. By and by naturalistic acting improved all round, until it reached the very high standard it is today.

While du Maurier was revolutionising acting, John Galsworthy, seconded by Granville Barker, set about the task of revolutionising plays and dramatic authorship. A little Galsworthy play called *The Silver Box*, produced at the Royal Court Theatre, was a landmark in our theatrical history. This and his earlier efforts, *Strife* and *Justice* patronised only by the limited intelligentsia of the London theatre-going public, heralded that sweeping change that I have mentioned, the take-over by the representation of life of the dramatisation of life. The change was not all that rapid; playgoers wanted their plays to stick to the good old tradition and to hell with this modernistic stuff. It is noteworthy that when an enterprising impresario experimented in producing a repertory season of new plays at the Duke of York's Theatre which included *Justice* (with a marvellous performance by Dennis Eadie as the original Falder), Shaw's *Misalliance* and Granville Barker's *The Madras House* among others, the whole undertaking was rescued from financial disaster by a revival of *Trelawny of the Wells* (with Sybil Thorndyke in an obscure minimus role) which alone played to anything like decent houses.

The old style play died hard; it was quite a while before it began to give place to the new. It continued to provide excellent over-material for a whole host of gifted and popular over-actors and over-actresses. Its characters were nearly always drawn from High Society or from the upper-middle-classes and the dramatist found a profitable line of business in what was known as the 'society problem play' (should the wife endanger her honour in order to prevent the husband from getting to see that letter?). Of the many plays which held me spellbound during that period, when I was about nineteen or twenty, one stands out above all others in my recollection. This was Alfred Sutro's *The Walls of Jericho* – a good example of how the dramatisation of life could, if dramatic enough, sweep aside incongruities and leave them unheeded or even unnoticed. Moreover it created a novel and genuine sensation (that oft-abused term) in going one better than the problem play and launching a virulent attack upon High Society itself.

The 'smart set', the cream of Edwardian society, whose denizens were wont to patronise the theatre in full evening dress and at ten shillings and sixpence a stall, suddenly found themselves denounced in the most scathing terms. How delightfully provocative. The smart set flocked to the slaughter like so many unblenching aristocrats in their tumbrils.

A rough diamond, Jack Frobisher, who had won for himself the nickname of 'Fighting Jack' (Mr Arthur Bourchier), having made a vast fortune in his native Queensland, comes to settle in the West End of London and marries the daughter of a Marquis, she being as ornate a smart settite as a vast fortune from Queensland can buy. (Miss Violet Vanbrugh.) The villain, Mr Harry Dallas, a young man about Society, does not get beyond making some rather tentative advances to her before his evil intentions become known to Fighting Jack. Fighting Jack exhibits surprisingly dignified restraint. He merely rings for the butler, 'Her ladyship will not be at home to Mr Dallas in future' but he subsequently delivers a long and bombastic denunciation of the wife and of the nauseating corruptions of the smart set in general.

All very dramatic, so dramatic indeed that the fact that Fighting Jack from the backwoods of Queensland was played by the orotund Mr Bourchier in his natural Old Etonian and Varsity urbanity of manner and without a trace of an Australian accent passed over the heads of critics and audiences alike. The phraseology supplied to him by Sutro, even in his tirade, emanated from Mayfair rather than from the bush. The nearest that Fighting Jack was allowed to appear in his true colours was in his final fling, always calculated to cause a flutter of trepidation among the hair-do's in the stalls; 'To hell with all this. You are my wife and not my mistress.' Poor Lady Alethea Frobisher did not get much chance of staying the flow; but her one protest was also in keeping with the stage dialogue of the Sutro period: 'You exaggerate grossly.'

I am not trying to debunk or to ridicule this and other plays of this same 1905 vintage nor myself and my fellow playgoers for delighting in them. Playwrights definitely catered for audiences who expected and wanted to be entertained by a race of small giants expressing themselves in dialogue of incredible flair and fluency. They didn't *want* real life; they wanted to get out of it for a couple of hours, to be stimulated or excited or to burst their waistcoat buttons in laughing, as the case might be. Some of the earlier specimens of the representation-of-life-play made them feel that they might as well have spent the evening at home wading through the family photograph album.

I saw *The Walls of Jericho* four times. I made a habit of paying two, three or four visits to plays which appealed to me. The gaffes only occur to one's mind when one reviews those old shows in the critical light of the present day. And oh, what splendid shows a lot of them were, gaffes and all.

Suddenly, unpredictably, the sun burst through the gloom of the City. I was rescued from the toils of commerce. I could heave my remaining parcels of sultana samples into the willing embrace of the City police and escape.

O. F. Odell was a gay, Irish chartered accountant. In Singapore he used to come into our office and perform the job of what was known as doing the books. He had first won my affection by telling that stinking manager that my enormity in mutilating the pineapple ledger didn't really matter a damn.

Now back in London, O. F. Odell listened to my tale of woe, took me to a Fleet Street pub and introduced me to W. Teignmouth Shore, a well-established freelance journalist who may be remembered as editor of some of the Hodge *Famous Trials* series and looked exactly like the accepted image of Pickwick. That very evening, an hour or two after he first met me, this splendid little man sat down and wrote a letter about me which wrought the miracle.

A few days later I was summoned to the Bodley Head, Vigo Street, for an interview with John Lane, who was by that time firmly established as the most individual and progressive publisher in the business. I don't think I shone very brightly at the interview but Lane must have spotted me as a likely candidate for apprenticeship. This, in my case, meant that my father had to fork out three hundred pounds in a lump sum in ready cash and that Lane paid me a salary, starting at a pound a week, which would just about work this preliminary payment off in the course of three years; in other words that old Lane would obtain my services, such as they were, for three years at a total cost to himself of nothing net.

I felt rather guilty (which is more than John Lane ever did) that, at the age of twenty-five, I had to rely on my long-suffering father not only to stump up what was in those days quite a lot of money to start me off again from scratch, but to pay for my entire keep for years ahead. But there was never the smallest sign of resentment on his part. Anything that brought me such new and tremendous happiness meant happiness almost as great to him; such was his affection.

He was duly compensated as he deserved. He lived to see me established as a successful playwright and found even greater reward when

34

my younger brother, Frank, joined the old firm and turned out to be as eminent a star-turn as I had been a flop. Eventually Frank became not only Chairman of the Company but, for the allotted term of three years, Chairman of the London Chamber of Commerce. My father had become Chairman of the Company in due course and my nephew, Roderick, Frank's son, later carried on the tradition. Commercial proficiency evidently runs in the family. Thank heaven it has given me a miss.

I joined the firm of John Lane, The Bodley Head, within a few days of my twenty-fifth birthday. Twenty-five years of late-Victorian boyhood and Edwardian young-manhood – if my memory tries to recall some of the personalities and topics of those twenty-five years an odd potpourri of random reminiscence comes to mind, regardless of values or selection or chronology:

'The Siege of Sydney Street', which I actually witnessed, with Winston Churchill, then Home Secretary, conducting operations from the cover of a doorway, wearing a funny hat.

An Australian lady, named Miss Annie Luker, diving in flaming sackcloth into a small tank from the roof of the old London Aquarium.

The London Hippodrome when it was indeed a hippodrome, half theatre and half circus, and its resident clown, Marceline.

And Dreyfus and German bands and ladies' cycling bloomers and halfpenny buns and D. L. A. Jephson, the Surrey lob-bowler.

And Phil May, the black-and-white artist, and Gibson Girls and the 'By the Way' column in the Globe and the smash-hit song, *The Honeysuckle and the Bee*.

And the Hon. John Collier's annual problem picture in the Royal Academy and Chappell's Ballad Concerts and early telephones with little handles which impatient male subscribers whirled like infuriated organ-grinders.

And George R. Sims and Sousa's Band and guttapercha golf-balls and the Dartmoor Shepherd, and the sweeping, precocious advent of F. E. Smith.

And penny-farthing bicycles and Talbot Baines Reed's books for boys (*The Cock-House at Fellsgarth*, etc.) and Selous (explorer) and Spurgeon (preacher) and the novels of H. Seton Merriman (*The Sowers*, etc.).

And the delectable series of musical comedy shows run simultaneously over the years by George Edwardes at Daly's and the Gaiety Theatres starring, at Daly's Evie Green, Hadyn Coffin, Huntley Wright, Ethel Irving, Gracie Leigh and Rutland Barrington; and, at the Gaiety, George Grossmith junior, Edmund Payne, Connie Ediss and Gertie Millar; lyrics at both theatres, by Adrian Ross, musical numbers by Lionel Monckton. I knew every number of every show by heart. Incidentally, Marie Tempest declined to play the title role in *San Toy*, because it would have necessitated her to appear wearing Chinese knickers.

But of all the characters who figured at the latter end of that quarter of a century the gold-medallist was the little anonymous man who walked down the highway carrying a red flag. Oh, nothing to do with Socialism: the little man with the red flag was there to warn the general public that at some distance behind him plonked the prototype of the horseless carriage, the earliest type of motor-car. It was he who unwittingly (and barracked by small boys) heralded that sudden unforeseen transformation in the conventions and motivations and destinies of the whole human race. He heralded the first glimmer of the dawn of Speed.

3

When I want to recapture (as I can) the newly-found interest and pleasure which were my twenty-fifth birthday present from Providence I find myself sitting in railway carriages. On my way to the City of mornings I had hated the sight of every station en route as being one step nearer the dismal day before me, especially London Bridge, the last short stepping-stone to Cannon Street. I cherished the coming of November, with its inevitable supply of mornings wrapped in fog, the long stationary stoppages and progress in brief jerks ahead as the train neared London. Now, O, superior and less-stopping train, bound for the heart of the delectable West End, hoot and hurtle ahead, propelling your passengers into soccer shoulder-charges at the bends in the track ('sorry; not my fault' to a male; 'I beg your pardon – really, this train——' to a female) – your destination was in easy reach of the Bodley Head, Vigo Street.

There the prospects of the day's occupation were so alluring that I once volunteered to spend a Bank Holiday on the premises to carry out some trivial but useful job and luxuriate alone amid shelves of books and manuscripts of would-be books, a blissful contrast to boxes of currants and packets of sultanas.

Not that this knocked the bottom out of my genuine ambition. I never for a moment settled for 'all right then, I'm going to become a publisher' instead of 'I'm going to become a playwright'. On the contrary, I felt encouraged; I was now at least an inhabitant of the literary world, however insignificant a specimen. My father had moved house and I was living with him in a delightful residence, Mole Cottage, Westhumble, across the road from the foot of Box Hill, where, up until a year before our arrival, George Meredith used to ramble around in his knickerbockers. In the privacy of my Mole Cottage bedroom I began to spend night after night into the small hours at my writing-table, struggling to begin a play. It never materialised; the night's work was invariably futile. Never mind, I'd make a fresh start on the play next night or better still scrap the whole idea and begin again on another play on entirely different lines. At least I was learning what has always been to me the first essential, to be immensely self-critical. I can't think of any play I have ever completed which hasn't been written at least three or four times. My Mole Cottage wastepaper-basket was the first of many wastepaper-baskets, including my present wastepaper-basket, destined to be filled with reams and reams and reams of rejections and revisions.

Fortunately for me the three years which I spent at the Bodley Head were during a notable period in the annals of literature – the H. G. Wells, Arnold Bennett, G. K. Chesterton era. I pick on the three leading authors whom I actually came across and who were just about the top-rankers at that time. John Lane had published the first efforts of both Wells and Bennett and some of the earlier prodigies of Chesterton. There was a Bodley Head legend about G.K.C. which sheds a pleasing light upon his singular personality.

Late one evening his massive figure stood outside the locked doors of the Bodley Head. Clad in his habitual flowing cape he must have completely overspread the narrow Vigo Street pavement. One can picture him puzzled rather than annoyed by the obstinacy of the door-handle and searching, in quick peering movements of the pince-nez beneath his vast canopy of a hat, to find the bell.

As it happened, Mr Harris, the accountant, was in a little room on the first floor, seated on an office stool and muttering over figures. Hearing the bell, he descended, unlocked the front door and confronted the formidable visitor. Chesterton carried a black Gladstone bag and from this he had already removed a set of proofs. As the door opened he offered this to Mr Harris.

'I have brought my corrected proofs,' he said in that near-falsetto tone which always seemed to emanate surprisingly from so gargantuan a frame. 'But I seem to have done so rather late in the day.'

'Oh, yes, sir,' replied Mr Harris, a rueful type of individual with an unkempt sandy beard and spaniel eyes. 'The office staff have all gone long ago. I'm just the accountant, you see. But if you care to leave the proofs with me I'll see they're handed to the right quarter.'

Chesterton presented him with the proofs. 'Thank you very much,' he said. 'I am greatly obliged to you for your courtesy. In fact, I would like to give a practical demonstration of my gratitude.' He drew a bottle from the Gladstone bag as he spoke. 'Will you join me in a glass of port?'

'Oh, thank you very much, sir,' said Harris, 'but I'm afraid I can't do that. The fact is I'm a teetotaller.'

'Good heavens,' explained Chesterton, the unnatural falsetto rising to a top note of horror. 'Give me back my proofs.'

In the course of my three years with the Bodley Head, most of the active literary celebrities of the period passed through the narrow outer office to and from John Lane's little private room, before my eyes uplifted in privileged curiosity. But the thumping personality of Chesterton looms up before any other when I look back to those Bodley Head days. He wasn't a frequent visitor and I myself only met him once or twice; but if I couldn't call myself an acquaintance of his I was, like many others, an eager devotee. He differed in a characteristic way from other celebrated wits who had preceded him, the Whistlers and Wildes and W. S. Gilberts. They produced comment and repartee in brilliant and often caustic flashes of inspiration. Chesterton always appeared to me to be like a large and leisurely and genial cook who kept the whimsical point of view and the quaint simile always on the simmer and ready to bubble over at the appropriate moment.

Once, during a conversation with him, a friend of mine made use of the adjective 'good' in a loose colloquial way – so-and-so was a good authority or such-and-such was a good policy. Chesterton disagreed, but expressed his disagreement with his customary moderation. 'Good? A word so freely used to mean such different things. If a man shoots his mother-in-law he is not necessarily a good man. But nobody can deny that he is a good shot.'

I once heard him speak in a debate on a favourite topic of his, the party system. His opponent was a young Irish peer who was gifted with the gab but who clouded the issue by a rambling diatribe on the parliamentary procedures in various European countries. Chesterton protested meekly. 'I am sorry to have made a foolish mistake; but when I was invited to discuss the party system I am afraid I assumed this to mean the party system in vogue in this country. After all, when a man says to you "Let's all go down the Strand", you do not leap to the conclusion that he means the strand of the Euphrates.'

John Lane was probably the most enterprising man in the history of publishing. But his enterprise had none of the spirit of adventure which one associates with enterprise in any physical sense. If taking a risk gave him a certain glee it was not because success would bring him a personal satisfaction, but rather the satisfaction that something which he knew to be good should receive its just reward. His soft voice and slow smile gave little evidence of his spirit of wild enthusiasm and impulse in the discovery and exploitation of talent and innovation. His head reader, Frederic Chapman, used to say that Lane had a sixth sense which enabled him to discern merit in a derelict manuscript or in some original and revolutionary project without himself ever reading a page or investigating a detail. He hated detail. The whole of his career as a publisher was one continuous flair.

He was short and jaunty with a neat grey beard which looked as though it ought to have been worn above a ruff. He had a perceptible west-country burr and a weakness of the eyes which tended to make them weep as he talked to you. This mild affliction only lent kindliness to his expression but many of his authors must have accused him of shedding crocodile tears and I certainly don't blame them. Most writers had to fend for themselves in those days, and in any case the very mention of a literary agent sent Lane hopping with indignation. I think that authors of first novels received a pretty good hiding from most of the other publishers, but John Lane remunerated them with scorpions.

The result was that some authors – H. G. Wells had been one of them and Arnold Bennett another – once Lane had brought their proficiency to light, had had no hesitation, nor, I suspect, the smallest qualm of conscience in breaking with him. During my years with him I met both Wells and Bennett in his company. Bennett, who was one of my fellow guests at a luncheon-party at Lane's house, only uttered one sentence throughout the meal, being obviously offended by the loquacity of some confident foreign gentleman who was another of the guests. The conversation turned to an anonymous article which had been published that morning in *The Daily Telegraph* and there was some speculation as to who had written it. Mrs Lane, an exuberant American hostess (and a fairly wealthy one too; I suspect old John had married her for that reason), thought this a good opportunity for wooing her disgruntled guest of honour. 'Perhaps you wrote it, Mr Bennett,' she said ingratiatingly. Bennett, in that remarkable voice of his which put one in mind of the sound of tyres on the road when somebody has suddenly jammed on the brake, made reply. 'I don't even read *The Daily Telegraph*,' he said and relapsed into silence.

By the time I joined the Bodley Head in 1911 the flair had been in operation for some twenty years. Some of its early products, such as the *Yellow Book* and Oscar Wilde's *Salome*, with illustrations by Aubrey Beardsley, had stirred the placid waters of the literary world of the nineties into a maelstrom of delicious consternation. When the Wilde scandal broke in 1895 one of Lane's office-boys figured in the charges. Lane found it essential to fulfil an urgent business mission in America during the turmoil.

But you could always find a reasonable and generally a worthy motive for anything John Lane did, however egregious. It is an interesting comment on his character to add that you always wanted to. It is an even more interesting comment to add that whether you wanted to or not he would always have expected you to.

The Bodley Head premises were – and remain – unique in being almost the only section of Albany ever to have been appropriated by commerce. How Lane had originally managed to effect this act of refined spoliation I don't know; but I suppose some impressionable authority had been successfully subjected to the burr and the pathetic eye-moisture at the critical moment. By the time I found my way into it the whole place was like an intellectual rabbit warren. But to me the hugger-mugger squash and inconvenience seemed part of my newly-found intimacy with happiness. It seemed as though the less room there was to move about in the more closely was I embraced by the buoyant spirit of delight I had at last found in my working hours. I loved every moment of it.

William J. Locke was a frequent visitor and I don't know whether his books (*The Beloved Vagabond*, etc.) are read nowadays but he was then one of the most popular novelists in the country and easily Lane's best seller. Perhaps in Locke's case shrewdness tortured Lane into an unwonted generosity in making terms; perhaps Locke's sense of rectitude prevailed. If this was reflected in his manners it was probably so, for he was, I think, the most courteous man I have ever known. In any case, he stuck to Lane, and I was told that Lane paid the whole of the Bodley Head expenses out of what he made out of Locke, which considering the salaries Lane paid was not unlikely.

Locke's urbanity was an exception to the general rule. The artistic temperament was a fashionable propensity and was freely exploited by those who possessed it and adopted by many who did not. William Watson, the poet, eventually knighted, was one of the genuine possessors. Shortly before I joined the staff, the Bodley Head had been the scene of one of his more dramatic displays of the temperament. Some unrevealed offence in connection with the publication or reception of one of his poems had been attributed by Watson to negligence on the part of Lane. He called to protest, swinging in from Vigo Street and taking up an intimidating stance in the midst of the outer office – a Titan of a poet in size and aspect. I can imagine Frank Baker, the bespectacled office-boy, rising from his stool with his air of take-'em-for-granted impassivity which never varied in the reception of any visitor from Thomas Hardy to a printer's tout. But Watson ignored Frank Baker and remained for a moment or two, erect and quivering. Then his eagle eye fastened on one of the chairs in which the less urgent visitors were wont to await their summons. He took a step towards the chair, seized it and raised it aloft. Then crash – fragments of chair flew in various directions in the midst of the already congested office. And Watson strode out again without having uttered a word.

The incident has always endeared Watson to me. There was a general popular theory in those days that if a man were a poet he was more or less lunatic.

One morning another poet arrived. I jumped to my feet and edged my way through the furniture to receive him with an alert 'bags-I' enthusiasm. His entrance had none of the Watsonian impetuosity;

he seemed to drift from Vigo Street into the Bodley Head as though from one portion of a dream to another. Nor, apart from his somnambulism, did he bear the appearance of a poet. He had a pallid sturdiness and looked like a bewildered edition of Napoleon Bonaparte. I recognised him at once. To me his importance was as a great man of the theatre. He had written a succession of plays beginning with *Paolo and Francesca* which had caused him to be hailed as the greatest blank verse dramatist since Shakespeare. (Well, there hasn't been much competition has there?) He was Stephen Phillips. Beerbohm Tree had found in those Phillips' dramas rich material for the gigantic prodigalities of production so dear to his heart and to the heart of the public; while the mellifluous empurpled period rolled delectably from the tongue. In the latest production, *Nero*, a speech describing the character of Poppeia had been originally allotted to the slave, Acte, played by Dorothea Baird; but the concluding lines so appealed to Tree that he removed them from their setting and appropriated them for his own Nero. They may be quoted as typical of the Stephen Phillips euphony:

> Yet fairer none has come into this world,
> Nor wandered with more witchery through the air,
> Since she who drew the dreaming keels of Greece
> After her over the Ionian foam.

Alas, poor Phillips – forgotten I suppose today; at any rate never produced and seldom mentioned. He outlived his popularity for a few years before he passed, still no doubt somnambulating inquiringly, into the beyond, though his final play *The Sin of David* was one of my favourite H. B. Irving productions. It was always an open secret that he sought even greater inspiration from Bacchus than from Calliope. He left five pounds and a lasting memory of the pleasure he had given me and many others.

During part of my second summer at the Bodley Head, London groaned and reeked with one of those rare and prodigious heat-waves which drive the statisticians to consult past records. I don't suppose I should remember this had it not coincided with the arrival, on a visit to this country, of Stephen Leacock. A year or so previously the *Spectator*, in a moment of exceptional but commendable levity, had published a contribution, written in an original and spontaneous vein of humour and called *My Financial Career*. Chapman had pounced on this article, discovered its author to be Professor of Political Economy at McGill University and inspired Lane to send off a cable to Canada, offering to publish this and a collection of similar articles in book form.

By the time of his visit, *Literary Lapses* and *Nonsense Novels* were on the market and Leacock was a great favourite with us at the office even before he arrived. Unlike other authors he treated us with a ready and jolly sociability, standing and sucking his pipe and rallying us with his impressions of London. His exterior was rugged and bear-like and he seemed to think that if Nature had endowed him with a crop of errant hair and a ginger moustache it was Nature's job to look after them. He was ill-prepared for a heat-wave. He wore a coarse serge suit and cumbersome brown boots typical, at that time, of the Dominions on tour in England. One day he came lunging in to the office from one of his stalking tours in the blazing sun outside. I think I have never seen a man in a state of such dilapidation from heat. The sweat poured from his face and had long reduced his stiff white collar to pulp. He stood mopping himself vainly with a red handkerchief, then swung round at me in an outburst of ferocious denunciation.

'Listen,' he said. 'I have just been around to your Piccadilly Circus; and stuck up there I see a notice "Gentlemen – Hot and Cold Lavatories". What shape should a man be in to need a hot lavatory?'

During the following year Lane took me to New York where he had a branch office. Leacock was there at the time and seemed to welcome my company on some of his stalking expeditions. He was a dogmatic man; he not only held strong convictions but was always ready to crack you over the head with them. Not that my head offered him much of a target. Humour was always uppermost in Leacock's mind and I often got the impression that he was trenchant and intolerant in his assertions and denunciations chiefly because he got so much pleasure out of ending it all in a chuckle.

He used to write to me occasionally. In reply to a letter in which I extolled an article he had written in appreciation of O. Henry:

Talking of O. Henry I met in N'York the other day a man who had known him and he told me that O. Henry
  (a) drank all the time, not part of it but all of it,
  (b) couldn't live with his wife,
  (c) probably took the money from the bank at Austin, for which
he went, as you know, to jail for 3 years.
But I don't care if he did. He was a great writer and a fine man.

In direct contrast to Lane's tendency to be parsimonious in the terms he inflicted on the tenderfoot novelist, was his insistence that every book he published, whatever its size, shape or content, should be turned out in the best popular style. Either in private libraries, where these still exist, or in the remainder shelves of Charing Cross Road, veteran Bodley Head publications can be identified at a glance by the elegance of their format and finish. And when the flair suddenly animated him with the idea of publishing a series of his

43

English translations of the works of Anatole France, his habitual economy was, for once, thrown to the winds. He produced a sumptuous edition of demy-octavo volumes at seven and sixpence each. I don't suppose that, even in those days, better first-hand value for money was ever offered to the book world.

This opinion does not seem to have been shared. On 10 April 1956 ten of these volumes were sold at Sotheby's for a total sum of £1.

But the general public had by this time become aware of Anatole France as one who must be sufficiently eminent in his own country to warrant attention in ours; and his decision to pay a visit to London was treated as an event of national importance. I think I am right in saying that Lane instigated the visit, though in the result it didn't matter much whether he did or not, because he certainly forestalled and appropriated all the kudos for it.

My impression of Anatole France throughout that visit was that from the first he tried nobly to disguise his regret for having made it. He seemed to be steeling himself patiently and politely to endure an ordeal of unutterable boredom. I imagined the relief with which he would find himself back in his villa, in his dressing-gown and skullcap, rubbing his great nose along the pages of some obscure codex of apocryphal lore and abstractedly accepting the ministrations of his elderly female companion. This lady accompanied him to London and followed doggedly in his shadow wherever he went. We, in the outer office, speculated eagerly on whether she was his wife, mistress, secretary or housekeeper. Her homely appearance and mute docility seemed essentially to suggest the last. The only certainty was that, whatever her functions, she wasn't his interpreter.

For the last night of Anatole France's visit Lane organised a dinner which assumed the proportions of a sort of literary state banquet. It was held at the Savoy Hotel and all authors who, in Lane's estimation, qualified for the honour were invited to come and pay at least a sufficient amount of tribute to the master to cover the cost of their meal. A few of the leading lights found they had previous engagements – some of them perhaps harboured a protracted if entirely one-sided antipathy to Lane – but it was a fairly representative gathering.

Having negotiated the primary arrangements and issued his list of distinguished starters, Lane, as usual, declined to be bothered with detail; and I was made responsible for the appalling job of arranging the seating plan for the various members of the congregation in order of precedence – Lane insisted on this. To be called upon to rank, in order of precedence, an imposing muster of contemporary authors of both sexes and of divers ages was about the most thankless, and indeed menacing, task imaginable and totally unrewarding. Add to which, Lane was certain to get belated, spur-of-the-moment notions about promotions and relegations he thought advisable or judicious, and would mess up the whole completed plan, probably after it had gone to press. Which, of course, he did.

Moreover, my allocations had to observe a tactful segregation of husbands, lovers, wives, mistresses, ex-wives, ex-mistresses, discarded spouses and co-respondents. It was the most formidable job of its kind that I've ever been called upon to do. Anatole France, inspired alike by the assurance that the end of his visit was in sight and by the plump and motionless proximity of his vegetative lady, rose and delivered a long and animated oration. I remember only his opening line, but perhaps that is because it was the only one I understood: '*Je ne sais pas que je ne rêve.*'

I never lost my first feeling of almost incredulous jubilation at being at the Bodley Head. But this was due, in part, to the Bodley Head being where it was. I can still feel the exhilaration with which I would step out of the office into Burlington Gardens and walk across Bond Street into Albemarle Street to spend my luncheon hour at the Public Schools Club, of which I was an original member. It always delighted me to realise that it was all part and parcel of my job to be situated here, in the heart of the West End, with all the delectable air of expansive Edwardian luxury which still clung to it; to know that I belonged to it and that it belonged to me.

I dare say some people may consider it incongruous that anybody should have been animated in this way by the surroundings when one views them today. Perhaps only those of my own generation (and sentimentalists at that) will appreciate my youthful exuberance. The Albany itself and Burlington House still present much of their sedate tranquillity to the pandemonium of a modernised Piccadilly, like two very old members blinking in stolid abstraction through their club windows at the extraordinary procedures of a changed world. Burlington Arcade, too, with its gay little shops tinkling with allurement as of old, still fills my nostrils with the nostalgic redolence of patchouli. Even Bond Street still seems to possess a portion of the spirit of my sumptuous days. Then the motor-car and the electric carriage had only recently arrived to challenge the brougham and the hansom cab for the right of way. Even now Bond Street suggests to my mind an aristocratic dowager (opposite number to the two old club members) preserving her spirit of dignity and nursing her poor worn-out old complexion among a charabanc-load of trippers.

In those its palmy days, what glorious and uplifting contrast it all was to the grim and greasy surroundings of Billingsgate. In the City everyone I had ever met had been elbowing his way through the day in the hustling contentions of trade. Here the whole of my working hours were spent in a realm of elegant hedonism. To this day my memories of the City are encompassed by an impenetrable

45

greenish murk; my memories of my three years with John Lane in Vigo Street are never out of the sunlight.

The Bond Street I knew then was the Bond Street where, only a few years earlier, the pony driven by A. E. Matthews had shied, throwing that promising young actor from his gig, which necessitated his carrying his broken arm in a sling when he appeared as the midshipman son of Aubrey Smith and Ellen Terry in J. M. Barrie's *Alice-sit-by-the-Fire*; the Bond Street which had been the beat on which a young Metropolitan policeman named Tom Walls enjoyed his preliminary experience of night duty.

Party politics (Liberal versus Conservative) were the subject of discussion and controversy to a far greater extent than ever before or since. They automatically cropped up as the natural and preliminary topic at every social function, at every dinner-table, in every railway carriage, in every barber's shop. Only some momentous event such as the sinking of the *Titanic*, or some really abnormal freak of the weather or some outstanding atrocity on the part of the suffragettes could temporarily supplant the rival policies of Free Trade and Tariff Reform or the question of Home Rule for Ireland as the universal, anticipated ingredients of conversation.

Although he never lost an opportunity of showing off his fervour for the Liberal cause Lane was not the man to let political bias interfere with a good bargain. No Conservative writer of the day was a better party marksman than H. H. Munro (Saki). Without going out of his way to lug a political allusion into his beautifully polished *Morning Post* stories he could release a brilliant occasional arrow of satire at the Asquith government and its ministers. But Lane, puckering his beard in forbearance, appreciated Saki and encouraged and exploited him for all he was worth.

I have asked the *Oxford Dictionary* what is meant by 'a wit' and I am told 'a person with the capacity for making brilliant observations in an amusing way', which is a fair description of Munro at a time when, it is interesting to note, Noël Coward, as a late-teenager, was one of his most fervent admirers.

Lane suffered from that ailment so common among the elderly, of being unable to remember people's names. This particularly applied to the names of authors, except for the chosen and familiar few. He had a quite automatic and unaffected habit of referring to authors by the titles of their books, but since he was often unable to remember the book-title either there were frequent occasions when the individual to be discussed had to be established by a process of deduction and elimination, in the course of which he would show increasing impatience with himself for his own lack of concentration, and even more with me for my stupidity in being unable to guess the name of the person he wanted to talk about. But on the whole

46

he was a good deal better at the book-titles than the authors' names. While we were in America he took a trip to Montreal and from the University Club in that city I received a letter from him which began:

'*Dear Ben,*
    '*I have lunched here with Leacock and I am to dine here with him and the husband of the Red Lantern tonight – tomorrow I dine at the Red Lanterns'.*'

I was with Lane for exactly three years before I went off in 1914 to serve in the war. I said that Teignmouth Shore's letter of introduction to Lane altered the course of my existence. It did. It is true that those three years were the whole of my experience in the publishing trade. Nor was my later career as a writer materially influenced by any of the Bodley Head authors; I had learned more in a few weeks from Pinero than in my three years of publishing. And at the time it was quite understood that I should return to the Bodley Head after the war, but destiny had other ideas.

My father was by now living, as I have said, at Mole Cottage, Westhumble, along with my brother and myself – in the circumstances which the fairly prosperous business man could quite comfortably afford. This meant that it was a spacious house with a billiard-room and a three-or-four-acre garden and a domestic staff consisting of a butler, Old King, and of butler's cook-wife and the cook-wife's housekeeper sister and two maids and a whole-time gardener and a chauffeur who drove an early specimen of Straker Squire car and had a letch on the prettier of the two maids, and I didn't blame him.

Old King was one of the now-vanished race of butlers, born to the job. Only once did his dignity forsake him and that in a moment of exusable excitement. He dashed into my bedroom early one morning crying wildly, 'Hairship . . . hairship.' I scrambled grumpily from bed and set eyes for the first time on an aeroplane. It was, of course, of the most primitive box-kite type and was staggering over the garden at a height of about one hundred and fifty feet.

I looked at it dispassionately. Interesting, yes – any phenomenon is interesting: but even such advanced prodigies of science and mechanics could never become any active concern of mine. I just wasn't made that way. I'd never even tried to learn how to drive the Straker Squire car. I thanked Old King rather curtly I'm afraid and went back to bed.

About a couple of years later I was, myself, a pilot – Flight-sub-Lieutenant B. Travers, Royal Naval Air Service – earnestly striving, as I had never striven before, to survive and succeed. I survived and succeeded. But it was all due to sheer persistent application – aptitude and ability both had to be strenuously acquired. Nobody less 'a natural for the job' can ever have qualified to become an air pilot.

Even in 1915 when I was flying my first single-seater box-kite around over my birthplace, Hendon, I had never yet taken the bother to learn to drive a car.

4

Mr Winston Churchill stood beneath the open cockpit of my aeroplane and looked up at me with the expression of a viva-voce examiner who isn't himself quite sure of the right answers. It was in the last days of May 1915; so he would have been about forty years old. He was First Lord of the Admiralty. Information had reached him that the Germans were about to launch the first Zeppelin airship raid on London. He had come to inspect the one Hendon aircraft which had been finally detailed and equipped to engage the enemy and to admonish its pilot and crew. I was the crew.

It was an exceptionally large and ponderous two-seater biplane known familiarly as the Sopwith gun-bus. It was of the pusher type, having its heavy stationary engine behind the pilot. The observer or gunner sat in front of the pilot and right out in the nose of the machine. So by standing and leaning over I was able to talk quite confidentially to Mr Churchill.

He questioned me about my armament and I exhibited the rifle with which I had been served out for the purpose of shooting down the Zeppelin. I didn't tell him that I had never handled a rifle in my life and hadn't the slightest idea how to reload it. He asked me whether it was conjectured that a rifle would prove an adequate weapon for shooting down Zeppelins. I leant a trifle farther over my cockpit and lowered my voice.

'It's got incendiary bullets, sir,' I said.

'Ah,' said Mr Churchill in a tone which seemed to imply that this settled the whole problem. He must have realised the pitiable inadequacy of the entire outfit but here was nothing in his demeanour calculated to dampen my zeal and optimism. On the contrary, as though satisfied with all he had seen and heard he changed the subject to ask after my cousin, Jim Travers, who was a pioneer of flying and with whom he himself had taken the air in a characteristic spirit of adventure.

There was less chance of my knocking out a Zeppelin than there was of my knocking out Muhammad Ali today. I don't suppose for a moment that this was in any way Mr Churchill's fault. He had, no doubt, taken office to find that, so far as the Royal Naval Air

Service was concerned, the preparations to meet the impending air attack on London were typified by the figure I must have presented to him, as I stood brandishing my rifle in the nose of the Sopwith gun-bus.

But the nod of encouragement Mr Churchill gave me also typified his strength of purpose in inspiring confidence at home and, with any luck, in intimidating the enemy. It had been openly stated that if a Zeppelin ventured to invade our skies it would fly into a nest of hornets. A small deputation of MPs had visited Hendon and had been shown a row of box-kite training machines, lined up in weather-bound and oil-stained dilapidation, some of them incapable of soaring beyond the few feet required for taking-off and landing practice. But the ordinary citizen knew nothing of types and performances. An aeroplane was an aeroplane. The MPs had gone away with winks and whispers of sage reassurance. It was true enough. The hornets were there. They'd seen them for themselves.

Flight-Lieutenant Douglas Barnes, my senior officer, was a big, slow, charming character of about my own age, which was eight or nine years above the age of most of the volunteers accepted for flying duties in the RNAS. He was invariably referred to and addressed as 'Auntie', a tribute to the benignity of his nature. He and I had been left at Hendon during a transition period in which our training squadron was being transferred to the neighbouring and affiliated station at Chingford. The authorities had recently selected and established the latter site as being ideal for training purposes, it being a strip of fogbound and soggy meadowland at Ponders End, situated between a reservoir and a sewage farm.

Auntie Barnes undoubtedly saved my life by exercising his authority as senior officer at Hendon. It had been originally laid on that in the anti-Zepp operations I should pilot a Caudron biplane, accompanied presumably by some ill-fated air-mechanic who was to crouch close behind me and direct a stream of incendiary bullets either through or just to one side of my shoulder. But I had never flown after dark and Auntie declared my Caudron unfit for flying. It wasn't; but no doubt he well knew it would have been very soon after my take-off; to say nothing of how unfit I and the wretched air-mechanic would have been. Grounded from my Caudron I compromised by persuading Auntie Barnes to cast me for the role of gunner in his Sopwith – and there I was, all made-up and accoutred, just in time for Mr Churchill.

It was late on the night of 31 May 1915, and darkness had set in when our signal came from the Admiralty by telephone 'Stand by and await further orders'. We stood by and awaited. The Zeppelin chugged its way to a destination somewhere over Victoria Station where it dropped a bomb or two and chugged away again, maintaining throughout a height of about 10,000 feet. Chingford duly received its further orders and some half-dozen pilots and their riflemen took off in a variety of training aircraft. One of them relied even on his box-kite and had to confine himself to a protracted series of furious circuits round and round the roofs of the Chingford huts.

At Hendon I waited with Auntie and eyed the silent telephone, conscious of a gradual evaporation of my urgent lust for battle. On the aerodrome miscellaneous air-mechanics made well-intentioned but ineffective efforts to illumine the ground for our take-off with acetylene searchlights which all spluttered out and contributed only an execrable stink. At length Auntie made bold to go to the telephone and prompt the hesitant Admiralty. 'What?' came the reply. 'Haven't you gone up yet? Go up forthwith.' I later ascertained that by this time the Zeppelin was well on its homeward journey somewhere over the North Sea.

I don't know how long we were in the air. I don't know at what height we cruised, peering in conscientious ineptitude through the mist. I suppose the gun-bus may have been encouraged by slow degrees to attain a ceiling of a sulky 5,000 feet. Eventually Auntie decided on a forced landing and nose-dived into a field at Hatfield. I had the presence of mind to slip out of my safety-belt on the way down and was shot like a stone from a catapult ahead of the wreckage.

It may seem strange and reprehensible that I can look back at the tragedy of that night with a light heart. Perhaps it is because my memory still hears the echo of the laughter and gaiety which inspired us all through our struggles with the risks and inexperience of those days. And, after all, if, when memory comes to rest on some old friend of the past, one's first instinct is to laugh, what more genuine proof can there be of one's affection?

Moreover, I myself went through the most ludicrous performance on regaining consciousness; one which should, I think, be briefly reported if only to show how odd may be the immediate effects of concussion. Perhaps the oddest feature of it all is that I have remembered many of the details so clearly, though only half my brain was functioning at the time. This half of my intelligence bade me first investigate what had taken place in the midst of the shattered gun-bus and struggled to release Auntie Barnes from the wreckage in his dying moments. Then for some time I was obsessed by a spiritual sense of duty in the tragic circumstances. This was quite as it should be, but my observances took the form of walking round and round in widening circles and singing a variety of hymns. Presently I found a stile and after gazing at it suspiciously for a minute or so I clambered with difficulty through the hedge alongside it. I found a cottage and my rambling soliloquies were heard by the inmates of the bedroom above. The husband naturally contented himself with sitting up in bed and shouting some terse and testy comments on whichever of his drunken neighbours was at it again. Fortunately the wife favoured more practical and energetic measures. She rose, pulled up the window and looked out, pausing no doubt on the way to arm herself with the water-jug.

She went and got hold of Mr Smith-Bingham who lived close by. He came and propped me up as we reeled along to his house. I was muttering all the time, 'I must telephone; I must telephone.' 'You shall telephone,' he said – I remember the quiet reassurance in his tone and exactly the position I sat in when I flopped into a chair in his study and every syllable that was said, and yet by this time I was hanging desperately on to the last shred of consciousness.

'Now – who d'you want to telephone to?'

'I can't remember.'

He asked to be put through to the Admiralty. 'Now, what's your name?'

'Barnes,' I said.

'Barnes. And what's the name of the other poor chap – the one we went and saw out there?'

'Travers.'

That was my last word for twenty-four hours or more. I didn't remain officially dead for long. Smith-Bingham must have seen the name-tabs on my clothes when he put me to bed and telephoned the Admiralty again. He and his wife put me up in their house until I was convalescent.

Some who are elderly enough to possess memories of those days may maintain that the administration and equipment of the RNAS were not so bad as this implies. After all, I myself, a few days before Mr Churchill's visit, had urged a Henri Farman biplane to a height of 7,500 feet, to beat the existing Hendon height record. And while I was yet on my three-week sick leave, Warneford actually brought down a Zeppelin in France and gained his VC. Even his achievement would have been forestalled if the bomb dropped by Bigsworth on a previous Zeppelin had hit something solid enough to explode it. So conditions surely couldn't have been as bad as I suggest.

But the fact is that, all through the war, the Army dominated the flying services; and when these were combined into the RAF in 1917, the RNAS was simply merged into the Royal Flying Corps and given military ranks. And this was because many of the senior officers of the senior service were stubbornly and foul-mouthedly shocked by the almost sacrilegious suggestion that these preposterous flying-machines, manned by a levy of lunatic landsmen, could ever aspire to render reinforcement to the Royal Navy. Some of them knew better and, later in the war, Admiral Beatty initiated, or at any rate approved, the formation of a squadron of land-based carrier-borne torpedo aircraft with the rather optimistic idea that they should undertake a surprise attack on the German fleet in Kiel Harbour. But many old sea-dogs, their judgment and tempers methodically undermined by gin, carried their grumbling resentment of the RNAS with them throughout the whole contest and, indeed, to their dying day.

Warneford trained with me at Hendon, a brash character, half, or perhaps wholly, American by birth. His cocksure and boastful nature annoyed us all and fairly infuriated the Naval Officer, Commander Sitwell, who had been transferred from the Fleet to instil service tradition and discipline into our uninitiated civilian understanding. Warneford's final offence was to land one precious training box-kite effectively on to another which was stationary on the aerodrome. He was forthwith dismissed the Station with a strong recommendation that he should be dismissed the Service. Instead, the Admiralty ordered him to France; a decision which, it was generally anticipated, meant only a brief postponement of his farewell to arms. A month or so later he was a national hero.

But I? Many of my associates have wondered what sudden incongruous circumstance – what sudden rush of fevered patriotism, whimsicality or wine to the head – induced the utterly incompatible me to become an air pilot. Some of the more candid have added, 'Even so, how the devil did you manage to remain one?'

It was November 1914. My brother and most of my friends were already in the Army. Why wasn't I? Simply out of conscientious allegiance to Lane. At the outbreak of war, three months earlier, he had once more beetled off to America. He had besought me to remain at the Bodley Head until he got back. He wouldn't be long. Oh, wouldn't he? The months passed. I became every day more conscious of my patriotic impatience and of the eyebrows of some of my father's acquaintances (themselves nicely beyond the age-limit) raised in exasperating unspoken comment. So I just quit, without notice to Lane, who was still maintaining his ostrich-act in America.

But I admit I nursed a certain foreboding. Army training involved, amongst other things, undertaking a continuous series of very long and very strenuous walks, a form of occupation which I had always regarded with the utmost reluctance and still do. Worse, I would frequently be commanded to double. Nor was I confident that I would take kindly to the use of firearms. Some odd little kink in my nervous system had always prompted me to shrink instinctively from firearms, rather in the way that one may shrink instinctively from snakes. I wasn't a coward. I could and would gladly overcome this aversion and brace myself to face the battlefield. It was just that

I deplored the dismal prospect of being taught, rather discourteously, how to get there.

But it was the unavoidable course which lay before me and patriotism reprimanded my qualms. Then, one day, when I was, as usual, lunching at the Public Schools Club, I met one of my fellow-members who was resplendent in a full RN sub-lieutenant's uniform. Full. None of your wiggly RNVR stripes.

'Good Lord,' I said. 'Where did you get that outfit?'

'Gieves,' he replied. 'RNAS. It's easy. They want chaps badly. I'll tell you how to apply.'

I applied, I was accepted. My medical examination held one awful moment when I was bidden to climb up a suspended rope. I waited until the supervisor was looking elsewhere and took a flying leap at the rope, landing over half-way up. The supervisor turned and saw me up there and said, 'All right, that'll do.' I went to Gieves. I walked down Piccadilly, myself in the uniform of a RN sub-lieutenant, varied only by the addition of a small gilt eagle on the left sleeve. I didn't know how even to exchange a Naval salute.

As for the perils of learning to fly – pooh. It wasn't peril I was secretly so anxious to avoid. It was that walking. I had dodged that anyhow. My lack of the first faint glimmer of knowledge of aeronautics dismayed me as little as my abrupt renunciation of Lane. But I must almost certainly have been the first individual who learned to fly an aeroplane before he ever learned to drive a car.

At the age of twenty-eight I found myself back in a classroom, learning logarithms, the theory of flight (I never got within a mile of that one) and navigation from a dug-out Naval Instructor and putting up my hand when I wanted to leave the room. Away flew all the intervening years, in Singapore, in the City, in the Bodley Head. Back came my boyhood with its obsessions and presentiments.

What was I doing here? My companions were hearty youths whose whole outlook and baffling technical conversation showed them to be well equipped for potential airmanship. I could have entertained them with a graphic comparison between the respective style and artistry of Clem Hill and Frank Woolley, or, if they preferred, could have quoted for their benefit the whole of Arthur Bourchier's acting version of *The Merchant of Venice*, with a critical commentary on the side. But they were concerned only with inlet-valve springs and ailerons controlling centrifugal force and Chinese of that sort.

My flying tuition was undertaken by Merriam, a name which will be familiar to collectors of flying memoirs and curios. I drove him nearly frantic. But here again I was handicapped by my inner sense of inadaptability rather than by lack of skill. Eventually Merriam's somewhat uncouth perseverance was rewarded; although, by the time I yanked my spluttering box-kite off the ground single-handed, I had been under instruction for what was then the preposterously lengthy period of two hours and six minutes.

Favoured as I was by an absolutely first-class ignorance of why and how aircraft flew – and consequently unaware of any probable source of disaster – I became an accomplished pilot. When, following my sick-leave, I reported back at Chingford they were on the look-out for instructors. A pilot of six weeks' standing, returning slightly haunted and unnerved by a narrow escape from death in an appalling crash, was held to be obviously the very man for the job. As it turned out I proved to be an outstanding success as an instructor and was retained at Chingford until the spring of 1918.

Ivor Novello, who joined the RNAS in 1915, was one of my pupils. He had just written *Keep the Home Fires Burning* and was welcomed as a promising recruit for the entertainments branch of the Station's activities, as indeed he proved. His first experience of flying entranced him to such an extent that it stimulated him into song. His voice trilled in ecstasy above the less dulcet roar of the engine. But after a few nerve-racking experiences I firmly ruled that, however lofty his artistic aspirations, as a pilot the ground was his limit. To have preserved the life of Ivor Novello at the outset of his career will probably be regarded by some as the one useful war job I ever did.

One morning at the outset of my training at Hendon the attenuated figure of a rather pallid eighteen-year-old trailed his long flying-boots into my company. I scrutinised him with that instinctive antagonism with which human nature is apt to prompt our first impression of any stranger of the same sex. 'They want chaps badly,' my club friend had told me. 'Indeed they must,' I thought.

But his conversation, conducted in a drawling tone in keeping with his stringy appearance, showed perspicacity and an undeniable sense of humour; and, after all, here we were in the midst of a war and it was necessary to associate and co-operate with various freakish assortments of one's fellow-man and I gradually decided very decently, if tentatively, to tolerate this springald youth. A few hours later it was revealed to me that he was the only son of my favourite actor, H. B. Irving. I adjusted my first impressions automatically. Here, surely, was one member of the Hendon party who might be able and willing to steer clear of thrust and dihedrals and centrifugal force and pitot tubes and all that gibberish, and to give me some really worthwhile information on the subjects nearest my heart. He became and remains the greatest male friend I have ever had.

Laurence Irving came back to Chingford from service in France in 1916 with a *Croix de Guerre* and impaired health. That in later years he developed into a man of such hale and striking appearance from the delicate creature he was then is a very good advertisement for something; enthusiasm perhaps. Even then his experiences at the front had not affected his inherent gaiety of spirit. Ivor Novello, now safely seconded to some essential but air-proof duties on the staff, collaborated with us in a revue and wrote some original numbers for it. We performed it at the air-station to the officers and their relations and friends and its success encouraged us to write a Chingford pantomime. But before this could be produced I was posted to East Fortune, not as may be supposed on account of my pantomime script but because Admiral Beatty's forthright plans for discommoding the German fleet were in process of gestation and I was to command one of the squadrons. These exercises in writing at odd moments when I wasn't engaged in teaching people to fly or when the aerodrome was under water or fogbound, as it often was for several days in succession, at least helped to keep the poor derelict old Ambition alive. They were, of course, essentially extravagant and local-topical, but this didn't make them any easier or less profitable as exercises. I still remember the concluding lines of the dismal soliloquy of the pantomime principal boy who had forced-landed in some god-forsaken back of beyond and was bewailing his impending fate:

> Marooned, without a drink, without a friend:
> And doomed, like Ponder, to a filthy end.

In the middle of the war, when air combat had become a regular and ferocious feature of hostilities, someone hit on the bright idea of inventing a parachute for the use of pilots in trouble. I was appointed to carry out some tests of this brainwave. An outsize toy teddy-bear weighted up to about fourteen stone, was strapped beneath the fuselage of a BE2C. A 20-foot coil of rope attached it to a parachute which was designed to open as it left the aeroplane. On the first test I released this elaborate bag of tricks at 1,000 feet. It worked perfectly and the teddy-bear sailed gracefully and without any severe bounce to the ground. I was then requested to repeat the experiment from 500 feet. They rewound and re-strapped the teddy-bear and parachute to the fuselage but they (and, needless to say, I) had failed to take into consideration the fact that the surface of Chingford aerodrome was in its normal state of soaking wetness. The rope had become saturated and although, on the second run, the teddy-bear duly fell out, the parachute refused to budge. I found myself flying around with a fourteen-stone burden swinging twenty feet below me. The only course was to make as slow a landing as possible, so that when the weight of the bear pulled off my under-carriage (as duly happened) I should avoid going over on my nose. It was a very minor disaster as it turned out but, when I sit and

56

watch TV films of operations which congest the skies with whole battalions of descending personnel, to say nothing of their guns, lorries and tanks, I recall with mixed emotions the aboriginal joint efforts of myself and Messrs Hamley. And apparently the teddy-bear put paid to any further wild-cat ideas of using parachutes for the time being – they were never in service during the First World War.

Frederic Weld-Blundell, a distinguished RN torpedo-man, had been transferred to the RAF (as it had now become) to take charge of the projective torpedo operations. I had taught him to fly and it was he who offered me command of one of the two squadrons in slow process of formation. The other squadron was allotted to Conway Pulford, who was destined long afterwards to be the ill-fated Air Vice-Marshal of the RAF in Singapore at the time of the Japanese invasion. Sopwith had designed a special aircraft for the torpedo job, the Cuckoo, probably to this day the largest single-seater machine ever put into service. We used Belhaven sands, near Dunbar, as an aerodrome and made practice runs, aiming at a stationary drifter and gradually working up into formation attacks on a co-operative destroyer steaming full-speed-ahead.

I initiated this enterprise when, on 4 July 1918, I deposited into the Firth of Forth the first torpedo ever to be dropped from a land-based aircraft. I hit the drifter nicely from about 1,000 yards. In a subsequent exercise an outsize wave caught my undercarriage and I was deposited tail upwards in the Firth of Forth. But the impact released the torpedo which made a perfect run and its dummy head biffed into a destroyer amidships. So like me. How odd it seems that so improbable a character as I should have figured in these elementary but portentous affairs.

The armistice mercifully curtailed our preparations but in the early spring of 1919, when I had got over the Spanish 'flu and my almost miraculous escape from succumbing to this ghastly scourge, I was sent on a mission to South Russia. This, I'm afraid, was not because a generous Air Ministry wanted to provide me with a rest cure. We were still – for some obscure reason which I forget now if I ever knew – lending military support to the White Russians against the Red ones. Someone in authority conceived the idea that we might torpedo the Red Russian fleet which was lying iced-up in Astrakhan harbour. The operation was not intended to anticipate a now popular form of entertainment and to be performed on ice; we were to be prepared to strike at the outset of the melting season.

Someone had to go and prepare the way for this nightmare sortie. If only the inspired and pugnacious Air Ministry chieftain had decided, as a preliminary, to consult the nearest geography master he would have ascertained that the Caspian Sea is a lake with a depth of about fifteen feet and was therefore impracticable for the reception of torpedoes. As it was, I was dispatched to spend three dilatory and excessively uncomfortable months of travel.

In the course of this I journeyed from Batum to Baku by the Trans-Caucasian railway in a train which covered some two hundred miles in a week. I was one of a British party recruited from all three services whose dozen members were making the journey impelled by a variety of biddings and motives. They ranged from an RN post-captain to a Scots private in a kilt.

The natives of Azerbaijan were enjoying a private feud with their neighbours of Georgia and our train was held up at the frontier by a hostile gang of Georgians, bristling with fur and firearms, who declined to allow an engine driven by an Azerbaijani to proceed along their territorial track. Our naval captain dealt with the emergency in characteristic style. He sent the Scots private along to the engine accompanied by a fixed bayonet and an interpreter. The interpreter was told to reassure the engine-driver that the Scots private would protect him from molestation; the Scots private was told that if we did not forthwith get up steam and blind ahead he was to give the engine-driver himself a good prod up the backside with the bayonet. We proceeded.

I eventually got home and issued to the Air Ministry my strictly confidential report on the depth of the Caspian Sea. I had been set several other questions as well. One, I recall, was 'What was the surface condition of Tiflis Aerodrome when you saw it?' the answer being 'I didn't. It was under eight feet of snow.'

My homeward journey brought me the second of two peculiarly eerie experiences which came my way during my war and post-war days with the RAF. This second one was on my homeward journey soon after my Trans-Caucasian train had jerked its laborious way into the first of its unpredicatable number of nights out. The RAF people in Baku had managed to get me installed in a specially-reserved and disinfected railway carriage and I was sitting in contented isolation when the train came to a halt – not one of its constant temporary halts with the engine alive and hissing but what appeared to be an exhausted, permanent halt. This impression was confirmed when the lights went out and I was left in complete darkness. Nothing could be seen on either side of the track except vast mountains of snow. I felt as if I had been lowered into a deep well and left there. The train must have collapsed somewhere just outside a wayside station because suddenly a posse of Russian soldiers marooned on its platform broke into song. They sang beautifully some tuneful chorus number, a performance comparable to that of a trained Russian male choir singing *The Volga Boat Song*. It was a glorious, awesome sound, half comforting, half menacing, as I sat there in eclipsed and snowbound vacuity. I forget what happened – the engine recovered with the dawn or they found another one or something; anyhow we proceeded on our spasmodic way to the comparative civilisation of Batum. Eerie experience number two.

Eerie experience number one was towards the end of my long spell at Chingford. A fellow-instructor had a crash and was killed. He and his wife were billeted at the same hotel as my wife and myself. His wife was in London shopping and my poor wife was given the job of breaking the news to her when she got back. She asked for her husband's sister to be told and to be brought down from London. I was appointed to motor to London to inform and convey the sister.

There was warning of a Zeppelin raid that night and the blackout regulations obliged householders in London to turn all their lights out for a while. I arrived during the while and was shown by a skivvy into a pitch-dark study. I stood in a state of rather nervous apprehension, trying to invent and rehearse my sympathetic opening to the invisible sister when a mongoose sprang from the top of a bookcase and landed on my shoulder. My heart stopped for what seemed like ten seconds. People shouldn't keep tame mongooses on the top of bookcases in air-raid blackouts. It wasn't made any better by the sister appearing to think that the catastrophe to her brother was all my fault. Quite excusably. Anger is often naturally one jump ahead of a sudden shock of sorrow.

I got demobilised. I closed my fifth and final Pilot's Flying Log Book with a hearty snap. Compared with that of hundreds of other pilots my war record was a very modest one; for one thing I had never, thank heaven, been called upon to engage in aerial combat. I had survived only eight crashes. But I had made 3,523 flights as pilot and had averaged three-quarters of an hour in the air for every day of the war. At the end of it all I found my sentiments towards aviation to be almost exactly the same as they had been on that early morning, some years before, when Old King had come panting into my bedroom with his precipitant 'Hairship . . . Hairship.'

Throughout the war I received many favours from Fortune or, as I prefer to believe, from Providence; but one of them was boundless and everlasting. Like my friendship with Laurence Irving this favour received a very lukewarm initial reception. At Chingford on Sunday afternoons accredited visitors were allowed to come and be shown round the place, but I could never be bothered with them. One day a lady and her daughter turned up to bring us news, which they had somehow or other received, of an ex-Chingford officer who had gone abroad and was a prisoner-of-war. It was a thoughtful action on their part, but when I, on the strength of having known the officer in question, was told off to greet and escort them I protested in brief, futile soliloquy and went to do so cursing my luck.

At the first moment of our meeting I uncursed it. By the time I had recruited some lounging nonentity to deal with the mother and had walked twenty yards with the daughter I was busily blessing it. We were married on 29 April 1916. If, as I honestly believe, I have spent a happier life than anybody else I know, that is the reason. The romance had one or two memorable features. As the result of that Chingford afternoon visit I was invited pretty readily to spend my next evening's leave with mother and daughter at their home in Elm Park Gardens (Father was doing some utterly futile regimental staff work somewhere in the north of England). I spent the evening with daughter – mother remained tactfully at home while we went to the pictures. By the time the picture, whatever it was, faded out we were engaged. We had only been alone together for an hour and a quarter, a pretty slick performance in those days.

I was duly summoned to interview Father who temporarily relieved his regimental staff of his presence for the purpose, though I don't suppose the staff noticed. I got on all right with him and he gave his consent on condition that the marriage didn't take place until after the war. Daughter, with a fine display of high spirits, said to hell with that, we were going to get married as soon as possible. The scene ended abruptly with Father in a tantrum leaving to go and spend the night with his mistress at the house he had bought for her in the rather improbable locality of Wyndham Street, Marylebone. But he soon relented – perhaps the outcome of the night soothed the tantrums. Anyhow, the marriage duly took place.

Father, having relented, did us proud. It is interesting, in view of the problems and miseries we endured during the Second World War, that there was no rationing at the time of my wedding during the First. The reception displayed all the traditional slap-up features of the normal pre-war wedding reception. Afterwards my wife and I drove to the Savoy Hotel, where I had booked, at the immense price of fifteen pounds for the night, a bed-sitter-bathroom suite which was usually reserved for the accommodation of Indian princes and the like. We dined (here's where the non-rationing comes in) on plovers' eggs, duck, asparagus and strawberries-and-cream. We then proceeded to a stage-box at the Gaiety Theatre and attended *Tonight's the Night* (Leslie Henson made his first West End hit in it). Next day we lunched at Prince's in Piccadilly, then the poshest of luncheon restaurants. After lunch we went by car to my newly-acquired billet at the Roebuck Hotel, Buckhurst Hill, and I was flying at dawn on Monday. A rare honeymoon.

'I am giving up,' said John Lane. 'I am turning the Bodley Head into a private limited company. Now – I will make you an offer.'

A brief pregnant pause. The lymphatic smile dwelt upon me with genuine warmth of affection. I wondered what the offer would be. From what I knew of him the old boy wouldn't be likely to be giving very much more than up.

The offer came. My father was to perform another modest exercise in stumping up to augment the capital of the private limited company. I was to work for the firm. I couldn't, of course, hope to participate in any profits but I would be paid a salary of five hundred pounds a year.

'My dear boy,' said my father when I told him about it, 'I can't possibly afford to raise ten thousand pounds.'

My father-in-law, Daniel Burton Mouncey, was a dapper, well-dressed, highly-coloured, sharp-tempered little man who possessed private means sufficient to enable him to live in comfort without having to earn his living. This was fortunate because I don't think he could have. Every hour of his life was regulated by a punctilious timetable, devised to enable him to spend each completely profitless day to his satisfaction. In London his daily programme never varied. He would proceed in his top hat and tail coat to his club, where he would read *The Times* and eat his lunch, before taking a taxi to join his mistress in Wyndham Street. My mother-in-law did not contribute much brain-power to the ordering of the methodical ménage, but she was the soul of good nature and enjoyed being laughed at, which always made her very easy for me to get along with.

It had been my father-in-law's pre-war custom to spend the late summer months, accompanied by his wife and daughter, at Burnham-on-Sea, in Somerset, where, to a strictly prescribed routine, he would associate with its disused residents and thrash its celebrated links.

I was now, of course, out of a job and circumstances seemed to recommend my finding one pretty quickly. Still, I had a handsome war gratuity and some savings. 'First of all,' I said, 'I mean to have a go at writing.' 'All right,' said my wife. 'Let's go to Burnham while you have it.' My wife (an only child) had become attached to Burnham as the result of these prolonged annual visits, and we had been there together on a week's leave during the war. We now rented a small furnished house there; but it can't have been so very small, for it accommodated us two, my one-year-old daughter and her nanny, a cook-general and, for many delectable weeks, Laurence Irving.

Under his influence the go at writing took a preliminary excursion into an exciting but unexplored line of country. Motion pictures, belonging to what are now referred to as 'the old silent days', were by this time so universal a form of entertainment that they had reached even Burnham. Laurence Irving was so obsessed with them

61

that he easily persuaded me to collaborate with him in writing a film script. All I can remember about it is that it was sternly and solemnly dramatic in theme, that it bore the title of *Priests' Land*, that it had something to do with an unfortunate priory house which had managed to land itself with a curse in the days of Henry VIII's abolition of the monasteries, and that its harrowing proceedings were presided over by a forbidding priest named Sarpax. I don't think the script ever got beyond our sitting-room until one day we decided to submit to the judgment of Laurence Irving's good-natured mother, Dorothea Baird.

She did me the first of two very good turns. 'For goodness' sake,' she wrote back to her son, 'tell your friend Ben to try his hand at something funny. I'm sure it's more in his line and there's always a much better market for it.'

But so long as Laurence Irving was staying with us the pictures were the thing. We used regularly to attend the abandoned shop which had been converted into The Majestic Cinema and sit gloating in an indescribable fug while the red-headed daughter of the manager accompanied the films on a piano. One particularly spectacular picture of the *Quo Vadis* species animated Laurence Irving's gift as a cartoonist. He depicted two lions leaving the Roman arena. One of them, wearing a very wry expression on his face, was turning to his partner and inquiring apprehensively: 'Did you notice anything queer about that last Christian?'

I had met Mrs H. B. Irving several times during and just after the war. Her extraordinary experience of having emerged practically from the schoolroom to create the part of Trilby and her long stage career which followed had left her the most untheatrical person imaginable. She was gentle and gracious, as, indeed, are a few other successful actresses, and I don't believe she had any great love for the profession. Later on I used to try to get her to come to one of my first nights, and she said she would for my sake; but she asked me to let her back out of it at the last moment. She said the environment of a first night made her feel physically sick.

She and my wife had been the only two feminine members of the audience at a memorable special performance of *The Bells* which H.B. had given to the troops in war-time and which marked the stage début of his daughter Elizabeth, Laurence's sister, who later married Sir Felix Brunner. Elizabeth Brunner has always presented a problem. Is she more beautiful in looks than she is kind at heart or the other way about? I think the only solution is that it's a dead heat.

The preliminary stage of my beneficial friendship with the Irving family was rounded off by my being taken with my wife to visit H.B. in his house at Harrow. There he was, sitting and talking to me, primate of all the high priests who had for so many years performed the rites while I had sat, an obscure little worshipper, embedded in the pit. I felt like Anatole France – *'je ne sais pas que je ne rêve'*. I was to experience this same queer sensation of incredulity on every occasion when I found myself for the first time in the company of others of the high priests – Hawtrey, Maude, du Maurier. They materialised into a still half-fantastic reality from the treasured mystery of my boyhood.

H. B. Irving died in early middle age and I was to meet him only a few times. I remember on this first occasion his asking me what impressions I had formed on my trip to South Russia.

I said, 'It's all very cold and uncomfortable. The food and living conditions are shocking. The country is crowded out with all manner of people of all nations and with nondescript refugees belonging to none. Their habits are indescribably dirty and their dispositions are most unreliable. You can never be sure whether anyone is your friend or foe.'

'H'm,' said H.B. 'It sounds very like England.'

Laurence Irving married soon after this and our friendship with him became duplicated. I have now known him for well over sixty years and to me his friendship grows a more valuable and dependable possession the older it gets.

'Something funny,' Mrs H.B. had said. A farce then, obviously. I had never envisaged myself as farce-writer but after all Pinero himself had explored and civilised that line of country before he discovered *The Second Mrs Tanqueray*. Moreover, I was under the delusion still shared by many people that farce was the easiest sort of play to write. I was soon to find out, and to continue finding out, that no form of stage entertainment is more difficult successfully to write, to produce or to act.

Anyhow, I knew the formula for farce – and here I was right enough. Act 2 – the sympathetic and guileless hero is landed into the thick of some grievous dilemma or adversity. Act 1 – he gets into it. Act 3 – he gets out of it. Right. Then what type of hero? Why not aim high? It was prodigious odds against my getting Charles Hawtrey even to consider my first and as yet unwritten farce, but he gave me a definite type to work on. And the particular form of adversity or dilemma? Suppose I myself were suddenly called upon to face up to some novel, topical, social obligation? Wasn't there one which would strike me as being peculiarly nightmarish?

Ballroom dancing of the sort known as 'specialty', originated by Vernon and Irene Castle and featured by their many proselytes after Castle's death in the war, was all the rage. What about a Mrs Vernon Castle, suddenly let down by her normal opposite number and roping in a kind and susceptible gentleman who undertakes to act as her partner before he realises what he is getting himself in for? Not bad for Hawtrey. The setting could be a county ball, given by an inflated, titled war-profiteer (another topicality). Once committed, the hero would, of course, remain loyal to the lady, engage in altercations with the host and in bewildered argument with the leader of the 'coon' band (popular coloured bands were always referred to as coon bands at this time). And no sooner has he scored in a comedy variation of the specialty dance than he is exposed by the belated arrival of the genuine husband. And is not his fiancée an unforeseen member of the house party?

I set to work. Pinero gave me my construction: the good old standard text-book still held good. But the West End theatre had become thoroughly du Mauriered by this time and there must be none of the Pinero grandiloquence. I started as I always went on all through my farce writing, making the characters recognisable types of human beings. The funniness must be in the situations and circumstances in which these human beings find themselves, and these are only funny because the characters are so recognisably human.

I finished my first edition of the farce. I didn't think it was bad but I funked the issue. A sort of lack of bounce and the sensitive apprehension of having my own feelings hurt, which were always lurking in my nature as the result of the timorous littleness of my boyhood, made me shrink from the prospect of having the ambition blighted in its first youth. But it seemed a pity to waste the material. What about writing it up as a novel? John Lane would probably be prepared to show a certain amount of indulgence in my case. So I wrote it as a novel, called *The Dippers* – the Castle characters in the story were named Hank and Pauline Dipper. And, sure enough, before long I had the curious experience of myself entering from Vigo Street and edging into the still teeming outer office of the Bodley Head to sidle my way through and be interviewed, as a prospective author, by John Lane in the doorway of his congested sanctum.

The private limited company did not seem to have materialised as yet and I wasn't altogether surprised. At any rate, Lane had given up giving up for the time being and was still running the business in exactly the same way. He produced a contract undertaking to publish *The Dippers* and five subsequent novels. That contract ought to be placed, as an historic document, on public exhibit in some appropriate berth, preferably the Black Museum at Scotland Yard. Down payment of a small sum in advance of royalties? Such an outrageous proposal simply did not exist at the time – at any rate in Lane imagination. On the contrary, the author had to forgo any royalties on the first one thousand copies sold, and a pretty meagre return after, as seldom happened, the first one thousand copies were sold at all.

But I signed it without hesitation. At least it meant my official acknowledgement and establishment as a professional author. I confided to Lane that I was toying with the idea of writing a stage farce on the subject of *The Dippers*. He looked at me as though he feared that the favour he had just conferred on me had gone to my head. 'Oh, I wouldn't try to do that,' he replied. I wonder whether he said the same to Agatha Christie, whose first novel he published on the very same day as he published mine. Already, since finishing the novel, I had rewritten the farce, and now another of Laurence Irving's visits spurred, or rather propelled, me to destiny. He put a stop to all my indecision and sent the script off to his mother. Before this happened we had temporarily left Burnham. My prolonged struggle with *The Dippers* had used up my war bonus and I decided that the time had come for me to get a regular job. *The Dippers* and others could continue their inconclusive antics, but this would have to be in my spare time. The trouble was that, at this juncture, it was nearly as difficult to find a decent regular job as it was to place a first farce. I scoured the publishing trade in vain and eventually had to agree to try my hand at the only available job, which consisted of touting a series of unwieldy and voluminous *Records of Varsity Sport* on commission. We took a small furnished house at Hayes in Kent while I endured this undignified occupation and my wife brought forth our elder son, Benjamin the Eighth.

One morning, some months after this event and early in the year 1921, I was in my bath before setting forth to fail to sell some *Records of Varsity Sport*. I heard my wife in conversation on the telephone below, and presently she paused to call excitedly up to me. 'It's about the play,' she cried. 'It's about the play.'

Like Archimedes in his moment of supreme enlightenment, I leapt from the bath. Unlike Archimedes, I stopped to wrap myself in a towel before dashing forth from the bathroom. By the time I reached her my wife had finished the telephoning and was on her way to bring me the news.

Who had been on the telephone but the invaluable Laurence Irving. But what had happened, what had happened? Just this.

Laurence had sent the script of *The Dippers* play to his mother. She had off-loaded it onto the leading play-agent in London, Golding Bright. Golding Bright, discerning in it potentialities for Hawtrey, had sent the script to Hawtrey. Hawtrey had read the farce and had considered it and had approved it. And at length, in due course, he had entered the building in Leicester Square and passed the ground-floor Leicester Galleries, and had mounted the stairs to the first-floor offices which later I was to know so well. And there he had finally clinched the purchase of *The Dippers* by presenting Golding Bright with two post-dated cheques.

The incredible had come to pass. My first farce – written for Charles Hawtrey – accepted by Charles Hawtrey. I swung the bath-towel round my shoulders with a sweep of triumph and embraced my wife. At length – at long length – I released her. And then I turned and shook hands with Pinero.

5

I soon proved myself to be about as good at selling *Records of Varsity Sport* as I had been at selling sultanas. I gave it up and spent all my time at Hayes writing. I tried my hand at some ready-money stuff, short articles and stories. A kindly editor, a friend of a friend of my father's, published a few in *The Referee* and *The Star* took four or five short stories but what gave me my greatest kick was the acceptance of my first attempt at a contribution to *Punch*. This was the one period in its history when, in its old traditional format and dignity, *Punch* was as funny as it used to be. It was in the Owen Seaman days. It was his custom as editor to send letters of acceptance in his own immaculate handwriting. Bernard Partridge was the chief cartoonist, a worthy successor to Tenniel, E. V. Lucas the sub-editor. Of all the regular contributors my favourite was A. A. Milne. Later he established himself as a classic writer as the author of *Winnie the Pooh* and those delightfully jingling children's rhymes. (I wrote a parody of them once, beginning: 'Winnie did a widdle in the middle of her pinafore') and he had great success as a comedy writer – no doubt Mr Pim still passes by the wings of Rep and Amateur productions. But I still think he shone at his brightest in those *Punch* articles. I revelled in them.

Destiny keeps some queer cards up her sleeve. Twelve years later I was to be sitting with Alan Milne watching a Test Match at Trent Bridge. I remember a characteristic comment he made to me, 'The sound of Hobbs' bat puts me in mind of vintage port.'

The Dippers novel was published and bought by so few people that I still wonder who they were. I expect my father surreptitiously accounted for a fair proportion of them. My father-in-law read it and expressed himself agreeably surprised. The surprise was mutual because his scrupulous design for living cannot have left him with much spare time for reading novels, especially during his afternoons. I am glad he made the effort because it was one of the last things he did. Early in 1921 this engaging character departed to his well-rehearsed rest.

This news of the acceptance by Hawtrey of *The Dippers* farce, this sudden heaven-sent windfall, meant more to us than a boost to my hopes as an author. Ever since we had left Burnham both my wife and I had nursed a longing to get back there. There are moments of memory that dwell in the heart rather than in the brain. One of mine is the expression on my wife's face as she spoke her first words after giving me the telephone message, 'Oh, back to Burnham.'

Burnham, Somerset, 1920. The local authorities whoever *they* were, tried to insist upon the place being labelled Burnham-on-Sea and the label has stuck. It is a rather pretentious misnomer because although situated on the shores of the Bristol Channel the town is often out of sight of the sea. It must be literally moonstruck, for at low-tides it becomes Burnham on a stretch of mud extending with a faint outline of sea on the far horizon. Not of sand, mud.

Nevertheless, Burnham has always claimed its right to regard itself as a seaside resort and as such remained, during the years we lived there, year after year, as an established and delectable flop. (It has now, since the innovation of motorways, become a featureless satellite residential area for people who work in Bridgwater, Taunton and Bristol.)

But back to 1920: failure has a strange fascination when it relapses into a state of stay-put, make-the-best-of-it resignation and contentment. We had become devoted to Burnham because it was so delightfully and comfortably wrong. Anything aggressively or permanently right would have been wrong for Burnham.

It had in those days a railway-station, the terminus of the Somerset and Dorset Railway which ran via Evercreech and Templecombe to Bournemouth. One of the small hotels situated on the mud-front ran a horse-drawn bus service which called for the passengers, if any, who wanted to travel by the one morning train. The bus was driven by an agreeable giant almost as large as his horse. He had a cheerful disregard for the timetable and was perpetually late for the train. The train-driver, never knowing whether he was coming along or no, didn't wait for him; unless the train-driver was late in getting to the train himself which was also often the case. I remember waiting agonisingly for the bus to call and pick me up (I am a fanatic about punctuality) and reprimanding the driver rather tersely when at last he turned up, 'Get a move on for God's sake; we're late for the train already.' 'Laate? No. Coople o'minutes maybe. Who caares for a coople o'minutes?'

Once jerked from the Burnham terminus the Somerset and Dorset Railway endorsed and amplified this contempt for the passage of time. My mother-in-law was at this time residing, like so many other people's mothers-in-law, at Bournemouth. I went to spend a day or two with her and was lucky enough to catch the morning train from Burnham. The journey involved a change at Templecombe and a wait there of forty minutes for a connection. Our progress to Templecombe became more and more laborious and intermittent. Outside one wayside station we came to a prolonged halt and I leaned out of the window to investigate. I found that the local station-hand and our guard were trying to drive a flock of hens from the line: a tiresome job, there was always one last misguided wrong-way screeching scuttler. But having at length passed by or over the scuttler we laboured still and the wait at Templecombe had dwindled from forty minutes to five minutes when at a further wayside stop I challenged the guard: 'Look here – we're going to make this connection, aren't we?' The guard gave me a confidential snigger. 'Wull, we missed 'er yusterday and we missed 'er day afore. And if we miss 'er now thut'll be three days running and thut'll be a reccud.'

And what about this as an example of the peculiar wrongness which made Burnham so appealing? A parishioner died expressing in his Will his desire to be buried at sea. This was optimistic on the part of a Burnhamite, but he was in luck because the freak tides were running exceptionally high just then, before ebbing as usual into miles of mud. So the vicar consented to accompany a couple of mutes and the coffin in a rowing-boat to a reasonable distance from the shore. But the sea was uncommonly rough that day and the vicar was seasick on and off during his administration of the funeral rites. The mutes, deciding to cut it short I suspect, hoisted the coffin and deposited it overboard. But the damn fools had forgotten to punch any holes in the coffin and it floated away, breasting the billows, with the boatman rowing desperately in pursuit. A vicar was not the most appreciative audience for what the boatman had to say, but perhaps the vicar was being too seasick to protest. They eventually overtook the coffin and the exasperated rower vented his feelings upon it with his boat-hook.

Even if we had known that for the next twenty-five years a great proportion of my time would have to be spent in London, we'd still have settled for Burnham. Where could the home be more ideal than in a place trailing the rest of urban England and a good lap and a half behind London itself? The fact that Burnham was a lasting joke simply established it as the lighter side of lasting contentment and happiness.

Reginald Golding Bright was a short pudgy man who looked like a peaceful bull-terrier. He was never perturbed. He had to deal with all manner of eccentric authors and vehement impresarios and did so with unruffled practice chain-smoking dispassion. He was secretive; he might confirm or deny information or rumour but he would never tell you what was going on until it had gone. It was this habit of his in the course of his dealing with *The Dippers* which was to bring me such resentment that I temporarily forsook his counsel; but I soon found myself back in his office and he received me with a bland amiability which seemed not merely to ignore my fit of pique but to be totally unaware that I had had one.

He was agent for nearly all the leading dramatists of his time; but it was not because he played so important a part in my own career that my thoughts of him always bring me an affectionate chuckle. Every first night discovered him in his stall and, by the time the play was halfway through, in an unvarying attitude, with his hands, encased in white washleather gloves, propping up his silver-knobbed cane, his chin resting on the knob and his eyes closed in apparent, and often genuine, slumber.

He enjoyed being a *bon viveur*, but in a strictly intimate fashion – one never seems to have heard of Golding Bright being at a party. He also delighted in exercising what he thought was his skill as a punter; though I suspect that his judgment in spotting likely winners was limited to plays. He had some remarkable theatrical treasures – once in his flat he showed me Barrie's original prompt-script of *Peter Pan*, with marginal comments and instructions as to how it should be produced and acted; and an eight- or ten-page letter written in red pencil on pages apparently torn from a child's exercise book, in which George Bernard Shaw implored the recognition and patronage which would promote him to success in the commercial theatre.

But my most impressive memory of that visit was gained by a glance into Golding Bright's bedroom. There is something engaging about a man whose bedside reading consists of only two volumes – the Holy Bible and *Ruff's Guide to the Turf*.

On my second visit to Bright's office I met Charles Hawtrey. He seemed to have stepped off the stage into the room and to be playing one of his usual characters: courtly, suave and complimentary. He congratulated me upon the farce. It was admirably conceived and well written. Indeed, he adjudged it to be quite perfect for his purpose. All that was required now was for it to be thoroughly and almost totally revised.

My memory is vague about the number of revisions I made and submitted to Charles Hawtrey in the course of the next few months. But I remember he arranged that I should be invited to meet him one Sunday at a luncheon-party given by Lord and Lady Tichborne at their house in the Thames Valley. I was to bring the first of the revised versions with me and Hawtrey and I could discuss it together after the meal. It was an extraordinary party with about a dozen guests so diverse that they might have been invited by lottery. They ranged from Hawtrey and Pouishnoff, the pianist, to Sammy Woods who was still at that time living on the reputation he had earned in past years as an outstanding Anglo-Australian cricketer. I had got to know Woods quite well at Burnham; he once caddied for me on a round of golf, his remuneration being a bottle of whisky. It was perhaps fortunate for him that modesty was not a game. He monopolised the conversation during luncheon with reminiscences of his prowess in two of the pastimes which had contributed to his fame, namely cricket and drinking, which he always referred to as 'lotion'. At the end of it all Pouishnoff was roused to challenge and in a tone of defiance to which his slightly foreign accent seemed to lend additional emphasis he cried, 'Mr Woods. In this cricket, no; I cannot compete with you. But please to take notice that I am willing to join issue with you at any time in the matter of this lotion.'

I suspect that Charles Hawtrey had been giving himself a quiet try-out as a potential rival to Sammy Woods in the course of the luncheon. At any rate, when he and I withdrew and he read through *The Dippers* again, he sat and laughed until the tears literally ran down his face. But more revisions were evidently called for. In a letter to me dated 4 May (1921) he wrote from the Playhouse, where he was appearing in *Up in Mabel's Room:*

'I am delighted to get your letter. I hope to read your new version this week'

which surely must relate to yet another revision from that which was the subject of another letter, written at the Orleans Club, Friday, whenever Friday was:

'If you get this in time will you look round at 37 Hertford St. to-morrow, Saturday? I have just got your new version and shall read it tonight.'

Eventually, however, a final pre-production new version was achieved and agreed.

Then suddenly one morning I had tidings of the Ambition's immediate prospects. My eye fell upon a headline in the paper:

Mr Charles Hawtrey for the Criterion

Ah. And then:

Mr Charles Hawtrey will shortly appear at the Criterion Theatre under the management of Mr T. C. Dagnall in a new comedy by Mr Walter Hackett, entitled *Ambrose Applejohn's Adventure.'*

Of course, it goes without saying that Golding Bright should have told me. But, as I have said, it was against Golding Bright's principles to tell anybody anything. I might have felt a little less aggrieved about it if Golding Bright hadn't been Walter Hackett's agent too, besides being the close friend and adviser of Mr T. C. Dagnall. I am not saying for a moment that they were not right to pick on *Ambrose Applejohn's Adventure* in preference to my farce or any other farce on the market at that time. It gave Hawtrey one of the best parts he ever had. That didn't alter the fact that every line and inflexion and reaction that I had written was perfect Hawtrey too. But there it was; and after *Ambrose Applejohn* had been running triumphantly for a month or two I was asked to call and see Hawtrey in his dressing-room. I went very despondently, knowing what was coming. He was going to relinquish his option on *The Dippers*.

I might have known Hawtrey better. Relinquish his option? When he's paid for it – with his heart's blood – with earnings hopefully to be filched from beneath the very noses of the bookmakers – to meet the two post-dated cheques? No indeed. But what Hawtrey could do was to *sell* his option on *The Dippers*. And had done so. It had all been most cordially arranged. Golding Bright, sitting pretty with the Hackett farce doing roaring business but saddled with *The Dippers* to sell for Hawtrey, had shrewdly sold *The Dippers* to Mr T. C. Dagnall as well. Mr T. C. Dagnall was looking for a new farce for Cyril Maude. So there it was. What could be better? To judge by Hawtrey's demeanour, cordial was an utterly inadequate word for the arrangement.

I knew I was still tremendously lucky – my first farce still definitely accepted, still definitely going into production. But it meant giving up what I had set my heart on – and not only my heart, my whole imagination and purpose. Every line, mannerism, glance had been devised for Charles Hawtrey, to say nothing of my devotions to the task and new versions and the glory of having had the last of them accomplished and approved and blessed. Even the two post-dated cheques had by now been duly honoured.

I stood in the dressing-room rather disillusioned and dubious. Hawtrey for the first time became a little testy with me. Clad, not inappropriately, in full pirate's rig, he spread his hands at me emphatically.

'Think, my dear fellow, think. Here am I – for another year or more – not a hope of doing your play, I'm afraid; not a hope. But Cyril Maude – an excellent fellow – and very popular – who better? And Mr Dagnall has agreed to buy the play from me. He wants to make it a condition that I shall produce it.' He sighed, as though he found this prospect a tedious obligation and the little matter of a producer's fee had not even crossed his mind. 'Oh, very well, I suppose if he wants me to – I *will* produce it. There. What more do you want?'

So it came about that one Monday morning in February 1922 I was again summoned to the Criterion Theatre – this time to attend the first rehearsal. I arrived late on purpose, being too self-conscious to face preliminary introductions and discussions. I found my way through the stage-door, down narrow stairs and along ominously silent inhospitable subterranean corridors (the Criterion Theatre decor is still not unlike that of a Gents' public lavatory), feeling rather like a lone passenger in the Ghost Train at a fair. I discovered the stage and halted, peering nervously from the wings.

The rehearsal had not yet started. The company was standing about in scattered little groups of twos and threes, engaged in subdued gossip. Seated in an upright chair mid-stage was Charles Hawtrey, shrouded in a heavy overcoat and a Homburg hat. Horn-rimmed glasses, resting almost on the tip of his nose, were bent over my script on his knees. A massive red pencil was in his hand and was methodically employed in scoring line after line of dialogue from the pages.

A sudden wave of resentment overcame my shyness. I advanced and inspected. On what passage of the play was the monstrous pencil at work? Yes – I might have guessed – one of my best scenes – and there it was going piecemeal – out – out.

This was too much. I had been belittled and ignored and treated as a cat's-paw for the Hawtrey–Bright machinations and had submitted pliantly. But at least the play had been there, completed and finally approved for them to do their surreptitious deals with. And here was Charles Hawtrey's endorsement of the completion and approval – in red pencil. So much for all his enthusiasm and delight and congratulations, my dear fellow. So much for the tears of laughter after the Tichborne lotion and fervid receptions of new versions from up in Mabel's room and from the Orleans Club Friday. I took a step nearer.

He didn't see me; he was too busy scoring out the dialogue – swish, swish. The next line? M'yes, swish. So naturally the dependent following line went too – swish. Another moment and that devastating pencil was hovering above my favourite line in the whole play – that brilliant riposte which had been chewed over and chuckled over in bathroom soliloquies for so many months past. The pencil duly hovered – struck. Out. A cry of anguish burst from my lips.

'Oh, Mr Hawtrey——'

He glanced up at me over his glasses. His countenance softened in a smile of welcome – 'Oh, there you are, my dear fellow.'

'Mr Hawtrey – that last line. Must that go? I'm sorry, but really I always thought it was – rather a good line.'

He gazed at me. He spoke in a tone of gentle incredulity.

'A good line?' he said, emphasising each syllable. 'A—good—line? My dear boy, it is an *excellent* line. Don't on any account lose it. Put it in another play.'

But whatever was retained or cut, it soon became obvious that the original Hawtrey farce was destined never to materialise. Cyril Maude's stage presence was that of the pathetic, appealing and unimpeachably respectable type which could never invest the part with the Hawtrey qualities of bemusement, blinking doubt about the causes and results of what he was doing and, above all, a subconscious awareness of possible amatory compensation for the same. Hawtrey's was the beloved tradition of the gay deceiver and sympathetic rake. Maude's was the established and incorruptible tradition of the *Flag Lieutenant* and *The Second in Command*. I don't think Maude was really a farce actor at all. I would add that, as leading man, especially in an anxious author's first play, he was a perfect godsend. From first to last he was unfailingly considerate and encouraging.

He maintained, unaggressively, the appearance and manner of the perfect private-life gentlemen in the plebeian off-stage theatre world. Some Green Room Club wag started the rumour that Cyril Maude always changed into his dinner jacket for his evening meal before a show.

The Dippers introduced a little song, whose melody was supposed to be overheard from the ballroom to be picked up and crooned by the leading lady in the preoccupations of her dressing-room. I suggested asking Ivor Novello to supply the tune and was duly sent along to discuss it with him.

Preserved from the carolling indiscretions of airmanship and any subsequent jeopardies of warfare, Ivor Novello had emerged to distinction not only as a composer but as an actor. He was indeed at the outset of a career which was to be outstanding in the history of modern theatre. At this time he was already playing juvenile lead, if only at the Kingsway Theatre and in one of those rather flaccid Anglo-Chinese pastiches of the 'Oh, my chelly-blossom' variety. I called to see him in his dressing-room after a matinée and he was as charming and co-operative as ever and asked me to sit down and write out the lyric of the song. While I was engaged in this the door opened and another very personable stripling of the theatrical world entered to salute his colleague.

I recognised him as the mature edition of a boy actor who had already blossomed forth as the author of a couple of promising light comedies, and as an occasional visitor to the Bodley Head in his Saki researches. His name escaped me for the moment – then, as Ivor Novello introduced me, of course – I knew I hadn't really forgotten it; Noël Coward. They left me to my writing and went into a little huddle of candid and completely genuine mutual admiration.

'You're wonderful Oh, I wish I were as wonderful as you are.'

'Oh, don't be so silly. You're much more wonderful than I am. You're marvellous.'

No matter which character spoke which line. They were both

74

equally sincere and, ah, how right. It amuses me to recall the three of us that afternoon in that poky little dressing-room, all as yet on the threshold of our careers. I myself was going to enjoy a certain distinctive measure of success in the theatre; but just think what the future held for the other two. Destiny must have peeped through the dingy window and lingered for a moment to dwell upon us with a knowledgeable smile.

Meanwhile, rehearsals – and there was Charles Hawtrey seated stolidly every morning on the Criterion stage, with me on the edge of an adjacent chair. He seemed rather bored and listless; I think he knew that the whole thing was doomed now to be a second-best. He groaned and grunted a good deal; though occasionally he perked up to treat me to some ripe aside. I recall Cyril Maude getting what he thought was a bright idea and Hawtrey obviously did not.

'Charles, wouldn't it be funny if I looked at her and said – so and so?'

'Excellent, my dear Cyril. By all means put that in,' said Hawtrey, beaming in approval. And as Maude left his side, Hawtrey turned to me with a poignant whisper: 'Christ'.

Once, when he caught some mumbled protest from my direction, he called a temporary halt to the rehearsal in order to forefinger me in admonition.

'My dear boy. I have been at this game for forty years. And there is one thing I have never finished learning and which I never will finish learning. And that thing is learning. Thank you. Now – come along then – who speaks?'

We had great difficulty in finding the right actress for the principal Irene Castle, or rather Pauline Dipper, part. The lady originally cast and two or three tentative successors had come, read and been defeated. One morning an attractive girl of a particularly dashing type arrived to try her luck. I had no idea who she was but I made a good guess about her favourite line of business; she was obviously a pantomime principal boy.

'What do you think of her?' asked Hawtrey aside to me.

I said, 'I think she would make a very good Dick Whittington. But I'm afraid she is not for us.'

Hawtrey seemed very struck by this judgment. He looked into my face as though he had suddenly discovered there a gleam of unsuspected intelligence. 'Yes,' he murmured, 'yes.'

A moment later the lady found a line in the script which she could really get her teeth into. She swung into an attitude and got them into it. Hawtrey clapped a hand on my knee and exclaimed excitedly, 'Thrice.'

'I beg your pardon?'

'Thrice.'

75

'I don't quite——'

'Thrice. Thrice, my dear fellow. Thrice Lord Mayor.'

A morning or two later a girl came along who not only made the part her own within five minutes but who brought fresh interest and hope to the whole rather bedraggled proceedings. She was Binnie Hale.

Binnie Hale may have inherited some of her talent but she herself has been responsible for most of it. Whatever her material has been she always used it to give the best performance imaginable. Others – Mary Martin in *South Pacific* for example – may have soared to heights which seem beyond the measure of comparison or even of calculation. But Binnie Hale was like the proprietor of some exclusive West End shop offering a wide variety of goods of which every specimen is the best on the market. In private life she has always loved to discard, not without conscious effort, the artificiality of her stage surroundings and to lapse into a natural enjoyment of being the relative-by-adoption of somebody's happy family.

She was just as clever and creative as a young girl as she was later on; and thank goodness she was. *The Dippers* was a moderate success and had a London run of 167 shows. But it was due to Binnie Hale that this, my first play, had any success at all.

Another lady who later achieved great esteem and popularity was in the company – Hermione Gingold. But at this time her gifts were only being employed as a walking-on-cum-understudy character, and her only marked contribution to the production was an occasional caustic estimate of it backstage.

When *The Dippers* novel had been on the market for a month or so, Jerome Kern came across a copy in New York and told the manager of Lane's American branch that he would like to use it as the theme of a musical comedy. The manager, knowing nothing about my aspirations as a playwright, naturally told Kern to go right ahead and cabled the glad tidings to the London office. But by this time the Hawtrey deal had gone through and the New York branch must have been devastated to receive a letter from Golding Bright telling them in the most unctuous terms that they were wasting their time. Whereupon Jerome Kern threw the novel aside (or, more probably, at the head of the New York manager) and there the matter ended.

I suppose I couldn't have it both ways, though I have never quite been able to see why not; but it was a pity. Jerome Kern had already established himself in England, where some of his numbers, beginning with *They'll never believe me*, had been introduced to bolster up some of our musical scores, and from then onwards he has always had my personal vote as the most delicious tune-composer of all the brilliant tune-composers of his time. My first four novels were published in America, but with remarkable non-success; and even later on when William McFee, who liked them, managed to promote a new uniform edition and got Thorne Smith to write a special introduction to one of them, they still fell completely flat. Nor was there ever a single professional performance of any of my plays in the States until late in 1975. An amateur society once produced *Rookery Nook* in Boston, Massachusetts; but the results seem to indicate that the operative word is 'once'.

The first public performance of my first play took place in what, for a farce, was not perhaps a particularly hilarious environment, namely the Theatre Royal, Liverpool, on the Monday of Holy Week. Liverpool tolerated rather than acclaimed the production. I sat with my wife in the stalls and endured the full ordeal, which I have always shunned ever since, of seeing the whole performance through, sensitive to the comments of unwitting neighbours, with my own lips muttering the lines a beat ahead of the actors, like Hamlet in the play scene, and breaking off to engage in frequent, hurried and intense moments of prayer. Later on, at the Aldwych and elsewhere, I always managed to get a box for first nights, so that I could sneak from the side of my unflinching wife in order to avoid any particular scene or episode which seemed likely to result in a foozle and to spend a few moments in consultation with some lurking commissionaire or, if the risk seemed really pressing, with the Almighty.

But the only vivid recollection I have of that Liverpool first night is the memory of my father. Since my dismal showing as a business man he had always been filled with an intense desire that – for my sake, not his – I should achieve a public success that would show the City that I wasn't such a damn fool after all. His anxiety on that first night was greater even than my own, for his hopes and fears had that special poignancy which springs from a parental love. He became almost assertive in his emphatic enjoyment of the farce and in his glances of challenge at any who did not seem to be sharing it. Later when the play was running in London, his pride and affection would bear him to the theatre in this mood of rapturous defiance. I remember sitting with him one night in the front row of the dress circle when, shortly before the play was due to start, a gentleman beside us remarked to his wife, 'H'm. Don't seem to be many people coming to see this.' An audible snort escaped my father. He allowed a minute or so to elapse; then half rose and, leaning over the front of the circle, surveying the stalls below: 'A *packed* house,' he exclaimed almost savagely and sat down again.

The Dippers staggered along to three or four provincial cities. I was too inexperienced to foresee the inevitable and, so far as I was concerned, unheralded arrival upon the scene – which was Brighton,

I think – of the jolly boisterous Sydney Blow, along with his accustomed partner, Douglas Hoare. They had established themselves as the accepted (and royalty-sharing) play-doctors of the period, their favourite patients being new-boy farce-and-comedy writers. Between them they had written several successes and were, no doubt, well qualified to resuscitate an ailing farce. Sydney Blow was, it seems, to perform the energetic and practical part of the job; Douglas Hoare appeared to fulfil rather the duties of bottle-holder and anaesthetist of the medical team. For Blow had been engaged not merely to overhaul the play but to reproduce it. He was a most amiable man; but I was indignant at having been left entirely in the dark about Mr T. C. Dagnall's quite justifiable decision and went speeding in hot haste to London to inform Golding Bright and seek his advice.

Golding Bright, of course, knew all about it beforehand. Hawtrey, who followed me into his office, knew all about it beforehand. I seemed to be the only person who didn't know the first thing about it beforehand. I asked Bright whether I ought to consent and he replied, rather more acidly than was his wont, that all depended on whether I wanted the play brought to the West End. Damped and somewhat despairing, I turned to Hawtrey for support. For he, too, was affected. Apart from what Blow was going to do to my script, he proposed to overhaul Hawtrey's production. What had Hawtrey to say about that?

Hawtrey said nothing about himself. Perhaps he knew that, whatever happened, Mr T. C. Dagnall would judiciously keep 'the play produced by Sir Charles Hawtrey' (he had recently been knighted) in the London programme. But so far as I was concerned his manner, like Bright's, was a trifle terse. 'My dear fellow, your name, as a dramatist, will be remembered long after Sydney Blow has been forgotten.' Did he really mean it? He seemed to. His tone grew more gentle and almost rhapsodical. 'Looking back over the wide vista of the years——'

He broke off with a friendly smile and we parted. I never met him again. Between the first exultant moment of its acceptance and the adequate success of its first night at the Criterion *The Dippers* had brought me a good few disappointments and frustrations, but in one respect it was the most rewarding play I ever wrote. To have known and worked with Charles Hawtrey, at his best moments and at his worst, must remain one of the richest experiences of anybody's lifetime.

I soon became infected with Blow's chortling enthusiasms. He and Hoare made a good job of reconstructing bits of the play while I wrote whatever new dialogue was called for. I had never had any real intention of opposing Mr Dagnall's abrupt ultimatum and it resulted in very few altercations for me to give way about. Binnie Hale made her big hit with the first-night audience at the Criterion and with the critics next morning; and the mangled but still animated *Dippers* had a very respectable reception. So I could afford to forget what might have been and to regard the whole long laborious and tantalising record of the production of my first play with grateful satisfaction. At least it assured me that I possessed two assets of great value to an aspiring playwright – a sense of the theatre and a weak nature.

I wonder how many people nowadays remember the Thompson–Bywaters murder case? I have always longed to know what Mr and Mrs Thompson thought of *The Dippers*. I don't suppose Mr Thompson laughed much at it; for he seems to have been a morose and captious man; but I hope it provided a certain exhilaration for him in the last hour of his life before Bywaters stabbed him on his way home. As for Mrs Thompson, it is obvious that unless she were definitely a party to the actual murder she should never have been executed. So, if the verdict passed upon her had the smallest iota of justification, she must have sat at the Criterion that night putting up a specious and discreet show of carefree merriment in order to conceal her Medea-like broodings over the forthcoming and pre-arranged assassination. What nonsense. It may be self-interest on my part, but I could never understand why the defence completely ignored the incredibility of her gratuitously seeking to face this frightful ordeal, which she must have imposed on herself had she really been a guilty accomplice.

Poor Edith Thompson – it has often intrigued me to reflect upon the association of her tragedy with my farce and I have journeyed specially to Ilford to have a look at the scene of the murder and at the house in which she sat and wrote her preposterous suburban fabrications. Ernest Trimmingham, a coloured disciple of Thespis who performed the extravagant duties of the leader of *The Dippers'* 'coon band', propounded a theory that the Thompson murder resulted in a hoodoo affecting the farce. After it, he declared, business was never so good either on stage or in front. I sometimes wonder whether Edith Thompson ever found cause to reflect on the last play she was ever destined to see and to decide that *The Dippers* had been a bit of a hoodoo to *her*. I hope not.

J. L. Sacks was a remarkable being who had originally issued from some Polish corridor and had found or wheedled his way, via South Africa, to the West End of London, where his transactions as a theatrical impresario remain a legendary joke. They were no joke to me.

He was short and hunched and his lower lip protruded almost to the level of his not inconsiderable nose. He could at least write his name but was reputed to be unable to read English which, however, he spoke with a fluent eccentricity. A blend of acuteness and effrontery soon gained him an impressive position in the musical-comedy world. He must have won the confidence of some of those mysterious men of substance who put up large sums of money to finance musical shows. His projects were exorbitant and in some cases ostensibly very successful. There was a sly, humorous philosophy in number which was appealing even when it was ludicrous and any number of people fell for him. Many of them fell with a wallop and I was one of them.

On one occasion he found himself in such reduced circumstances that he had to resort to a fruit machine in order to raise his railway fare from London to Manchester, where he bought up (with goodness knows whose money) an enormous musical play which subsequently had a long run in the West End. But it was common knowledge that the current state of J. L. Sacks' finances at any given time was somewhat suspect. It certainly must have been so when I encountered him.

He or some beguiled backer had bought the English rights of a comic opera by Franz Lehar. This was to be produced in London by Tom Reynolds, who was Binnie Hale's uncle and an old hand at this sort of game.

In the autumn of 1923, some months after *The Dippers* had surrendered to the hoodoo, Tom Reynolds asked me whether I'd like to have a shot at supplying the English libretto of this opera, *The Three Graces*, for which Sacks had already secured an option on the Empire Theatre. Impulsively I replied of course I would. I rather fancied myself as a librettist and the vision of taking a bow at the dazzling Empire as collaborator with Franz Lehar was, to say the least, exciting.

But there was an unusual feature about the proffered task. There was nothing to serve as a basis for adaptation. The original German libretto had apparently been so unspeakably awful that the opera had either been stillborn or had died in earliest infancy – nobody seemed quite certain which. Never mind – I felt confident I could devise some story to fit the vocal characters and some appropriate words for them to get vocal about in Lehar's numbers.

My enthusiasm was irked by misgivings about the trustworthiness of Mr J. L. Sacks and I told Tom Reynolds I had better consult Golding Bright. Tom Reynolds, who himself possessed something of Golding Bright's habit of thinking more than he said, but in a humorous and philosophical sort of way, said he was afraid that would mean the end of it. He had a presentiment that Golding Bright would not favour my undertaking a commission for Sacks. But he quite agreed that I'd better take due precautions. By this time I was so eager to begin that I was incensed by the very thought of opposition. I recalled to myself my resentment of Bright's secretive manipulation of *The Dippers* and now it exaggerated itself almost to the proportions of a feud. All right then – I was through with Golding Bright anyhow. I'd consult my solicitor and get him to draw up a good stiff contract with Sacks.

My solicitor was one of those solicitors who was my solicitor because his father had been my father's solicitor. He is long dead now and I will not say anything derogatory about him except that I wish he had been dead then. He received my apprehensions with a derisive smile. He knew how to deal with people like Mr Sacks. Leave it to him. And sure enough the good stiff contract was duly drawn up and delivered, bearing J. L. Sacks's outlandish autograph.

I worked away and eventually completed the most difficult and painstaking job I have ever known. I laboured for months inventing a story, writing the play, and scribbling nonsense words to indicate the intricate metre of the required lyrics while an obliging lady thrummed the tunes on an office piano. Presently I inquired of my solicitor whether he had completed his difficult and painstaking job too. He had not. There was no sign of my cheque for advance royalties from Mr Sacks.

I attended rehearsals and watched the promising preliminary efforts of such considerable contemporary performers as Winifred Barnes, Thorpe Bates and Morris Harvey. The leading comedian had been recruited by Sacks from America and appeared somewhat distrait but said he would be all right on the night. Meanwhile whole ranks of immense but symmetrical show ladies posed to order; chorus singers trilled my distinguished lyrics; male and female dancers bounded and twinkled. The American comedian still said he'd be all right on the night and everybody seemed to be going ahead splendidly – with one exception. My solicitor wasn't.

On the day before the show was due to open – cold – at the Empire I called on my solicitor and told him he'd better apply for an injunction. The costumier had just done so and had been paid on the nail. But my solicitor thought it would be as well to give Mr Sacks a last chance. This he gave him in the form of some facetious sarcasm over the telephone. It was all very exasperating, but I decided that it might be well to refrain from taking any action which might mar the prospects of the morrow's triumph. Better, perhaps, triumph first and injunct later. Even Sacks would be bound to have some cash by then.

He had certainly put the show on regardless of somebody else's expense. The sets and effects and costumes were superlative. The orchestra was too large and too noisy. My poor lyrics were utterly inaudible; but perhaps this didn't matter much. I re-read and re-wrote the whole libretto not long ago at the request of the George Dance Company and, having seen a production with the present script substituted for the precocious original, I realise that the triumph might well have come to pass. For Lehar had written some beautiful numbers, though, with the exception of the still remembered *Gigolette*, they didn't seem to make much impression on the rather saturnine first-night audience. Morris Harvey had some funny moments as a Dutchman and got the one big laugh of the night with my original version of an oft-repeated joke about his encounter with a Highlander in a Scotch mist: 'So thick was the mist that at first I did not know whether he was a short man with a beard or a tall man with a sporran.' But gradually and unmistakably I felt the icy presence of failure pervading the huge auditorium and, at the finish, the booing from the gallery drowned the polite half-hearted applause from the stalls. Lehar was mistaken enough to make an appearance and the booing waxed in an angry crescendo. I wasn't such a fool as to venture from the wings. My first and only essay in musical comedy was a decisive enough flop without my being personally informed by the audience. On the second night a modicum of disgruntled advance-bookers and curiosity-seekers duly corroborated the press notices.

The American comedian was not as all right on the night as he had hoped to be. It transpired that the well-established Broadway comedian whom Sacks had engaged had decided to stay put and to send his inefficient brother to Sacks who never found this out until it was much too late to do anything about it. He was soon replaced by W. H. Berry, complete with Arthur Wimperis and Nat Ayer as his song-writers, and although between them they greatly improved the show they couldn't redeem it. Morris Harvey was extremely piqued by the introduction of Berry. Harvey had practically monopolised what laughs there had been and he objected to a star comedian being brought in to raise some bigger and better ones. 'After all,' Harvey protested to Sacks, 'I saved the show on the first night.' Sacks snapped back at him. 'You did, eh? And who saved it on de second?'

The failure evidently confirmed Sacks in the opinion that I need not, and had much better not, be paid anything. The show ran for altogether 130 performances and I never received one single Polish rouble. In view of my solicitor's confident contempt of my qualms at the outset I thought his final pronouncement on the disaster was particularly choice. 'Let this be a lesson to you never again to have any dealings with a man like that,' said my solicitor. But there – he is, as I have said, long dead. The longer the better.

So is Sacks. In his old age he was sustained and provided for by Jack Hylton and he still shuffled round the fringe of the theatre world and past the buildings where, to give him his due, his name had shone in lights above the titles of many musical shows renowned in their time. My own association with him had finished up, all those years ago, in a heated and futile exchange of abuse in a café. But I am sure that had I met him again in his latter days I would have yielded once more to the subtle appeal of his quaint personality. And this would not have been in any spirit of heaping coals of fire. For the very improbity of Sacks had in it a whimsical and mischievous attractiveness which awakened in one an instinct of illogical charity and even of indignant affection.

Some years after the Empire disaster, when I was fairly established at the Aldwych, a friend of mine happened to mention my name to Sacks.

'Him?' cried Sacks. 'I made him. I gave him his first yob. But for me he vill never have been heard about.'

And a little later still I was dining one night with Harry Graham, whose many successes as author and librettist never robbed him of the appearance and manner of some traditional Guards' officer engaged in a rather bewildering but tolerable civilian enterprise.

'Has it ever struck you,' Graham suddenly asked me, 'what really quite extraordinary people one is called upon to deal with in the theatrical profession?'

'Yes,' I said. 'It has.'

6

There was one old lady who played an important part in my life though she had been dead for a good many years before I ever heard of her. She was my wife's father's mother. I don't know what terms she had been on with her only son, methodical Lazybones, but anyhow she had wisely decided that he already had enough money of his own with which to enjoy his pursuit of nothingness, so she had left my wife a legacy in trust as from her twenty-first birthday or from the date of her marriage. My wife was married on her twenty-second birthday so she could claim it either way, and it brought in an income of about a thousand a year. It was mainly this that had kept us going during the first years of our married life and financed the going-back-to-Burnham business. Even when I started earning money the earnings were pretty modest from my first two plays. From Mr T. C. Dagnall (he was always 'Mr' for some reason) I received in royalties for *The Dippers* thirteen hundred pounds in all, and from Sacks for *The Three Graces* nil. Needless to say, the latter sum applied also in the case of John Lane, The Bodley Head.

In the interim periods away from the theatre I had been busy with my second novel *A Cuckoo in the Nest*. This had now been published and had made quite a hit with the book-reviewers, who began to sit up and take notice of me as a genuine contender in the humorous fiction line. It sold moderately well; well enough even to reach the figure at which a John Lane author began to participate in the returns. But if so the author's share did not present any problem in mathematics to our old friend and Chesterton's, the bearded teetotal accountant, Mr Harris.

Oh well then, if I were going to be accepted as a humorous novelist the material offered by egregious Burnham was surely money for jam. Burnham became Chumpton. I wrote *Rookery Nook*. This when published (under the handicap of a ghastly jacket) confirmed rather than boosted my reputation as a humorous novelist though it never caught up with the *Cuckoo* in this respect. This was especially true when, a good many years later, both novels appeared in Penguin editions. Personally, of the two, I have always had a rather warmer feeling for *Rookery Nook* but perhaps that is because it was about Burnham.

The residents of Burnham, needless to say, simply lapped it up – a new subject for gossip in a community where gossip was the staple industry. Everybody started to recognise their neighbours in the *Rookery Nook* characters and the recognisers were duly recognised by the recognisees. I was, I admit, guilty in one instance. One particular specimen of the several retired, blasted-short-putt-missing, Bridge-wrangling inhabitants appeared thinly disguised in the novel as the fire-eating Admiral Juddy. To my dismay, this formidable model halted me one morning in the main road and squared up to me in a very challenging manner.

'Now then, young feller – this book of yours. That admiral. Damn bad form. Libellous. Eh? What have you got to say for yourself?'

I murmured some lie about being sorry but I didn't know what he meant.

'Oh, stuff. That won't wash. That admiral, he's nothing but a damned caricature. The whole place is saying so. Everybody knows he's meant to be poor old Hart.'

By now, after two or three full length experiments, I had got the stage version of *A Cuckoo in the Nest* into shape. I couldn't bring myself to show it to Golding Bright. I had seen him on the first night of *The Three Graces* sitting as ever with his washleather gloves clasping his cane and his chin resting on its knob, immobile in repudiation of what he was or was not seeing and hearing. My resentment of him had lapsed into shame-faced timidity. I was afraid that he would have written me off as a failure and that any further offering of mine might be automatically referred to the attentions of the mice in his office cupboard.

Then, one morning at Burnham I received a letter from Australia. It was a letter which was ultimately to trigger off my successful career as a playwright. It was from Lawrence Grossmith, a name which will be as unfamiliar to the general public today as that of Golding Bright or of Mr T. C. Dagnall or, if it comes to that, of poor old Hart. But this is my story and Lawrence Grossmith played a short but very significant part in it.

He was the younger son of George Grossmith who created the Gilbert and Sullivan Bunthornes and Kokos and wrote *The Diary of a Nobody*. Lawrence's elder brother, George junior, played a leading part in a string of Gaiety Theatre musicals and was the stage-essence of the type known in those days as a fop. (My father hated the very sight of him.) George senior's brother, Weedon, was just about the best light-comedy-farce actor of his time, Hawtrey always excluded. My chap, Lawrence, was a competent straight comedian but that was all. He had figured in one or two West End plays which had been successes but not for that reason. Like many near-leading actors but not quite, he was extremely vain.

His letter from Australia was to tell me that he had read the *Cuckoo* novel and wanted to acquire the stage rights. Impetuous as I was and still am, I immediately sent him a copy of the farce and it was only when I had a letter back readily accepting my adaptation that I began to relent my impulsive response and wondered whether I couldn't have made a better choice.

The one good thing about it was that I could face Golding Bright without any squirmings and entreaties. On the contrary, I could walk into his office in a pretty cocksure manner and say 'Oh, hallo, Golding. Look. Here's a farce I've sold. Would you care to handle it for me?'

I didn't do this of course, but if I had my cocksureness would have evaporated rapidly. Golding, apparently unconscious of the fact that there had ever been any rift between us, said he'd certainly handle it but he obviously took a very poor view of my having fallen for Lawrence Grossmith.

When I think of the benefit I derived from having done so, it seems mean to deride Lawrence Grossmith but he had a lofty self-sufficiency and disdain about him which was really rather ludicrous. He regarded any stroke of good fortune that came his way as his normal due. Soon after we met he informed me that he would like me to meet a great friend of his who had read the farce. The friend had been greatly tickled by the farce and wanted to be allowed to direct it. Oh? Who? Grossmith told me who in the same casual tone. Gerald du Maurier. His manner suggested that it was only being a friend of Lawrence Grossmith's that qualified Gerald du Maurier to direct the farce.

So for the first time I met Gerald du Maurier. The *Cuckoo* seemed particularly to appeal to him because it would be a welcome change from the sort of play he was generally concerned with and he appeared to look forward to directing it in a holiday spirit.

In his discussions of the farce with me the one idea was that we were in for a bit of fun. He smiled his slightly crooked smile and twitched his nose in that particular way of his in keeping with a pleasing thought. He was anxious to get the play launched as soon as possible and I went with him one afternoon on a visit to some likely theatres. At one of these, the Kingsway, there was a matinée in progress of a play in which Tallulah Bankhead was appearing. She came to the stage-door to see du Maurier and he asked her whether it was true that she had become a lesbian. An obvious leg-pull which she ignored.

Our round tour did not result in our finding an immediate vacancy but I was greatly consoled when Gerald du Maurier, noticing my dis-

Above: My father

Below: Bromley, about 1895, my mother sitting under the parasol, my sister Muriel, with my brother Frank and myself in front

Above: Myself aged about seven
Below: Charterhouse 1900, Baden-Powell, just after the Relief of Mafeking laying a foundati
stone. I am the very, very small boy above the woman on extreme right of picture and next
a lady in a boa

Early 1915, a Bristol Box-kite aeroplane

Above : My wife
Below : My wife with my first grandson, Andrew Morgan

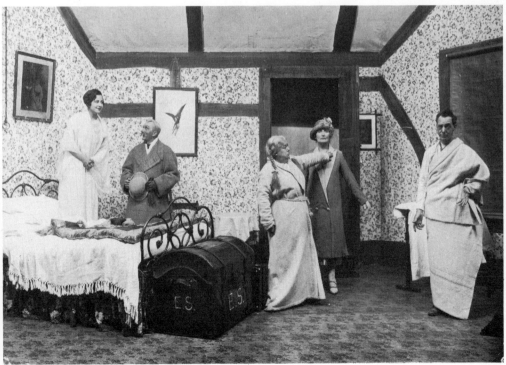

Above: 1922, Criterion Theatre: *The Dippers* starring Cyril Maude and Binnie Hale
Below: 1925-6, Aldwych: *A Cuckoo in the Nest*, Act III, Yvonne Arnaud, Tom Walls, Mary Brough, Grace Edwin, Ralph Lynn

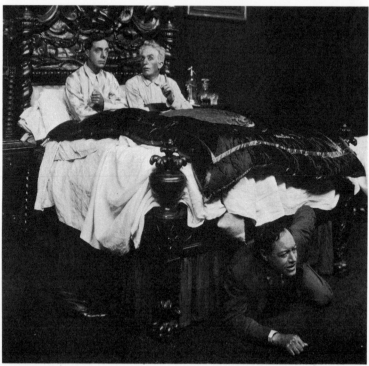

Above: 1926, Aldwych: *Rookery Nook*, Act I, Robertson Hare and Winifred Shotter
Below: 1927-8, Aldwych: *Thark*, Act III, Ralph Lynn, Tom Walls, Hastings Lynn

bove: 1928, Aldwych: *Plunder*, Act II, Robertson Hare and Mary Brough (L) Archibald
atty, Tom Walls and Ralph Lynn (C), Winifred Shotter and Doreen Bendix (R)
elow: 1928, Aldwych: *Plunder*, the Scotland Yard scene, Herbert Waring (seated at centre
ble), Tom Walls and Ralph Lynn

Above: 1930, Aldwych: *A Night Like This*, Act III
Below: Ralph Lynn and Tom Walls in the film of *Plunder*

Tom Walls, Jane Baxter and myself on the film set for *Second Best Bed*

Above: With Sybil Thorndyke, a snapshot taken at Ion Trewin's wedding reception
Below: 1965, at an exhibition to celebrate the Diamond Jubilee of the Aldwych with Sir Feli
Aylmer and Lady Hicks (Ellaline Terriss). She was in her late 90's and lived to be over 10

5

1969, watching cricket in Melbourne

With Lindsay Anderson and the cast of *The Bed Before Yesterday* during rehearsals

Zoe Dominic

Zoe Dominic

Zoe Dominic

Camera Press

The Four Almas in *The Bed Before Yesterday*, *top left:* Joan Plowright, *top right:* Sheila Hancock, *below left:* Judy Cornwell, *below right:* Carol Channing

Above: The *Evening Standard* Special Award presented to me in 1975 by Rex Harrison
Below: Myself with Edna O'Brien

Above: A visit to the Aldwych in company with Richard Briers and Arthur Lowe
Below: 1976, a ninetieth birthday celebration at the Lyric with Sheila Hancock and
Robert Morley

Three generations of Ben Travers

appointment at this, said to me, 'All right then, I'll promise you something. I promise you this play will be done in the West End.' That was good enough for me. I went back to Burnham to await, like Browning's Artemis, 'in fitting silence the event'.

Daphne du Maurier's biography of her father shows very candidly that he wasn't a genial and easy character with everybody, but he always was with me. I loved him.

The event took an unexpected form. A wire from Grossmith bade me come up and meet him at the Badminton Club next day, for a preliminary discussion before Tom Walls came along to join us for luncheon.

It was in keeping with Lawrence Grossmith's personality that he was a past-master of the cliché. His conversation coasted smoothly along the centre of the well-beaten track of stereotyped expression. Our preliminary Badminton Club discussion gave him full scope.

It had come to his knowledge that Tom Walls at the Aldwych Theatre was in pressing need of a successor to *It Pays to Advertise* which had outrun its popularity. Grossmith had accordingly submitted the script of the *Cuckoo* to Walls, intimating that should it find favour he might be prepared to surrender his option for a reasonable consideration. Those who exercised any authority at the Aldwych in addition to Walls had signified their approval of the script to a man. Walls himself was straining at the leash to set the ball in motion. Gerald du Maurier had been acquainted with the proposed transaction which he applauded to the echo.

I listened to this exposition of ordered English with mixed feelings. When I think of what the acceptance of that proposal was going to mean to me for the whole of the rest of my life I realise that it only goes to show that I've always been a mug in these matters, headstrong in accepting a doubtful offer, hesitant about accepting a good one. But, after all, walking out on Gerald du Maurier, at that stage of my career, seemed absolutely suicidal unless the compensation was going to be something really terrific.

I had my doubts about the compensation. I hadn't seen *Tons of Money* or, at that time, *It Pays to Advertise*. By now, in 1925, they had established the Aldwych as the focal point of broad farce with Tom Walls and Ralph Lynn as its star comedians. *Tons of Money* by Will Evans, a funny and unpleasant music-hall and pantomime performer, and one Valentine, whoever he was, had in its original form, gone the rounds of theatre managers and had finished up through the letter-box of Walls and Henson (Leslie, of Gaiety Theatre fame) who had started out in business together running summer shows on piers and that sort of thing. Their office-boy, Reginald Highley, read the script and found it funny enough to recommend to Tom Walls, who spotted that it had a good basis for a farce and got Ralph Lynn and Yvonne Arnaud to adapt it to their own purposes and play the leads. It was produced one night in 1922 at the old Shaftesbury Theatre opposite the Palace in Shaftesbury Avenue (senile playgoers will remember *The Arcadians* there). It scored one of those rare, genuine, overwhelming first-night successes which drive minor critics to their dictionaries to check up on how to spell 'unparalleled'. *The Dippers* was then in its provincial Blowing and Hoaring stages and I remember reading the notices of *Tons of Money* with pangs of jealousy. The *Daily Mail* even had a leading article about it.

The Aldwych Theatre was rather off the map at that time. During the First World War it had been a YMCA headquarters. Walls and Henson secured a long lease of it on good terms, transferred *Tons of Money* there and settled down in rooted occupation. Eventually *It Pays to Advertise* had succeeded it and ran for eighteen months. So the prospect of having the *Cuckoo* as the next Aldwych production was indeed pretty terrific.

But I had a notion, not priggish or bumptious, but a justified notion, that my type of farce was a cut above the larger-than-life absurdities of the Aldwych. I had visualised and written my characters as genuine human beings. What about these two comics who apparently specialised in the grotesque?

Tom Walls. I had seen him sometimes, an unfunny and over-red-nosed comedian playing small parts in musical shows. The father-in-law who was the leading support character in the *Cuckoo* called for a straight comedy actor and I had suggested to Gerald du Maurier that he should cast Charles V. France for the part. The idea of Tom Walls red-nosing and reeling his way through it dismayed me for a start. (The glorious, restrained study that Tom made of the befuddled Major Bone surprised me as much as it gratified me.)

The other and more conspicuous Aldwych attraction, an individual named Ralph Lynn, I had seen only once and that in a very silly music-hall sketch. He typified the contemporary monocled 'nut' and had gained a moderate reputation as such when he suddenly, that night in 1922, sailed up to stardom.

But there again – wouldn't this mean that the conscientious young husband of my farce would be caricatured and nincompooped into fatuous unreality? Oh, my poor little fastidious rueful reservations – I was about to join forces with the greatest farce actor of our time.

Tom Walls arrived at the Badminton Club and within five minutes my mixed and indefinite feelings had ceased to count. The terms of Lawrence Grossmith's reasonable consideration must have been settled in advance, for Tom Walls made it clear that he had decided on the *Cuckoo* and that was that. I learned for the first of many times that once Tom Walls decided on anything that settled it. This was a Wednesday. The *Cuckoo* went into rehearsal on the following Monday morning.

I was surprised to find that Tom was so young – it turned out that he was only two or three years older than I. The shape of his head and one or two misfires in his pronunciation made it unnecessary for him to confide to me, as he did at a later stage, that he came from yeoman stock. But whatever his stock I was soon to discover that so far as the Aldwych Theatre was concerned he was the sole and absolute dictator. Chairman, Managing Director, head of every department, general supervisor, in complete charge of productions, star actor (it was always Tom Walls and Ralph Lynn, not Ralph Lynn and Tom Walls). He had to have someone to help him spell and add up, but that didn't make him any less the boss.

I will have a lot to say about him and although to the present generation he, like so many others of his period, has faded into oblivion, Tom Walls not only made a great impact on my professional life, but was, without exception, the most extraordinary man I ever came across. But leave him for the moment and accompany me running from the Badminton Club to tell my news to Golding Bright.

Golding waved the cigarette smoke from his line of sight and received the news with a nonchalant satisfaction. News? Golding didn't tell me so but of course he had initiated the whole thing. Being the agent of Walter Hackett, one of the co-authors of *It Pays to Advertise*, Golding had been well aware of the state of affairs at the Aldwych and had pulled the strings accordingly.

I regret that I saw but little more of Lawrence Grossmith. I hope I have not been unkind about him and his clichés. I really liked him very much. After all it was he who twigged the dramatic possibilities of the *Cuckoo* novel. He earned my eternal gratitude and his two per cent of the play's gross receipts at the Aldwych.

Tom Walls gave me my first experience of some of his singular methods as actor-producer (play-directors were called producers in those days). For the first two of the three weeks' rehearsal he sat and directed the rest of the company, including his understudy. At the beginning of the third week he resigned himself, with a groan of effort, to participation in the acting. But during the past fortnight he had, of course, been much too busy to study his lines; and when the play started out on its one week's probation at some provincial theatre his performance was liable to hiatus. This didn't embarrass him at all. He would cross to the prompt corner and rally the dithering stage-manager with a rasping and resounding aside – 'Come on, Bobbie – let's have it, can't you?' Bobbie was Bobbie Dunn, the father of Clive of *Dad's Army*, etc. Bobbie philosophically survived years of torment at the hands of Tom Walls. Tom had no shame or compunction about not knowing his lines during the try-out week. He took a contemptuous view of audiences at the best of times. But it is only fair to say that on first nights in London he was not only word-perfect but gave what was probably his best performance of the entire run of a play. 'In every play there's only one show that really matters,' he used to say; a candid admission of his cynical outlook on the whole concern. But he was always ready to see the funny side of his own discomfitures.

Another of his peculiar practices was to ignore the third act completely until the last week of rehearsals. In the case of the *Cuckoo* this resulted in the most distressing ordeal for me. By the end of the second week the first and second acts had been cut, re-invented, transcribed, gagged and generally tinkered into fairly promising shape. On the Saturday – or was it the Sunday? – morning the company read through the original third act. What they read or the way they read it or both made it sound like a prolonged incantation to Gloom. I sat squirming in self-conscious anguish. The material had been in keeping with the original first two acts, but by now the first two acts had been translated into Aldwych.

At the end of the reading Tom handed me a copy of the original third act. 'Go back to your room,' he said, 'and rewrite the whole bloody thing. Don't strain yourself. Thursday morning will do so long as you get it right.'

Don't strain myself. My three children had just got over whooping-cough and were down at Burnham being looked after by a nanny, but they had handed the whooping-cough on to me. I was with my wife in London, in some bed-sitter suite I can't remember where. I sat up for the next fifty-four hours without a thought of sleep, jumping up every few minutes and pacing the room, beating my chest and fighting for breath. My wife ministered patiently and without any of the 'I don't care what happens; you can't go on like this; you *must* be in bed' business but just quietly watchful – but for her tender commonsense the job would never have been done. But done it was. Tom got his new third act by the middle of the week and it turned out to be a great success and called for scarcely any alteration in its performance. But that doesn't mean that the lodging-house wastepaper-basket wasn't as full of discards as all its mates before and since.

Tom always gave Ralph Lynn a free hand in the way he played his part, though both of them never missed the opportunity of being critical of each other to me on the side. At the very start of the *Cuckoo* rehearsals Ralph told me that he'd agreed to play it after reading only the first act. His reason was that the character didn't try to be funny but just walked rationally and naturally into trouble. I was tremendously elated – so much for my apprehensions about that 'silly ass' approach. In one moment the monocle was transformed from an evil omen to a lucky charm.

In all the many farcical plays and films we were to do together I took care that the troubles and embarrassments he got into were actuated by reasonable and acceptable motives. He was an ideal farce actor to work with. I have never seen or heard of any actor in any field with such an instinctive and unerring gift of timing. I soon learned to exploit another distinctive and inimitable feature of his, the throw-away line – or perhaps what, in his case, would more aptly be called the give-away line. He made deliberate, unfunny, definite and convincing declaration; then, unable to contain his self-satisfaction, he ruined its whole effect by some ill-considered after-thought.

He also always relied to a great degree on instinct and impromptu, taking the form of a sudden whim during any one performance, momentary and almost unintentional. Often in the course of our long years together I looked into his dressing-room after a show and said, 'That was a lovely bit of business tonight in the second act. Don't forget to keep it in.' And he asked blankly. 'Why, what did I do?' The bit of business or the extraneous remark may not always have been so lovely, but he only had to be told that it was out of character for him to cut it out. When, before I became acclimatised to the Aldwych, I sat at rehearsals of the *Cuckoo* racked with suspense and whooping-cough, I listened to Ralph's interpolations with aversion. Some, admittedly, were good; but I felt uneasy about taking the nominal responsibility for a line like this: when, having written a false name in the inn visitors' book, his entry is inspected by the puritanical landlady:

'You don't write very clear.'

'No, I've just had some very thick soup.'

I gently protested but Ralph said he'd like to try it, and it always got a big laugh. And after all it's exactly the sort of thing Ralph himself would have said in the circumstances.

A Cuckoo in the Nest was topical in a way. It was a comment on the contemporary (1925) state of the divorce laws. It had always been taken for granted that any unmarried couple who spent a night together in an hotel must, incontestably, be guilty of adultery; as in most cases no doubt they were. But at this time divorce judges were beginning to get rather restive and inclined to hanker after some pretty solid evidence. I thought it might be a good idea to show a couple fortuitously separated from their respective spouses and compelled by circumstances to spend a completely blameless night together not only in the same inn but in the same bedroom. And a good idea it was, though little did I foresee in my Badminton Club moments of misgiving – that the essential absurdity of the situation could not possibly be better brought out than by having Ralph Lynn and Yvonne Arnaud as the joint occupants of my bedroom.

The credit for getting them there must go entirely to Tom Walls. He had an extraordinary gift for sensing the potentialities. I think he must have persuaded, or perhaps even bluffed, Yvonne Arnaud into accepting her part in the *Cuckoo* on the strength of her successful association with Ralph in *Tons of Money*; for it wasn't worthy of her. But the fact that she was little better than a picturesque foil for Ralph never seemed to occur to anybody, except to dear Yvonne Arnaud herself, which only goes to show how accomplished she was.

All she had to do was to sit up in bed, looking very attractive in the midst of her primitive and forbidding surroundings, and complacently to read a book, while Ralph wandered about, irresolute and woebegone, with a blanket and a pillow. Nobody but Yvonne Arnaud could have conveyed so perfectly the sheer impossibility of there being anything morally wrong in the situation and at the same time her mischievous amusement at their joint dilemma. And yet almost every line she was given to speak was a feed line:

'My husband hasn't got a nasty mind. Has your wife got a nasty mind?'
'No, but she's got a nasty mother.'
'To any decent-minded person there's nothing wrong in your sleeping on the floor of my bedroom, is there?'
'No. But where's the decent-minded person?'

The Lord Chamberlain's Office expressed great concern about this bedroom scene when the script was presented for consideration. So much so that, for the only time in my experience, a special (and very inconvenient) rehearsal was called for inspection by a representative of the Censorship Department. The genial major detailed to pass final judgment did so without hesitation and almost apologetically; which was in itself a further unspoken, and perhaps unconscious, compliment to the art of Yvonne Arnaud. The genial major confided to me that the Lord Chamberlain 'simply had' to check up on the second act because bedroom scenes in plays were frowned upon in 'certain quarters'. The certain quarters could only mean Buckingham Palace, where Queen Mary was now in stately residence.

The first night in London took place during a violent thunderstorm, which must have upset the calculations of any Roman augurs who happened to be about; for the farce was a definite success. Tom Walls did not discard his red nose; but his glorious study of a Major of Yeomanry in decay quite justified this. He was the sort of old fellow who would be bound to have had a red nose in real life. Mary Brough had been in *Tons of Money*, but it was her landlady in the *Cuckoo* that constituted her an indispensable member of the Aldwych team from this time onwards. She was in all nine of my Aldwych farces and had one remarkable trait. She always retained and observed the traditional but by this time archaic attitude of deference to the author from the actor when on duty. All through the nine years, once we were in the theatre she would address me as 'Sir'. I never told her not to; I knew that would be asking her to forsake her principles. It must have been Mary Brough, or someone very like her, who inspired the original use of the term 'trouper'.

She lived – the object I am sure of enormous local esteem – at Clapham. Every night during the run of the *Cuckoo* she used to be hoisted into the sidecar of a motor bicycle and conveyed to her home by a young member of the company, who was no less a person than Roger Livesey. He played Alfred, the inn barman and general factotum – another example of Tom Walls' genius for casting. I always remember Roger Livesey in one particular moment, typifying the obstinate density of my home-grown Somerset chawbacon at cross-purposes with the hero's clamorous mother-in-law:

'Where is the landlady?'

'Gone to get some milk.'

'Where from?'

'From the cow.'

'Yes, but where *is* the cow?'

'Being milked.'

'Yes, but *where* is the cow being milked?'

'Wull, you knows whurr to milk a cow, don't 'ee?'

There were two others in that cast who, with Ralph Lynn and Mary Brough, were to appear in all nine of my Aldwych farces. One was Ralph's elder brother, Sydney Lynn, who acted under the name of Gordon James. The other was, at that time, a conscientious and punctilious little support-player named Robertson Hare.

People of middle age and upwards still sometimes talk about the Aldwych of those nine years as a landmark in theatrical history. My own memory dwells perhaps less on the plays themselves than on my association with Tom and Ralph and, beyond everything else, the participation in their laughter. Tom might be despotic and arrogant and quick to assert his position as the boss of the place, but he would no more let this interfere with his laughter than he would let it interfere with his methodical, and apparently quite innocuous, patronage of the bottle. As for Ralph, he always had a nimbleness of wit as individual as his methods on-stage. He not only saw the ridiculous side of things; he searched for it. His first instinctive thought was to spot something funny in anything he saw or heard or read. Usually his sallies were as unpremeditated as his stage gags; but sometimes he would remain silent and pensive for a moment or two, looking as if he were trying to work out a sum in his head and then suddenly produce some odd quip. He originated, in the course of everyday conversation with me, one now familiar joke – the one about the Elephant Old Bailey, with the disreputable-looking elephant accused of giving evidence on his own behalf and, asked what he had been up to the night of the crime, protesting, 'I can't remember.' I was always fond, too, of Ralph's bookmaker caught in a shipwreck on board a liner, running up and down the deck and shouting, 'Women and children third.'

I once spent a few days with Ralph in Paris. Oh, *mon Dieu*. Ralph understood only one attitude towards France – I don't think he knew that any other existed. This was the splendidly insular, Gilbertian 'darned mounseer' attitude, which considered that the sole function of Paris was to serve as a playground for the light-hearted English visitor and that its citizens were the natural and legitimate butt for his persiflage. He sidled up to respectable middle-aged Parisian lady window-shoppers with a toothsome smile and remarked, 'Kiss pussy?' But my worst moment with him was when he noticed a gendarme on duty in the middle of one of the busiest avenues, armed with truncheon and whistle and trying to regulate the Paris traffic with the non-stop vigour of a frantic marionette. Ralph immediately stepped into the road and began dodging his way towards him. I felt bound to follow, and both of us, after escaping death by inches from a dozen hooting cars, eventually arrived intact beside the gendarme. He was too busy whistling and flourishing his truncheon to give us more than a fleeting and furious glance; but at length, during a momentary lull, he turned his head and shot out a sharp interrogation. At this Ralph performed the elaborate gesture of the conventional stage Frenchman, with the high-shouldered shrug and outspread palms. He leaned towards the gendarme and spoke in confidential and expectant inquiry, 'Feelthy pictures?' he asked.

But Ralph was always painstaking about his work. He was never satisfied so long as there was a single line in any of his scenes which wasn't right. All through the run of a farce he would worry and experiment until he got the thing to his liking. In those moments there were none of the waggeries and wisecracks of his leisure hours; we were concentrating on the solemn problem of creating laughter. Nobody ever appreciated so well as Ralph how intensely serious is the job of being funny.

When the general strike of 1926 closed the theatres for a week or so, Tom and Ralph motored down to stay with us at Burnham and I read aloud to them the first act of *Rookery Nook*, which I was re-adapting for them on Aldwych lines. They were by this time labelled and regarded as co-star comedians of equal standing, and the first result of this was that they had become, and were always to remain, extremely sensitive and wary – not about their own individual material so much, but about each other's. I had not merely to write farces containing two leading male characters of equal importance, but to organise my scripts so that in their scenes together, if one were given a line calculated to raise a laugh the next laugh had to go to the other. Or, if unavoidably, A got two laughs in succession B must forthwith be allowed to bring the score level. It was an intriguing exercise and proved very beneficial to the farces. Tom and Ralph soon learned to rely on me to observe the fifty-fifty rule but at the outset they kept a pretty sharp look-out about it. The only time I was interrupted in my reading of *Rookery Nook* was when, at one point, I had given Ralph what sounded like three to nil, and my drawing-room rang with Tom's quick challenge: 'Hi, hi – what's all this?'

There is some peculiar quality about *Rookery Nook* which has made a lasting appeal to the British public. I will not divulge what this quality is, but only because I don't know. It has been acted by repertory and amateur companies all over the country and in the Dominions, more or less habitually for the past fifty years. I have no idea how many times in all it has endured the inspection of urban and rural district audiences, but the total number of its performances has been many times greater than that of all my other plays put together. And yet it might not have survived if my gate at Burnham had not opened one morning at the psychological moment when the 'Hand ever above my shoulder' gently pushed into my front garden a girl we knew named Betty Tucker, selling flags for the lifeboat.

The first two acts, as written, had been accepted as quite promising. They planted and developed the situation of the innocent maiden, driven from home by her Anglo-Prussian stepfather and forced to seek sanctuary, wearing only her pyjamas, with our old friend, the migrant but loyal and well-intentioned husband. But the third act, when at length Tom consented to get to it, just ambled along, limping as it went and showing ever-increasing signs of fatigue. It was Ralph who hit on the idea of enlivening the proceedings by introducing a new and unheralded young woman, to be inveigled into the house as a substitute for the original refugee, without the knowledge of the husband. As usual, I agreed readily to experiment with any suggestion offered, without pausing to calculate the problems it involved. The procedure of the new young woman had to be odd, to say the least. She had to pay a morning call at the house of a man who was a complete stranger to her. Once inside, she had to agree to lend her frock to another girl whom she'd never met, and to remain there to explain. Well, I felt I could account for her behaviour when she'd got into the house; but her motive for coming along there in the first place had, in keeping with my principles, to be unimpeachably reasonable and probable. Perhaps I was rather dense, but I couldn't for the life of me determine what that motive could be. Then – click – the gate; and in walked Betty Tucker.

I jumped up, hurried out and must, I think, have aroused suspicions in the breast of Betty Tucker by the lavish abandon with which I purchased her flags for the lifeboat. Festooned and elated I returned to my study. The rest was easy. Poppy Dickey arrived and knocked at the front door of Rookery Nook, and the whole situation blossomed forth into what proved to be a really triumphant dénouement. It was one of the best bits of farce-writing I ever brought off; but it would never have materialised (quite apart from Betty Tucker) if it hadn't been for that vague and speculative inspiration of Ralph's.

I have often been asked how Winifred Shotter came to be discovered for the leading girl's part in *Rookery Nook*. It was due to Leslie Henson, who had been a management co-director with Tom Walls ever since the start of *Tons of Money*. Winifred Shotter was in the chorus of one of his musical shows and he thought she looked the sort of girl for the part. He thought rightly; she looked ideal for it. But it wasn't just a matter of looks – the way this part was played affected the whole action and justification of the story and the humour of the situations. The girl had to be seductive enough to justify the gossip of the 'residential seaside cats' but at the same time quite without guile and, as the Ralph Lynn character asserted, 'like Potiphar's wife – above suspicion'.

Winifred Shotter brought exactly the right blend of charm and naïveté to the part. She immediately won the approval of critics and audiences and very soon was commanding a record proportion of wall-space in Service quarters, Varsities and Sixth-form studies at Public Schools. Today, whenever I meet some veteran who remembers the Aldwych farces, his first remark is invariably, 'What's happened to Winifred Shotter?' It became taken for granted, rather than decided, that she should stay on and appear in future Aldwych productions. It was a useful additional asset to have a young and very attractive leading girl; especially as Ralph invariably stuck to what are known as 'juvenile' characters, and whatever the juvenile in any of the farces got up to was inevitably the outcome of romantic feminine inducement. But, although this turned out to be a very useful and delightful arrangement, I don't think it did justice to Winifred Shotter. It resulted in her becoming 'typed' as some ingenuous fiancée or engaging young person of unassailable virtue in urgent need of equally decorous male championship. Only in *A Cup of Kindness* did she get the chance to show how good an actress she was. Perhaps, however, her having had to impersonate a succession of young women of undesigning maidenhood is one of the reaons why she looks very little older today than she did then.

The success of *Rookery Nook* seemed to confirm the appointments, as it were, of several other members of the company. The farces that followed it were, to a large extent, cast before they were written. They had to contain worthy or suitable parts for Ralph Lynn, Tom Walls, Mary Brough, Robertson Hare, Winifred Shotter, Gordon James and Ethel Coleridge. Another standard feature of the future Aldwych farces had its origin in *Rookery Nook* – namely the traditional victimisation of Robertson Hare.

So far as *Rookery Nook* was concerned, his character of the intimidated little male relative who becomes entangled in the trouble was written as a subsidiary 'feed' part. I had certainly no idea of exploiting the personality of Robertson Hare. It never crossed my mind that he would be given the part; and, in view of the results, it is interesting to record that he wasn't Tom Walls' first choice for it.

But he played it; and the fact that he played it initiated and practically dictated a new feature in Aldwych policy. The farces thereafter generally had to contain a situation in which he stood between an inexorable Walls and a more plausible but no less ruinous Lynn, to be fleeced of his fair repute, of his cash and of his trousers. In *Turkey Time* the biggest laugh of the whole play was when, Tom and Ralph having rehearsed their fell designs upon him, he made his entrance and duly arrived, beaming and unsuspecting, for the slaughter.

I am quite convinced that this standard victimisation joke would never have found its way into the subsequent farces if the third person had been any other actor than Robertson Hare. There is nothing the farce-going public loves to laugh at more than the sight of the familiar, next-door-neighbour type of earnest little citizen in tribulation or being 'put upon'. Some years ago I was asked to write about Robertson Hare, and I can only repeat what I said of him then. He has been endowed by Nature with the personality and physique of the ideal 'put-uponee'. And he lives next door to everybody.

'The lack of inches – offset by a cocksure sort of confidence that he is as big as they come; the lack of hair – offset by a cocksure sort of confidence that he is bald because he prefers to be; the pedantic, almost clerical intonation in which he voices his ready assent to some calamitous proposal or his bootless distrust of the same; the expression of his face, puckered in instinctive doubt about the integrity of some interlocutor (and pucker in doubt well it may after all he has been through) – yes, Nature has certainly contributed ...'

97

In farce the object of the audience's derision quickly becomes the object of its affection. With *Rookery Nook* Robertson Hare rose from being one of the useful Aldwych hangers-on into becoming one of its popular attractions.

The bare subject of my third Aldwych farce was suggested to me by Tom Walls. By this time I was intimate with him, had got his measure and knew all his foibles and he knew I knew them and trusted me. And, notwithstanding the abrupt word of command regarding the subject of the next farce, he was always, from now onwards, readily prepared to accept any major projects of mine; and his imagination and sense of humour would often improve on them. So long as I didn't try to improve on *his* projects all was well. I have said he trusted me; and one of the things he trusted me not to do was, ever at rehearsals or in company, to say anything which might appear to challenge his judgment.

He wasn't just a crude egotist – it wasn't as simple as that. And he didn't mind so much having his decisions criticised or opposed. What sent him up in a blaze was to have them criticised or opposed in front of other people. For this might lead the other people to think (and perhaps to whisper) that somebody else knew better than he did.

At one rehearsal (of which of the plays I can't remember) I felt convinced that he was all wrong in his direction of some important piece of action. I was determined to get it done my way. If I had said, 'Tom, don't you think it would be better if——' that is as far as I would have got. He would have said quickly, 'All right, all *right* – d'you think I don't know what I'm doing? Who the hell's producing this play?' So what I did say was this:

'Tom – half a tick. You've forgotten something.'

'Eh? I've forgotten? What d'you mean?'

'Last time we did this bit you said you were going to alter it and have so-and-so do such-and-such.'

'Eh? I don't remember that.'

'Yes, you *do*. I said at the time what a good idea.'

'Oh? Oh, yes, I think I remember now. Hold on then. Here – Coley – go back to where you were. I've decided to do this another way.'

I was undignified and obsequious? Never mind – I wanted the thing done my way and I knew that, with Tom Walls, this was the only way of getting it done.

Tom's gift for getting the best out of my farces was an absolute revelation. It didn't show itself in flashes; he had a steady almost lazy application and foresight in discovering possibilities which had never occurred to me. Frankly, I think my Aldwych farces were excellent material which owed a great deal to Ralph's preliminary help; but the material could not have been more keenly appreciated or put into better trim to be presented as a finished article. And never, never did Tom fail to give me full credit for my efforts.

Tom hailed from somewhere in the hinterland of Coventry. I never discovered where, if anywhere, he was educated but I would guess that his schoolmasters, like my own, decided to call the whole thing off at the earliest convenient opportunity. In his early twenties he decided to come to London. He applied for a job in the Metropolitan Police and was duly given it. Even at this early stage his self-confidence was so bloated that, as he told me himself, his motive in joining the police was that he knew damn well that within about three years he would have become one of the big noises at CID headquarters. That things didn't turn out that way was due primarily to his already insatiable delight in sexual intercourse (and who's to blame him for that). At this period and for many years later the northern pavement of Piccadilly was crowded with prostitutes, upgrading in glamour, hauteur and price according to their beat, from the Circus westward towards the Park. By some incredible act of miscasting the newly-joined Tom Walls was allocated to night duty in Bond Street. He loved to relate how he would select some promising candidate, lead her into a sequestered side street and interrogate her against the wall. Tom Walls' career in the police force did not last very long.

Quite apart from his talent as a producer Tom was the actuating force which drove Aldwych farce to flourish as it did. Nor could it have done so had not Tom Walls been exactly the Tom Walls he was. That same self-protective arrogance was an essential and guiding factor in the character of this rather coarse, wrong-shaped-headed, ruthless, dissipated, utterly extravagant, optimistic, entertaining, laughing, irresistible man.

Once, at the Garrick Club a distinguished actor dismissed Tom Walls to me as a 'beggar on horseback'. Well, a beggar on horseback he may have been. But nobody ever gave him a leg up – nobody could. He alone hoisted himself to the saddle. And even the horse won the Derby.

7

The Aldwych farces were no *Mousetraps*. The length of their respective runs seems rather paltry nowadays. But the fact is that each of them played to pretty nearly capacity business for practically the whole of the run. At the first sign of a definite falling-off in the takings Tom Walls would say, 'This is it. Our number's up. Let's get back to the big stuff. Come on, Ben, when will you have the next one ready?'

Ben always had the next one ready. Directly one farce was successfully launched I was back at Burnham busily overloading the waste-paper-basket again with the rudiments of another. I knew that the current runner would be smartly exterminated directly it showed the first rheumatic symptoms of its autumn.

For the record (that 'record' again – 'Is your record really necessary?') here is the rather mediocre-looking tally of my nine Aldwych farces:

PLAY	PRODUCED	PERFORMANCES
A Cuckoo in the Nest	22 July 1925	376
Rookery Nook	30 June 1926	409
Thark	4 July 1927	401
Plunder	20 June 1928	344
A Cup of Kindness	7 May 1929	291
A Night Like This	18 Feb. 1930	268
Turkey Time	26 May 1931	263
Dirty Work	7 Mar. 1932	195
A Bit of a Test	10 Jan. 1933	144

Tom Walls did not appear in the last two. He did not appear in a good many performances of the others. In *Turkey Time* Archibald Batty, Tom's understudy, engaged by Tom on the strength of his having been Prince Arthur of Connaught's aide-de-camp, was called upon to play Tom's part no fewer than ninety-five times.

I supplied the first six of these farces in a row; then in the autumn of 1930 Golding Bright got an offer from Gilbert Miller to produce *Plunder* on Broadway. By that time Tom had acquired the talkie rights in *Plunder*, refused to negotiate with Gilbert Miller and in fact put his fiery kibosh on the whole project. I knew nothing of what was going on (Golding as secretive as ever) but Tom apparently thought otherwise. 'I'll teach Ben Travers', he told Golding and immediately accepted a footling farce called *Marry the Girl* to follow *A Night Like This*. I went to the first night and had a job to conceal my delight. The expectant Aldwych audience was coldly disillusioned by a flop which evoked occasional comment from the gallery. Tom, being Tom, quickly switched horses in ebb-tide. He made a curtain speech entirely about me. 'There has been some rumour that I have fallen out with Ben Travers. Nothing could be further from the truth. It was simply that Ben hadn't got a new play ready in time,' and so on. I knew my cue and my Tom. I hurried back to Burnham and started writing *Turkey Time*.

But this little espisode belonged to the years ahead. In 1926 and 1927 *Thark* was the job in hand.

There were three postmen at Burnham. One was our children's nanny's brother-in-law who had a cleft palate. One was a shell-shocked war victim who used to umpire our local side to victory in village cricket matches. The third was elderly and lame. It was beautifully in keeping with Burnham to employ a lame pedestrian postman.

Easeh week one of the three brought me a fat envelope from Golding Bright with details of returns and a cheque for royalties. As the run of a farce progressed the cheques increased because the former farce had no fewer than three touring companies doing their rounds of the provinces. I think the reason for my being able to recall the complete happiness of my married life is that we couldn't be bothered with any sort of reckless experiments in extravagance, but never spared a penny over anything that brought us additional comfort and contentment. We upheld the congenial oddities of Burnham. Our cook was almost stone deaf. Our old gardener, Stacey, could only have been a native of Burnham. He came to us daily on a tricycle and his manner of speech was the purest Somerset. On one occasion, having slain a poor old doe-rat bulging with progeny, he held her up by the tail for me to inspect – 'Ahh – a good catch, she be. Thur be more'n one rat inside of he.' When requested by my wife to transplant some specimens of growth from her botanical border, Stacey complied with contempt for the intruding blossom. 'I done un,' he duly reported. 'I put un longside o' rubbish-heap. And thur they can wrangle so fur'n they please.'

Our children's nanny (we had a second son in 1922) was an import to Burnham but soon became acclimatised to its anomalies. She was the perfect prototype of her vanished race from the hairs on her chin to her troublesome feet. She returned on one uncommonly sweltering

101

summer's afternoon from trying to cope with the three children on a visit to the Manor Gardens, sank into a hall chair and sighed, 'I'm prostitute with heat.' I remember overhearing another nice Nanny-ism, when she was trying to exert what she called dipsipline. 'Josy, Josy. Be a little lady, do. Keep your legs together. The boys are growing up.' Eventually she lived well into her nineties and my daughter, over fifty herself by that time, paid her a visit. Nanny wrote to me expressing her appreciation, 'I think Josy is improving.'

I seem to have come across authors' wives who have stated confidentially with a simper, or blatantly at cocktail parties, that it isn't easy to be an author's wife. My wife found it easy enough because she never interfered or investigated. She just left me to it and when it was over for the day it was never discussed – it was done with for the time being. Not that I was ever one of those authors who get disconcerted or exasperated by interruption. I can still picture myself, showing not the least concern, because someone had managed to take time off from nanny and had looked in to drive a train round my study table. But I always had the habit (and still have) of speaking my lines of dialogue aloud as I compose them or experiment with them. My Burnham home used to resound with animated stage conversations. My wife and the domestics got quite used to it (the cook was deaf anyway, wasn't she). But casual visitors would often appear startled and somewhat apprehensive. My wife would reassure them with fond unconcern, 'Don't take any notice of that. That's only Tom Walls having a bit of an argument with Ralph Lynn.'

One morning in January 1927 I had a telephone call to tell me that my father had suddenly died from a stroke. The last time I had seen him had been a month before when he shared with me a small box designed for two, tucked away alongside the circle at the Aldwych. Ours were the only two seats in the house that hadn't been sold; so there was no need for the dear old man to reconnoitre anxiously and to direct fierce glances at his neighbours and announce emphatically 'a packed house'. He had been loyal and loving to me all through the years when I must have been a rankling disappointment to him and it had given him great glee to have been able to say, 'There you are – a genius – absolute prodigy. Good God, d'you think I didn't always know the boy had it in him?'

He had the further satisfaction of knowing that I was already busy writing my third Aldwych farce. If anybody is curious to know how *Thark* came into being (as well anybody may be) the answer is that it was ordered to be written – ordered, needless to say, by Tom Walls.

It was soon after the successful production of *Rookery Nook* that Tom said to me, 'The next one's going to be about a haunted house.

So go on, get busy with it.' Though this was the only occasion when Tom told me what I'd got to write about, I cottoned on to the idea at once. It would involve Ralph Lynn in an exercise in ghost-laying against his will – a promising theme.

So – an isolated haunted house – where? In some rather remote countryside – Norfolk seemed to offer a likely location. An old Norfolk manor with a name implying bleak, stark boginess. Thark. I decided on it the moment I thought of it. As in the case of *Rookery Nook* the first word I wrote of *Thark* was its title.

The Aldwych regular patrons were rather perplexed when this title was first announced. The theatre libraries sent a bunch of representatives to call on Tom to expostulate and to tell him bluntly that he couldn't hope for much of a deal for a thing called *Thark*. I don't know what Tom said to them – I wish I did. I only know that the librarians immediately surrendered, turned their tails and retreated with them between their legs. In many ways Tom Walls was a splendid man to work with, just as in some ways he was a vainglorious, implacable dunderhead.

So long as there was plenty of money about Tom never spared expense in staging, costumes and effects. The set of the dining-hall at Thark was the most elaborate ever built for the Aldwych. This scene called for the appearance of a sepulchral, nightmare-ridden old butler, Gordon James (James Agate in his *Sunday Times* notice described him as 'Brontë-esque') who had to intimidate Ralph Lynn. One point in their exchanges was the cue for a loud and prolonged roll of thunder. This was the context:

'You – let me see – what's your name again?'
'Mrs Frush wouldn't call me by my real name, sir; so she calls me Jones.'
'Oh, a sort of pet name. But what is your real name, Jones?'
'My real name, sir?'
'Yes.'
'Death.' (*Thunder*)

Tom decided that he was going to promote a roll of thunder which would put paid to all rolls of stage thunder for all time. He happened to know that my first cousin, Dan Burges, VC, was at that time Governor of the Tower of London. I was commissioned to visit my cousin and apply for the loan of two dozen cannon balls. Tom erected in the wings a steep and solid flight of wooden stairs. The cannon balls were discharged from aloft, one by one, by a couple of stage hands, down the wooden stairs, and collected by a hard-pressed fielding-side of stage hands at ground level. Other stage hands performed simultaneously on thunder-sheets for good measure. Tom got the effect he wanted.

Rehearsals of *Thark* were conducted as usual with the result that at the opening of the try-out week at Southsea, Tom had a very vague idea of his lines. In the last scene, in which nephew and uncle share a double bed in the haunted room, Bobbie Dunn, the stage-manager, remained hidden under the bed with the script in one hand and a flash-lamp in the other, doing his tormented best to keep Tom informed of what he had to say next. But this scene was always liable to be interrupted by incidental impromptus. On one night during the run Ralph completely dried Tom up with laughter by informing him apologetically that he had let a soft fart. 'Oh dear, I'm sorry, Tom; but I'm afraid I've cut one.'

The name of Kenneth Kove will be remembered by mellow Aldwych farce-goers. He drifted back into the company for the run of *Thark* and it was he who had received and foolishly declined the original offer of the Robertson Hare part in *Rookery Nook*. He had a pallid, weedy personality and a piping monotone which set him apart from any type of actor, or indeed individual, I've ever come across. He trailed his thin umbrella in and out of three of my farces – an odd exhibit rather than a recognised member of the team.

Plunder followed *Thark*. It got unanimously what today are termed 'rave' notices. The story was straight drama and it had the distinction of being the first farce in which the action involved a death – some time before *Arsenic and Old Lace* and so on. Its current revival at the National Theatre makes it unnecessary for me to say much about the play itself but the really effectual thing about it is its period. In 1928 the perpetrator of the most serious crime in the catalogue, wilful murder, usually finished up by being escorted (as I was by Mr Gulliver) to the 'gallers'. If Tom and Ralph were to be grilled by Scotland Yard it must be because they were suspected of a crime involving the maximum menace; only the maximum menace could provide maximum laughter. So the charge had to be wilful murder and the penalty the rope. Ralph could not have got the last ounce of comedy out of the situation if he hadn't stood to be hanged.

Tom, of course, revelled in playing a character in flat undisguised defiance of the moral principles. And he agreed with me that in order to get full value from the Scotland Yard scene, the personnel, setting and procedure must all combine to give a lifelike reproduction of the real thing. Before I wrote the scene Tom got an introduction from a friend of his, Stanley Wootton, the trainer, to Chief Constable Wensley and we went and spent a couple of hours in consultation with him. Wensley had risen to his high position from the ranks and was by this time in middle age, a man of slow impressive speech, a ponderous, almost mournful manner. He might have been a successful undertaker, as in a sense he was.

He took the utmost pains to instruct us. 'I've seen Scotland Yard on the stage before now – terrible. Inspectors with their feet on the table and so forth – nothing like it.' He told us he never acted as the chief interrogator of any unfortunate suspect. He contented himself with offering him at the start the most comfortable – in fact the only comfortable – chair in the room and studying the victim's reaction to this unexpected courtesy. 'I see you casting an eye on that screen in the corner. They all do that. No reason to. It's put there to hide a wash-hand-stand. There's nothing like that goes on. No Sherlock Holmeses either. It's jest all hard sloggin'.'

I told him I wanted the two characters suspected of joint participation in a crime to be interrogated together. Wensley shook his head. 'You can't do that; it's always one at a time. No, now, hold on. You could have the Chief Inspector Detective say to the individual under suspicion, "I fear I don't believe you're telling me the truth. I will have your friend in and ascertain what he replies to that question." 'I recall,' Wensley added, and his eyes seemed momentarily to grow watery with crocodile-tears, 'we had to do that in the case of Mrs Thompson and Bywaters.'

That unhappy pair again. I glanced at the comfortable chair, now occupied by Tom, and pictured poor Mrs Thompson seated there and savouring very little of its comfort.

When the play came on Tom offered Wensley and his wife a stage box at a matinée show. Wensley solemnly confirmed that the Scotland Yard scene was the right thing at last. On the last night of the run I walked on as the stooge who sits and takes shorthand notes during the interrogations. Tom and I kept this a secret from Ralph which gave Ralph the opportunity for some flighty gags. 'Go on, you. Put that down. Oh, he can't – look at him. He's blunted his pencil.'

A great actor, who still lives vividly in the memory of those of his time, made a spectacular comeback to the West End theatre at about this time. I've always been proud to think that I was responsible for this. *Plunder* was tried out at Southsea for a week in the middle of June and Tom transported his spacious Rolls-Royce one day to the Isle of Wight, luxuriously to patrol its pleasant leas. Personally, I don't care for motoring for so-called pleasure, but I do like shellfish; so I went with him, as did my wife and Golding Bright. As we purred along, piloted by Tom's chauffeur, who bore the appropriate name of Pacey, we approached a signpost which stood on a little island of grass at a fork in the road. On the grass was stretched a strikingly picturesque figure. It was that of a lightly-clad bronzed, gipsy-like and remarkably handsome man, lying there oblivious of cars or anything but an opportune place in the sun. I remarked, 'Look at that chap – he looks like Harry Ainley.' As Pacey slowed down to something like 40 mph in order to select the right prong of the fork, I said, 'Hold on – it *is* Harry Ainley.' We halted. Golding dismounted and trudged for a considerable distance back to the grass plot. Next day he told the Haymarket management that Henry Ainley's long rest-cure was complete and that their problem of finding the right actor to play opposite Marie Tempest in *The First Mrs Fraser* had been solved. Henry Ainley duly returned to the theatre and, for some years, to what the world regarded as his rightful place in the sun. Later on he faltered again; his nerve forsook him at a critical moment; the sun went down. The last I saw of him was in a film production of *As You Like It*, when in the minor part of the Banished Duke he outclassed everybody else concerned.

Plunder was a big financial success all the time. Why, then, should it have come to an untimely and premature end? Simply because all profits were going down several drains.

If in some ways Tom Walls was a genius, he was no genius of finance. But what about myself? I invested and lost two thousand pounds in the company Tom formed to take a lease of the Fortune Theatre on lunatic terms, and thousands more in another company he later formed to purchase some infernal quarry somewhere or other. I could therefore myself claim distinction as a mug of the very highest order and Tom's was, after all, the mastermind of muggery which originated these lamentable ventures. And I never really had any sound belief in them; it was simply that I let my disgustingly weak nature be dragooned into participation. But Tom thought he was infallible; and when he began his Fortune Theatre tenancy with the successful run of *On Approval*, by Frederick Lonsdale, he thought so with even greater ease than before.

When I say 'successful' run, *On Approval* may have exemplified Lonsdale's peculiar skill but not mine. I never got a penny out of it. And when the play chosen to succeed *On Approval* turned out to be an utter flop and had to be withdrawn after losing money steadily for six weeks, the Fortune Theatre, if still a going concern, showed pretty clearly where it was going to. But I couldn't very well complain about this, because I was the author of the flop.

I knew that a new comedy would soon be wanted for the Fortune and therefore I greedily and far more hastily than usual adapted some of the main incidents of *Mischief* into a mistake in three acts. It had a brilliant first scene which did it more harm than good; because Yvonne Arnaud came on and delighted everybody with a matrimonial squabble; but from then onwards what I had intended to be sophisticated and amusing became unsympathetic and irritating. It was a meagre and inconclusive little affair in any case. Perhaps I, too, had begun to think I was infallible.

So that prize misnomer, the Fortune Theatre, swallowed my two thousand pounds. I could afford to write off the loss. *Plunder* was bringing me in ample returns and was so settled a success that it couldn't fail to do so for another year or more. Just as well – because I had planned to go to Australia in the winter of 1928–9. I also had to face the prospect of sending my daughter, Josephine, to an expensive school for girls and my son, Ben, to old Tom Pellatt's school, Durnford, near Swanage; and there may still be about some poverty-stricken old gentlemen who will remember what that used to cost, even in those days. My second son, known as Burtie (he was named Daniel Burton, after that master of applied indolence, his mother's father), would be following along there in another year or two – yes, it was just as well that I had dug my heels in so firmly at the Aldwych.

But if the Fortune Theatre dealt a painful glancing blow to my financial resources, what did it mean to Tom's? He still carried on there and produced several more unsuccessful plays; but already the project must have cost him a weighty packet. He was to lose plenty more in the years to come. That damned quarry hadn't yet hove in sight; and, however gruesome was the appearance of his banking account at any given time, Tom always pursued a mode of life which was an unvarying pattern of glorious extravagance.

He must, however, just about this time, have been called upon to face one of the more vexatious of his many crises. After the Christmas holiday season of 1928–9 the returns from *Plunder* began to show a slight falling off. That could augur only one thing, especially when Tom's finances were in such a chaotic state. Back to capacity at the Aldwych – Goodbye, *Plunder* – another new farce. Come on, Ben.

By that time I was in Australia, enjoying myself and thinking about the subject and story for the next farce only at odd, disjointed moments. I could think it out on my way home and write it when I got there. It didn't matter how long it took. *Plunder* would still be running. As it turned out, I was cabled for at the end of January, snatched some last-minute non-starter's berth in an Orient liner and spent most of the homeward voyage looking for inspiration. I had carefully labelled the inspiration 'wanted on voyage', but it had disappeared.

Tom said, 'This has got to be the cheapest production we've ever had. Just one set throughout and a pretty simple one. The smallest cast you can manage,' I said. 'After *Plunder* they'll be expecting something elaborate.' He said, 'I don't care what they expect, they're not going to get it.' I said, 'All right; we'll go for contrast. Something domestic.' It suited my book. The only time when I had discovered anything like an idea on board ship was when I suddenly recalled a subject I had experimented with in the old old days. On one of those evenings, nearly twenty years before, when I had come back from giving sultanas to City policemen and had settled down to the real business of the day, I had written the first three pages or so of a play which was to treat of a perfectly innocuous young man being arrested at his wedding reception. The idea had been consigned, like so many others, to perish in its infancy. But now, with Ralph on hand, it resurrected itself and throve.

A Cup of Kindness fulfilled all Tom's stipulations and gave him the results he wanted. I made it a Romeo and Juliet story of the suburbs. The Montagues were Tom Walls, as Mr Tutt; Mary Brough, as his wife, Mrs Tutt (an ex-barmaid) and his two sons, played by Ralph Lynn and Kenneth Kove. The Capulets were Robertson Hare, Marie Wright and Winifred Shotter, as Mr, Mrs and Miss Ramsbotham respectively. There were also a revolting old invalid Mr Ramsbotham, senior, with bits of pineapple on the front of his dressing-gown, for Gordon James; an elderly skivvy for Ethel Coleridge; and a good-looking nurse who was supposed to attend to old Mr Ramsbotham and was attended to in her turn by Tom Walls. The arrest of Ralph for an unintentional breach of the law governing outside brokerage was timed to take place just as the parties were posing for a wedding group, and to throw an already restive interfamily party into absolute chaos.

The by now traditional Aldwych favourites were all well catered for and it was, as intended, a very funny little farce on frugal lines. During its run, there occurred a minor incident which provides a good example of how Tom Walls could combine his sense of authority with his sense of humour. It came to his ears (everything came to his ears) that Kenneth Kove was going about saying that the people who really contributed most to the success of the show were some of the support players, including, naturally, himself. Kove was perhaps betrayed into this assumption by the laughter throughout the scene of his first entrance. Ralph was just on the point of persuading his stubborn and irascible father, Tom, to give his approval and financial aid to his (Charlie Tutt's) marriage with Betty Ramsbotham. At this moment the lamentable younger Tutt son arrived, in the shape of Kenneth Kove, having just been sent down from the Varsity.

TOM: What for? What did you do? And who is she?

KOVE: A girl called Robinson. I met her and her people last year at Winter Sports.

RALPH: The Swiss Family Robinson.

TOM: Shut up, you. Well?

KOVE: They found her in my bathroom, but I wasn't there at the time.

TOM: Why not?

At the end of the scene Kove concluded that he had better leave the Ramsbothams' house and return home. To this Tom had, of course, only one answer – 'Go to hell.' 'Right-ho,' said Kove. 'Then I'll see you later.'

His exit on this line always got a good laugh and a round of applause. On the night when Tom had heard of Kove's indiscreet remark he refrained from comment; but when the cue came for him to say 'Go to hell', he contented himself by saying 'Go away.' 'Right-ho,' replied Kove, somewhat flabbergasted. 'Then I'll see you later.' He withdrew without a sound from the audience. A few minutes later, the picture of wan and injured perplexity, he was confronted by Tom in the wings. 'Now who contributes the big laughs to the show, you tuppeny-halfpenny little bugger?'

This was 1929. The picturehouses, still displaying their visual wares in an atmosphere of orchestral decorum, were destined in the near future to be rent asunder by a cacophony which sounded like machine-gun practice in a parrot-house. The first 'talkies' arrived.

Herbert Wilcox may have been a loss to the diplomatic service but I am one of many who had cause to be glad that he took to the motion-picture business. He seized on Aldwych farce as being the most promising material for the new medium. I know little about the course of his negotiations with Tom Walls, but I do know that Tom would only come to terms on condition that he should take command of the shooting. He entirely lacked experience but the results of his first and subsequent efforts, though often assailed by critics and rivals, provided picturehouses all over the country with customers for years to come. But it was characteristic of Tom that on the first occasion he entered a film studio it was to direct a picture. *Rookery Nook* was the chosen subject. It was the second talkie to be made in this country. Our cameraman, efficient from the start, was destined to become one of Hollywood's leading lights in his line of business – Freddy Young.

For my part I, for once, insisted on something. Although it may now seem past belief, my suggestion that it would be effective if there was musical accompaniment to some of the action was regarded with disfavour. The introduction of musical noises into a straight farce would be inappropriate and unrealistic. But I eventually prevailed and Tom and I interviewed, on Wilcox's recommendation, a man I had never heard of – a gentle, modest, stammering American named Carroll Gibbons.

Twenty-three years later, in 1952, after the first night of *Wild Horses*, I took my family and Laurence Irving and his wife to supper at the Savoy. When he saw me there, Carroll Gibbons delivered from his piano a long impromptu calypso about me. We had made friends over that *Rookery Nook* film all those years before; and once you became a friend of Carroll Gibbons you stayed his friend for good.

I saw a public try-out of *Rookery Nook* with the Aldwych company while we were in Glasgow for a preliminary week with my next farce. It filled me with horror and headache. It was a great success all over the country and later was used as the opening attraction of the largest picturehouse in the Empire, the State Theatre, Sydney. To me, the film always remained a painful, distorted version of the genuine article, even when I had to walk on to the stage of the New Gallery in Regent Street with Ralph Lynn and Winifred Shotter and receive a prize for my contribution towards the best British talkie of the year. The prize was an inscribed scroll and I haven't the slightest idea what has become of it.

There was no further call for immediate frugality at the Aldwych now; *A Cup of Kindness* had paid off well and there was plenty of money around. *A Night Like This* was an elaborate affair with a large cast and six sets. One of these represented a London exterior in a thick fog which was well suggested by means of a gauze curtain and skilful lighting. An old-fashioned growler with a real cab-horse was discovered and, the cabby having temporarily deserted it, the horse moved off at a given moment and was supposed to home, like a pigeon, to its mews, carrying Ralph and Tom inside the cab. This was easily managed, with the genuine cab-driver in the wings to instruct the horse; but the poor old horse, though otherwise an excellent actor, persistently declined to control itself on stage and before long we had to appoint an artificial substitute. Regrettable – but the genuine horse's offence not only embarrassed the audience but prolonged the interval during a quick change. Besides, it always tempted Ralph to stray beyond the recognised bounds of impromptu.

Soon after the opening performance of *A Night Like This*, Queen Mary attended a special matinée which was given for some distinguished charity or other. I was commanded to be received in her box during the second interval. This interval immediately followed a scene in which Ralph and Tom, desirous of keeping Robertson Hare imprisoned in a room, decided that the best way of doing this was to remove his trousers and take them along with them. This was the farce's moment of most blatant frivolity and a good deal that had preceded it had not been exactly puritanical. I awaited the comments which Her Majesty might graciously be pleased to make, with some disquietude.

She said, 'It is very amusing and very interesting.' I bowed my acknowledgement, though I couldn't help wondering whether 'interesting' was a compliment to myself or to Robertson Hare. Then, with a slightly quizzical look, she added, 'Is it an adaptation from the French?'

As time went by the ill-feeling between Tom and Ralph at the theatre became more acute and more persistent. They weren't jealous of each other; each had quite sufficient confidence in himself to prevent him from resenting the other's success. But they bore an irksome grudge against each other. I think the real trouble was that they had got weary of their long year-in, year-out stage partnership and by the perpetual pinpricking differences in their characters and standards. Ralph's approach to his work was intensely and unceasingly conscientious. Tom's was blasé and feckless. He would constantly prolong the interval between acts while he entertained aristocratic guests in his dressing-room, leaving Ralph and the others – to say nothing of the audience – chafing to get on with the job. Ralph loved to make his laughing comments to me on Tom's ambitions as a social climber and of where he had climbed from. Originally in *Turkey Time*, I wanted Tom to appear in another of his elderly character parts. But he wouldn't; he said he wanted to play a man about town. 'That's what the women like me to be.' I said to Ralph, 'I had that good part for Tom but he won't play another old man. He says he's got to be a man about town.' 'Oh indeed?' said Ralph, 'What part of town?'

Turkey Time was a good farce but designed and produced on the old elaborate scale with quick inter-act changes of set and all the rest of it. This is perhaps the reason why it has become a relic of the distant past. We were busy in the film studio by day. I endured hours of tedium there, waiting for the next thing to happen; but Tom wanted me there because I had written the whole shooting script on my own. This meant my having to spend so much of my time away from Burnham that my wife and I decided to rent a flat in town. It was a nice little flat in Knightsbridge opposite the French Embassy. The daily woman was still very much in existence and we possessed an affable member of the tribe in Mrs Scott. I treasure her memory for what must be the prize non-sequitur even in the records of daily women. I secured seats for herself and her husband towards the end of the run of *Turkey Time*. She arrived next morning wobbling with pleasure and gratitude. 'Oh, it was lovely, reely lovely it was. But Mr Walls, he wasn't there acting last night.' (This didn't surprise me.) 'And Scotty, he'd seen it before. And he said that the gentleman last night wasn't as good as Mr Walls was. It's a small world, isn't it?'

The success of the *Rookery Nook* talkie brought Tom a big offer for a sequence of further film versions of the farces. He forsook Herbert Wilcox and teamed up with the Gaumont British company. But Wilcox had faith in Ralph's popularity as an individual comedian,

111

especially with Winifred Shotter as an added attraction. I wrote two very successful talkies for them. The first was *The Chance of a Night-time*, an adaptation of *The Dippers*. The second was *Mischief*, which stuck to the novel and redeemed the wretched little stage failure. Wilcox had an outstanding gift for showmanship. He organised one of those ostentatious full-dress charity crushes for *Mischief's* first showing at the Carlton and somehow managed to get the Duke of Windsor, who was then Prince of Wales, to come along. The whole thing was a tremendous success and the Press enthusiastic. But, oh, wait a minute – what did Tom Walls have to say about all this?

He rang me up two days later at Burnham. He had already told me that he would produce (direct) the next of my Aldwych farces but wasn't going to appear in it himself. This telephone call was to inform me that he had now further decided to sack Miss Winifred Shotter.

What a bastard you say. And so at that moment did I. How much longer was I going to put up with him – sitting there tamely while he directed the next farce; waiting day after day for him to turn up late at a film studio, so that I could tell him what we were going to shoot and what it was all about, while he got made up and then went to see yesterday's rushes before he postponed any further activities until the afternoon? Not only that. Look at the way I'd been let down over the Fortune Theatre and that blasted, or rather un-blasted, quarry. Oh, and don't think these were my only grievances. He had taken a night off from the theatre (you don't say) to take me to the first inaugural greyhound-racing meeting (it was at the White City I think). Tom had been impressed; so over-impressed that he proclaimed, 'This is going to sweep the country. It's going to knock provincial tours endways.' He thereupon, the very next day, cancelled all the prearranged dates for future tours. The boss. In one of his many headstrong myopic moments.

But now – this blatant exhibition of jealousy of Ralph and myself and of getting at us by an act of revengeful injustice to Winifred Shotter – that surely called for my parting of the ways with Tom Walls, didn't it? If it came to that, how could I have put up with him as I had for so long?

Was it because it was worth my while to put up with anything so long as it ensured my present and future prosperity? I sometimes used to ask my conscience that question and my conscience had no hesitation in replying, 'Yes, of course that's why. You can't kid me.' But my conscience knew that there was a good deal more to it than that.

I've told you once already, this man was irresistible. His vices out-numbered his virtues by the score and although he enjoyed the vices more than the virtues the virtues still came out on top. Jekyll was such an hilarious, entertaining devil-may-care delight that within five minutes of his company you forgave all the offensive and destructive infamies of Hyde. When I went to visit him on his death-bed he talked exclusively about fucking. But I don't mind betting that he got round St Peter all right.

Meanwhile there he was directing rehearsals of *Dirty Work*, the farce that followed *Turkey Time*. Ralph and I thought that Winifred's successor (recommended to Tom by C. B. Cochran) was a pretty inefficient subsitute and Ralph persuaded me to tell Tom that we didn't think she'd do. Tom, of course, brushed me aside. 'Oh nonsense – leave her to me. She'll be all right; she's clever as a monkey.' I reported this to Ralph. At the next rehearsal he sidled to my side, stooped and whispered, 'Some monkeys are not so bloody clever.'

But Ralph and I were wrong. The girl was Constance Carpenter who took over the lead in *The King and I* on Broadway when Gertrude Lawrence had her fatal illness. I am reminded of my one and only interview with Gertrude Lawrence. Herbert Wilcox had arranged for me to visit her in her dressing-room after whatever London show she was in, to try to get her to star in a talkie.

Miss Lawrence received me graciously and asked me to wait until she had changed out of her stage costume. Her elderly dresser drew a curtain across the centre of the room to debar me from the pleasure of witnessing this procedure, but, having mislaid something or other, the dresser pulled back the curtain and crossed the room, leaving Gertrude Lawrence to confront me with nothing on above the waist. I laughed. She said, 'It's nothing to laugh at.' I said, 'Isn't it? I'm getting for free what some old West End gentlemen would give fifty pounds for.'

Dirty Work did well enough considering that Tom was now a permanent absentee instead of being a slip in the programme. Bunny Hare was promoted to the position of joint leading comedian opposite Ralph, the first time his bald head became airborne to stardom. Margaretta Scott joined the party, full of the bouncing enthusiasm of the up-and-coming. We called her the Labrador puppy.

Another up-and-comer played a small support part in my next and final Aldwych farce, Wilfrid Hyde White. His somewhat sedentary methods were already in evidence and he was known to the company as Dasher White, which I call him to this day. In this farce I forsook my principles of depicting the characters as familiar true-to-type human beings, since Bunny Hare was England's cricket captain on an Australian tour and Ralph the leading batsman. They had to be kidnapped by bushrangers in the middle of a Test Match and rescued by Mary Brough in riding-breeches. The whole thing was really a topical burlesque, written to coincide with that tour which gave rise to the historic body-line row. It had a limited public but many people thought it very funny except in Australia. When some optimist produced it there it was regarded almost as a profanity and was quickly slain. If I had been in Australia at the time I might well have been slain too. I had dared to joke about cricket.

With Tom Walls giving his attention exclusively to the film studios my Aldwych farces expired, I, too, had rather lost the incentive – they were never the same without Tom Walls.

So, not long afterwards, did dear old Mary Brough. Her funeral in a large suburban cemetery, became quite inadvertently rather like a scene from one of the farces themselves. The public came in their thousands and the early-doors occupants of the crammed chapel feasted their eyes on Tom, Ralph and Bunny Hare, who sat with me in the front row. They were used to this at race-meetings and in restaurants but not at funerals and we had a job to appear duly reverential. Ralph didn't help by observing between clenched teeth, 'The second choir-boy on the right is like Madge Saunders.' We had a prolonged wait in the porch after the service because Ralph had left his wreath in the car and insisted on going to find it. No sooner had he got back than the hearse ran over the foot of an over-zealous Press photographer. Finally as we followed the hearse, four abreast, to the place of burial Tom turned suddenly on Bunny Hare, pistoned him in the ribs with a forefinger and spoke in a tone of savage command: 'When we get alongside that grave don't you dare get photographed between me and Ralph looking as if you were being bullied. They'll think it's a publicity gag.'

Whenever I look back on those nine years at the Aldwych and on all my associates there – Ralph, Tom, Bunny Hare, Sydney Lynn, Yvonne Arnaud, Mary Brough, Winifred, Coley – there is one who outshines them all in the contribution made to my success story, a quiet unobtrusive one but my guardian angel throughout. Vi, my wife. She was the most untheatrical person imaginable. She never had any desire or curiosity to participate in the professional or technical side of the theatre, but the human side interested her enormously. For this reason she was of immense help and value to me at the Aldwych and in any of my subsequent plays. Theatre people soon found out it was no use trying to talk their eternal shop to her. It wasn't due to any lack of sympathy; simply she didn't pretend to know anything about it. On the other hand she loved nothing better than to spend an evening backstage and have a good old gossipy and not necessarily very decorous discussion about mutual domestic affairs with anybody who was glad to escape from the artificiality of their surroundings. And oh, how they all delighted to escape into her company.

There was never a suspicion of insincerity about her. She didn't bother about who the people were or what they did; she just enjoyed the people. She was equally at ease and natural and good company when Tom Walls entertained us on a Sunday evening at his house at Ewell and escorted us round his stables – with a good deal of formal inspection of the horses, which bored me no little – as she was when one of the dressers at the theatre was telling her about her daughter's expectation of her third in four years. When my wife joined me at the Aldwych towards the end of a day's rehearsal, she would leave with very little idea of what had been perpetrated on the stage but full of the latest information about the understudies' dogs.

She was beloved by everybody in the world of the theatre who ever knew her, from her close friends like Binnie Hale to the stage hands and the cloakroom women.

When, many years later, in 1951, Ralph Lynn heard of my wife's death, he sent me a telegram which summed it all up in four words – the telegram simply read: 'Oh that lovely woman.'

8

Ever since I was first invited to occupy a small autobiographical space in *Who's Who* my favourite recreation item has remained the same – watching cricket. In 1905 I had read a book called *How We Recovered the Ashes* by P. F. Warner and had vowed a vow that if ever I got the chance I would go and watch a Test series in Australia. In 1928 when I was forty-two and *Plunder* was going strong at the Aldwych I sailed in an Orient liner with England's team.

My wife came with me as far as Colombo where we left the ship and toured Ceylon for a fortnight. She loved cricket as much as I did but she went back home to the children for Christmas and I pursued the England side and caught them up in Sydney. On the way from Colombo onwards a fellow-passenger was one of Australia's greatest cricketers of all time, C. G. Macartney. When we got to Melbourne he took me to the offices of the Victorian Cricket Association and introduced me to the Secretary. In the first Test I had ever seen, on the tenth to twelfth of August 1896 at the Oval (my father took me there – 'Tea-time; come on; let's pump-ship and have a bun'), that Secretary took 6 for 59 and 6 for 30 – Grace b. Trumble 9. F. S. Jackson b. Trumble 2. Abel c. Griffin b. Trumble 21. Hayward c. Trott b. Trumble 13 and so on. Hugh Trumble, a gentle old character. Then in came another celebrity, not so gentle – Warwick Armstrong. I sat with three of the greatest Australians in cricket history. I had that same feeling of incredulity as when I had first met Charles Hawtrey and Gerald du Maurier in the off-stage flesh – *je ne sais pas que je ne rêve*.

Nobody but a well-heeled fanatic travelled from England to Australia to watch cricket in 1928. I and my only fellow maniac, a plump and convivial individual named Colin Maesmore Morris, became privileged camp-followers, unofficial members of the team as it were. Percy Chapman was captain of probably the strongest England side that ever won the Ashes over there. Only three of them survive, Larwood, Geary and Ames. Douglas Jardine, still preserving his high-nosed superiority as an amateur (he wouldn't sit at the same table as the pros at breakfast), got a terrible pasting from the Hill at Sydney and it was mainly this which instigated his bitter

116

enmity when he was captain four years later and body-lined his revenge.

In contrast to the hullabaloo from the Hill at Sydney a brass band played (inevitably) a selection from *The Gondoliers* and there was a special Ladies' Enclosure, which was a good idea, as it allowed the male spectator to feast his eyes on a cross-section of the most beautiful feminine race in the world without having to listen to its conversation. Wally Hammond, who was the star English batsman of the tour, liked to spend most of his not-out luncheon intervals in sitting beside me and borrowing my powerful field-glasses.

Cricket enthusiasts with their age-old and often inherited collections of *Wisden's* can review for themselves the record of that tour. In the course of it I once rather unwisely tried to conciliate an attractive Australian girl on our way from the ground. 'Oh, well; cheer up – cricket's a funny game, isn't it?' 'To you it is,' she replied snappily. I have further memories of my sojourn with the team which *Wisden* would eschew. One night when I was returning very late with Patsy Hendren to our hotel at Melbourne we encountered a sozzled Australian gentleman and his equally sozzled lady friend on their reeling way out. They came to a sudden halt and the male challenged his mate. 'Wai——minute – your wrap thing, you know, scarf thing. Wheresit? Did you leave it dine-room, clo-room some place?' To which the lady replied, 'Fruit tart'. As a result of this the expression 'fruit tart' became a catchword with the England side. For years afterwards I used to send and receive post-cards and Christmas cards simply inscribed 'fruit tart'.

I don't suppose that any cricketer will be more fondly remembered by all who knew him than Patsy Hendren: he was in his best form on this tour off the field as well as on it. There was no covering of the wicket then and during the third Test at Melbourne a terrific thunderstorm looked like putting an end to England's hopes. (We eventually won through a superhuman effort by Hobbs and Sutcliffe.) After a long day in the field when Bradman made his first century against England the thunderclouds burst and our side trooped in, exhausted, dripping with sweat and for once dispirited and inclined to be acrimonious. There was only one man who could put things right. And he did.

In the course of the stripping and cooling-off stage Patsy, stark naked, began to imitate a monkey searching the likeliest portions of its anatomy for fleas. Within a couple of minutes he had everybody in the dressing-room roaring with laughter.

The Australian crowds loved him too. He was the favourite of the Hill. Once when he was in the outfield with his back to the Hillites, an untoward and over-beered barracker made insulting remarks about his size – 'show-off squit' or some such pleasantry. Patsy backpedalled to close quarters with the detractor and replied in the friendliest tone, 'I'll run you, I'll fight you or I'll fuck you.' This concluded the conversation.

I made friends with most of the Australian cricketers too – Vic Richardson (grandfather of those Chappells) and Alan Kippax and Bertie Oldfied. Kippax was the most stylish batsman in the world. If I were given my choice of watching anybody I have ever seen in my life play a long innings I would pick on him and most old cricketers I have known agree with me, especially Australians. The first match I saw in Australia, MCC v an Australian eleven at Sydney – an Aussie try out before the first Test – brought me into contact with the youth whose name was on everybody's lips, the Bowral boy wonder, Don Bradman. He played an innings which won him a place in the Test side. But – to show how the Aussies honour their great departed – when Bradman made a particularly brilliant shot one enthusiast in the members' stand yelled 'Trumper'. He was in momentary danger of being lynched. Time marches on.

Don Bradman and I have kept up with each other ever since. On one of his latter-day visits over here (his latest I think) I was lunching with him and said something which impressed him. (*I* said something about cricket which impressed Don Bradman – it seems to put me in the Muhammad Ali class of big-mouths.) I said, 'I think there are two categories of really great batsmen. One says to the bowlers, "I'm going to slaughter you." The other says "You're never going to get me out." You, Don, are the greatest ever in the first category. The greatest ever in the second was Jack Hobbs.' Don Bradman said he'd never heard it put like that before. And now he came to think of it I was dead right.

But that Australian tour brought me one of my greatest and truest friends in this life and for evermore – Arthur Mailey. I never met anybody who set my mettlesome impetuous nature a more valuable example in contrast. He viewed the world at large with an impassive sense of proportion, which means, of course, that he had a natural and unobtrusive sense of humour. He was the true philosopher. He treated the rush and turmoil of the modern, hurry-along-there-please way of life with quiet impracticable practicability. I needn't elaborate on his standing as a great Australian slow-bowler (*Wisden* again). But if he had worked away trying to lure a batsman into making a particular faulty stroke and the catch was dropped he wasn't unduly upset – he'd got what he was aiming for. If he wanted to go anywhere by train he didn't consult any timetable; he just went to the appropriate station – after all, that's where the trains went from. I often think of him when I'm getting into a frenzy about something which isn't really all that important. 'Mailey yourself,' I say. 'Mailey yourself.'

He was naturally generous: 'All right, Ben, we'll meet the girls outside in the lunch interval. I'll bring the champagne; you bring the pies.' He was a perfectly inoffensive debunker. In his early days when he emerged from some humble industrial job to bowl against England, the Australian side were invited to a reception at Government House in Sydney. The wife of His Excellency chose to be somewhat patronising. 'I suppose, Mr Mailey, you've never been in Government House before?' 'Yes, madam, I have. I was here about a year ago. I came to fix the gas.' He was almost as good a self-taught cartoonist and artist as he was a bowler. Queen Mary, inspecting one of his landscapes, remarked, 'Is not your sunshine rather faint, Mr Mailey?' Arthur replied, 'Perhaps it is, Ma'am. But here in England we have to paint the sun from memory.'

In these days when Australia's attitude towards the poms is that of a flourishing offspring tolerating a decrepit parent it is amusing to recall the assiduous and challenging desire that used to be shown to impress the English visitor. On that visit I had to endure an endless invitation to admire Australia's climate, scenery, cattle-stations, sheep-stations, cricket grounds, race-tracks, score-boards, Bradman, the way the people sing, the way the people bet, the athleticism and physique of its young men, the superlative beauty of its young women and various other amenities in comparison with my home products. I agreed, quite sincerely on the whole, especially about the score-boards and the young women, but there were limits. One of these urgent Aussie friends took me and parked me in his car on a vantage point from which I could view the whole range of Bondi beach in its full Sunday morning glory with thousands of young males with bronzed torsos and of their girl friends sporting, even in those days, the two-piece swimsuit. My host rallied me enthusiastically:

'There. You've nothing like that in England.'

'I'm afraid my Burnham doesn't quite compete.'

'Just look at that clear sky. The blue of that sea. The whole thing – you've nothing to compare with it. And those boys and girls, their splendid healthy bodies. Look at 'em.'

'Don't worry; I'm looking.'

He couldn't resist a crowning pious claim, 'Hygiene, relaxation – that's all they're here for. There's not a man or girl among the lot with a thought of sex in their head.'

I got back at him at last. 'Oh, bollocks to that,' I said. 'I'm here for one.'

The cricket spectator and those who spend long hours of discomfort watching tennis (a form of fanaticism verging on lunacy) at least have one great advantage over golf-followers; they spare themselves the tribulation of having to go for very long and often futile walks. I say futile because whenever I have been cajoled into taking this kind of exercise I have never once been able to see where anyone hits his ball to. And yet I have been more closely associated with golf and golfers over the years than with cricket and cricketers.

Burnham's one redeeming feature was its golf-course or rather links (natural hazard as in Scotland). The Burnham-and-Berrow club boasted a semi-championship standing and the English Amateur Championship was played there occasionally. In 1927 J. S. F. Morrison, an Old Carthusian, whom I had got to know when we were flying trainees together at Hendon in 1914, invited himself and his half-brother Dale Bourne, to stay with us for the meeting. Bourne was a brilliant golfer and won the title. He was a very gay and irresponsible character and, as his host, I had a stiff job in catering for his diet and timetable. As a result of my successful efforts I was enlisted as trainer to the Old Carthusian side which competed annually for the Halford Hewitt Cup at Deal. In 1928 and for some years ahead Charterhouse, with such players as C. V. L. Hooman, John Beck, Victor Longstaffe, and Morrison and Dale Bourne, had a winning side. The annals have been admirably chronicled by Henry Longhurst, who was soon himself a playing member of the OCs. I achieved quite a reputation as a trainer and deserved it. At the outset I conceived the bright idea of taking up my station at selected points on the course with a bottle of gin in one pocket and a bottle of kümmel in the other. Apart from this I won my reputation without much undue labour, though I do remember having to take Dale Bourne his breakfast on the first fairway.

My own attempts to play golf may best be described as a floundering and exasperating waste of time. They were put a stop to some forty-odd years ago in a very unexpected way. Tom Webster, the *Daily Mail* sports cartoonist, who was a friend of mine, was eagerly sought after by the leading professionals who played anything, fought each other or rode horses (is Tishy still remembered?). Tom took me with him to play golf one Sunday afternoon at some suburban course. At lunch we were joined by a stranger whose name I didn't catch. Tom Webster told me he was going to play with us. I naturally concurred amiably and it was only on the way to the first tee that I discovered that my threesome opponent was George Duncan, the reigning British champion. I said, 'Oh, thank you very much; I'll watch', but Duncan would have none of it. He insisted on at least an inspection, so I unwillingly prepared to have a bash. He foreclosed on this; 'No, no; you're standing all wrong.' He was in dead Scottish earnest. 'Stund to pee,' he said, 'and in imagination let your urine fall sex inches behind the ball and you'll be in the

120

correct stunce for the drave.' I obeyed orders and hit the ball about thirty yards along the ground. He sighed deeply – 'No, no, no – *sex* inches, I said, *sex* inches.' I asked him whether he taught many ladies to play the game and became a privileged spectator. But it was indeed a valuable lesson. It taught me to stop trying to play golf for ever after.

But especially in the years following the finish of my run at the Aldwych I took little time off for watching cricket or anything else. I was hard at work in and out of the film studios. I dry-nursed two of Tom Walls' productions of talkies I wrote for him, *Lady in Danger* and *Dishonour Bright*. Yvonne Arnaud co-starred with Tom in the first of these. In the second Cecil Parker got his first real chance and a support part was played by George Sanders, who had been spotted by Tom as a promising exponent of naughty-boy parts. I got the idea for the film when Tom and I were invited to go and supply the inaugural programme of Radio Luxembourg. The story was about the queen of a small European country caught up in a revolution and conveyed to safety in England disguised as a nun and shepherded by a benevolent English visitor. (With Tom Walls as the latter 'shepherded' is obviously a mild way of putting what happened to her.) I had originally written the thing as a comedy for Tom and Yvonne Arnaud but Tom had given up the stage and wanted it for a film. This upset Golding Bright who said it was the best play I'd ever written. He stuck to this opinion with the result that a few years later, on 11 December 1936, Yvonne Printemps and Pierre Fresnay opened at the St James's Theatre in the comedy, renamed *O Mistress Mine*. Yvonne Printemps couldn't speak English and had to be taught – by Fresnay – to deliver her multiplicity of lines phonetically, like an enchanting parrot. Fresnay, the most charming, generous-minded chap, was badly miscast and the play would have been doomed to failure in any case. But a strange coincidence gave it a sensational kick in its ill-fitting pants.

The eleventh of December 1936, its first night? On that day King Edward VIII abdicated the throne of England. There was a scene in the play in which every accursed line might have been a satirical commentary written by some republican poison pen. The audience sat silent and aghast. Some of the more sensitive of its members crept away. I was one of them.

I don't suppose many people read the Apocrypha of the New Testament but I did. In it I found the fascinating fable of Thekla, the girl who fell in love with St Paul and had to be counselled rather disappointingly to cool off. I wrote it up as a play and Ronald Adam put it on at the Embassy Theatre. The author's name was kept anonymous and the company entreated not to let on. There was some speculation in the Press about it and when a disgruntled member of the cast got the sack and spilled the beans I got an item of rather flattering prominence on the front page of the *Sunday Despatch*. The result was that the critics, while quite kind to the play, suggested that a farce-writer should keep within bounds. I resented this. I will lay odds that I'm more religious than any dramatic critic alive or dead. Moreover, not one of them would ever have guessed who dunnit. Margaretta Scott, now emerged from the Labrador puppy stage, was an ideal Thekla and successfully conveyed that St Paul must have been hard put to it.

But it was films, films for most of my time during that period. I wrote well over twenty shooting scripts on my own. They all did quite well or at any rate got by when they were shown in the West End which, along with my author's fees, was some consolation for the hours of tedium in benighted studios. And there was another pleasing feature – several of my favourite stage performers were roped in to boost the productions – Marie Löhr several times; Charles V. France and, above all, Diana Churchill, my brightest star of all in her theatre days. Now, crippled by arthritis, she can only employ her talents occasionally to bolster up the secondary (and often dreadful) fabric of radio plays.

My wife and I went one evening to see *A Cup of Kindness* done by the Bristol Rep. Mervyn Johns, who played the lead, told me he had been at Bristol for ten years and had played hundreds of leading parts. Soon afterwards he came back to London and gave a performance as Sir John Brute in Vanbrugh's *The Provoked Wife* which drove James Agate into a state of ecstasy. I had persuaded Tom Walls to give Mervyn a small part in a film of mine called *Foreign Affairs*. (It was typical of British film mentality that, without my being consulted, it was renamed *Foreign Affaires*.) Mervyn Johns so completely stole his one scene with Tom and Ralph that his part was almost completely cut out of the finally-edited version. But I am always pleased to have given Mervyn his first job in the pictures.

I never had any ambitions or ideas about Hollywood until one day Sam Goldwyn paid a visit to London and stayed at the Ritz Hotel. To my surprise Arthur Hornblow sought me out and took me along to the Ritz. Sam Goldwyn was discovered reclining on a richly upholstered divan in his private suite. He looked at me and then at Hornblow, of whom he inquired bluntly, 'Is this for Eddie Cantor?' as though I were some questionable form of diet. Hornblow told me to go ahead and tell about myself. I did myself ample justice for some minutes. I ceased. Mr Goldwyn did not make verbal comment. He shifted his position on the divan and gave vent to a loud and prolonged fart. I took this as my cue for exit. That was the nearest I have ever got to working in Hollywood and from what I've heard I'm very glad it was.

After the Aldwych days Robertson Hare had teamed up with Alfred Drayton, an excellent actor and a big, raucous man, admirably equipped to pursue the popular pastime of bullying Bunny Hare. They had been together in three or four successful farces at the Strand Theatre under the management of Bill Linnit and his partners, O'Bryen and Dunfee. Linnit asked me to provide them with a new farce, so I wrote and, as usual, rewrote and rewrote *Banana Ridge*. It was agreed that the three sets should be designed by Laurence Irving, who over the years had established himself as a front ranker in this line and produced a most convincing verandah of a Malayan bungalow. All promised well but we couldn't find an actor who could gabble the Malayan language in the part of the Chinese servant. A few nights before we started rehearsals I was having dinner with Bill Linnit and he said the only way out was for me to play the part myself. We signed an agreement on the back of a menu and left it on the dinner-table.

It took me a good deal of preliminary ground-work and three-quarters of an hour before every performance to transform my face into anything that might pass as that of a Chink, even a half-bred Chink of obscure half-parentage. But at least I rather staggered the first-night audience by shuffling on and saying '*Tuan tada sini, mem, dia dalang pad ang. Mem mau sia panghil.*' A *Daily Express* man who was standing with Bill Linnit and who had been born and brought up in Malaya remarked with surprise, 'Good lord, that bloke's talking the genuine stuff'; to which Linnit coolly replied, 'Well, what do you expect in one of my productions.'

Alfred Drayton was scornful when he first heard that I was to play the part. 'Pooh, you amateurs – you'll be sick of it in a fortnight and get someone else.' I bet him a fiver I wouldn't miss a performance. On the last night of the run on my last exit he was waiting for me in the wings with a five pound note. 'Here y'are.' Poor old Alfred, it was a bitter farewell. He was fond of fivers.

I deserved that fiver. I played the part over four hundred times without a break. It entailed some sacrifices. I only saw Burnham for the whole of Sundays and half Mondays. I had to leave Vincent Square for a matinée at half-time when my elder son was playing soccer for Charterhouse against Westminster. Again, I had to quit the Oval when Hutton and Leyland were batting in that Test in which Hutton made his record score, but I dashed back after the matinée to find him and Leyland still hard at it.

Banana Ridge cheerfully survived the 1938 Munich crisis but my next Drayton–Hare farce, *Spotted Dick*, was one of the first theatrical war-victims. It opened to as enthusiastic a reception from the first-night audience and critics as one could set heart on and its first innings lasted for nine performances. War was declared and the West End theatres automatically put the shutters up (all except the Windmill, the pioneer of bare bosoms, 'we never closed'). A little later, when the air-raid menace was still in the simmering stage, *Spotted Dick* put in another three months at the Strand. My daughter, Josephine, played a small support part and was singled out by some of the critics. She had been an understudy in *Banana Ridge* and had been sent a note of congratulations by Gladys Cooper, who didn't know her or me but had watched her from the front. A rare compliment, for when I later met Gladys Cooper and reminded her of it, she told me she had only done such a thing about twice in her life. Josephine then toured for a year with Ralph Lynn in *Rookery Nook* and she was the snappiest Poppy Dickey I've ever seen. She married during the war and settled for motherhood and domesticity. I am mentioning all this only because one of our best character actresses hasn't been on the stage for thirty-five years.

During the pre-war years Gerald du Maurier gave up a good deal of his time to the running of the Actors' Benevolent Society, in aid of which the annual Theatrical Garden Party was a special feature. One of its attractions was what was termed the Grand Giggle play, a half-hour rag performed by a cast of stage stars three or four times in the course of the afternoon. Du Maurier asked me to write one for him, with the result that he himself played the lead, the Rasping Kid, a prizefighter. Noël Coward played his fiancée, Edmund Gwenn his mother, Cedric Hardwicke the Chinese villain and Charles Laughton his Chinese girl-friend. Some leading actresses also participated in some of the male parts, Dorothy Dickson, Marie Löhr, etc. It was all like the brief fevered dream of some aspiring playwright and I remember little about it except that I rather ingeniously made Cedric Hardwicke commit hara-kiri by knifing himself from stomach to throat up a zip-fronted leather waistcoat and that Noël Coward especially appreciated my naming my White Star liner 'The Pedantic'.

From time to time all through my play-writing obsessions I had been writing some odd bits and pieces as contributions to magazines. For several years on end *The Tatler* commissioned me to write a short story for its Christmas number and these stories got a special boost because part of the standing order was that they were illustrated by H. M. Bateman, the leading humorous artist of his time. Another artist who ran him close was Heath Robinson and he illustrated two series of things I wrote for *The Passing Show*. The first of these offered modern versions of old fairy tales, retold for the benefit of up-to-date children. 'There was once a certain king. He died. That'll teach him to be so damn certain.' – That sort of thing. And the Jack-and-the-beanstalk giant's 'Fee–fi–fo–fum – I smell the blood of an Englishman' which was rendered as:

Fee–gee–fi–fo–fum –
It's a boy, some boy, I think;
for my cute old smeller is the dandy of a teller
Of the claret of an Albion gink.

John Lane's successors at the Bodley Head (the old boy had at long last given up by now) published this series and the second, dealing with Misguided Lives (Antonio, Merchant of Venice, the Excelsior youth with the banner, Ethelred the Unready and others) and they also got me to select and edit a Stephen Leacock anthology, which was a nice job as it enabled me to include some of my favourite snatches which had always been rather overlooked, such as Leacock's Ibsen play, *The Sub-Contractor*. Here is the song which bursts from the lips of the heroine 'in a moment of peculiar access of gaiety':

Was ik en butterflog
Flog ik dein broost enswog,
Adjo, mein Hertzenhog,
Aje, Adjo.

I also recalled a gem of Leacockian Scandinavian lampoonery which has been, and shouldn't be, neglected:

THE FRAM. August 20th, 1896.
(Fridtjof Nansen's ship, *The Fram*, returns safely to Skejervoe.)
What a glorious day
For old Norway,
When *The Fram* came sailing into the Bay
To the dear old fjord,
With its crew on bjord
All safely restjord
By the hand of the Ljord;
And they shouted 'Whoe
Is this Skejervoe?'
And they rent the ajer with a loud Hulljoe;
While the crowd on skiis
As thick as biis
Slid down to the town on their hands and kniis.
And oh, what cries
When they recognise
A man with a pair of sealskin pants on
And thjere, I decljare, is Fridtjof Nansen.

John Lane had brought his nephew, Allen, to London and had installed him as one of the directors at the Bodley Head. He had specially requested me to make friends with Allen Lane, which was as easy a job as I've ever been asked to do. I have always been glad to have been a rather mature friend of his youth, particularly on one memorable occasion a few years later. He had conceived an original, enterprising and hazardous enterprise which his co-directors at the Bodley Head had turned down flat. He came to ask me what I thought of it. He showed me a list of ten books, all published by Jonathan Cape, who was willing to do a deal with Allen for the hitherto unconceived paperback project. They were the first Penguin Books. Utterly unqualified to advise, I encouraged Allen to go ahead. At least, I knew the Lane flair when I saw it.

I began this rather rambling chapter with cricket. I have said that cricket brought me in Arthur Mailey one of my few really great male friends (they are badly outnumbered by the female ones). It brought me a second in Raymond Robertson-Glasgow. He will be well remembered as a cricket-writer with a predominant sense of humour all his own; moreover for Charterhouse, the Varsity and Somerset he was quite a good fast bowler. One of his less successful experiences as such was when he spent one exhausting and unprofitable morning against Hobbs and Sandham at the Oval. On his way up the pavilion steps at lunch-time he paused to make a brief confidential report: 'It's like bowling to God on concrete.'

One of my many happy memories of him was when he was staying with us at Burnham and we spent the evening with the two boys playing that delightful game, stub-cricket. When the boys had been bribed to go to bed we hit on the idea of playing a match between the contemporary England side and a team composed of notable figures in the world's history whom we would relish watching at Lord's or the Oval. Our joint selection of the world team resulted in a tantalising miscellany. The opening batsmen were Beethoven and St John the Baptist. (Beethoven was run out for nought, failing to hear a call for a sharp single on account of being stone deaf.) Others in the side were Attila (fast bowler), Torquemada (spin and googlie expert), Landru (the French bluebeard) and Sir Redvers Buller, of Boer War fame. I forget the rest, except Robertson-Glasgow's choice of Mrs Hemans (authoress of *The boy stood on the burning deck*) as wicket-keeper – the only wicket-keeper, he affirmed, who had ever been able to take the ball without the use of gloves or pads. I remember the umpires too. They were Pontius Pilate and Judge Jeffreys.

It is not often that one is given the opportunity to indulge in the appreciation and delight of utter and genuine absurdity. In my lifetime there have been only two supreme absurdity-caterers. Lewis Carroll stands unchallengeable (Lear never got within miles of him). My other absurdity champion is a music-hall comedian, Harry Tate: elderly laughter-lovers may be lucky enough to recall him. He specialised in jollying our popular pastimes – motoring, fishing, golf – into complete sabotage. His extraordinary voice, which I can best describe as a sort of rolling croak, was not assumed, though augmented on-stage by a gymnastic property moustache. In private life his sense of humour was less in evidence. Meeting him in Tom Webster's flat one night I had some good reason or other to ask him his address. His reply was a nice specimen of anti-climax. 'My address? Harree Tate; Veeeel Franche; Purley.' No absurdity about that: in fact a touch of pomposity.

I dare say Charles L. Dodgson was a rather frumious edition of the beamish Lewis Carroll.

9

When war was declared in 1939 I was getting on for fifty-four but I was self-employed and active, so it was up to me to do some sort of official war-work, wasn't it? Yes, I suppose so, but it was an upsetting, incongruent prospect. Another of those pregnant telephone calls from Laurence Irving decided my fate. He was back in the Air Force doing a uniformed job and begged me to come along with him. But what a job it turned out to be. It was at the Air Ministry in the section responsible for Security – A126 sub-section B. I spent my first week there trying to remember where I belonged.

Up to then no-one had bothered his head about air-security. Then Lionel Heald, a man of enormous perspicuity, took it in hand. Working under him was like panting after a running-coach who shoots ahead and waits patiently at the next corner for you to catch up with him. He was responsible for discovering and defining what air-security meant. What did it mean?

It meant fighting not so much the Germans as our media, though that revolting term hadn't been invented then. It meant imposing secrecy concerning anything that hadn't already been published about operations present and projected, types of performances of aircraft, equipment, personnel, establishments, casualties, armament, bombs, weather, and everything else. And to draft and issue in terms of prescribed restraint the daily Air Ministry communiqués, ensuring that we stopped the enemy from getting to know what they had done themselves if there was any chance that they hadn't found out – in fact to stop them thinking that we knew anything about anything we knew about them if they didn't already know they knew we knew.

But the worst of my duties was to arrive, after an occasional weekend's leave in the paradise of Burnham, back into the blank blackout of Paddington station to begin another haunting spell of security.

About two years of this was enough. I wangled a transfer to the Ministry of Information as one of the Air-advisers to the Censorship. There I further wangled a duty-schedule which gave me longer spells of respite at Burnham. The job did mean my having, on frequent occasions, to stay awake all night, but I was so seldom disturbed that I read the whole of the Bible, the whole of Shakespeare and the whole of Gibbon's *Decline and Fall* during those hours of duty (and still stayed awake? You don't believe it and, in retrospect, I'm not sure that I do).

One of my nights at the M. of I. was rather more excitable than Gibbon. A telephone call from the Air Ministry reported a sensational news item just received and I went to see whether I could check up on it. In a hallway I met Walter Monckton, who was the Minister of Information at that time. He said, 'Yes, I have just had a personal call from Winston. He said, "It's true Walter. Hess has landed in Scotland. The bug is in the apple."'

By the time America had been in the war for about six months their Army–Air-Force Intelligence had got into a rare muddle over their Security system, passing what we were stopping and vice versa. Someone had to be sent from our side to Washington to try and get the thing sorted out. I was sent there for three months and stayed six.

When they first saw me the Security Section of the AAFIB didn't think I looked a very good pick. Who can blame them – an elderly and bent little man in RAF Squadron-Leader's uniform with only about four medal-ribbons – is this what the Air Ministry, London, England, has sent us to think he can teach us our job goddammit? But I soon got them where I wanted them. They knew about as much about security as I know about the Koran. Within a week I had them laughing at me to my face and before long they were actually coming to me and asking me what to do.

They turned out to be a very friendly bunch and since, like myself, they were civilians in uniform their lack of proficiency was excusable as they were never let into any top secret. Even if our Colonel in charge got entrusted with one he was very guarded about letting on about it. On one occasion he summoned the whole section to be informed of some vital hush-hush operation impending. We congregated and awaited him, agog with speculation. The Colonel entered, a bristling little man with a snappy, impressive manner. He sat. We stood. He compressed his lips. He closed his eyes. A tense portentous pause. He opened his eyes and looked keenly at each of us in turn. He undid his lips and spoke.

He said, 'Gennelmen, this is it. Right now is what we've been waiting for. Yes, gennelmen; we're going to town.'

That was all. All his men looked at each other with a wild surmise. Some indulged in whispers of triumphant relish – 'Gosh, feller, you hear that? We're going to town.' Nobody knew what he meant. I'm not sure the Colonel did himself. Nobody asked him. I even resisted the temptation to quote Ralph Lynn and ask him what part of town. It didn't matter because nothing happened except that soon afterwards the Pentagon building was opened and we were transferred there; so perhaps that was it. I was perhaps the very first Englishman to occupy the Pentagon. I was suddenly back in my childhood, a little boy, bewildered in the maze at Hampton Court.

The bristling Colonel had been allocated a single-engine two-seater Harvard trainer for his own personal use, which he appreciated to the full because he had a girl friend who was one of the many supernumerary film actresses in Hollywood. So the Colonel consequently found it essential to fly his Harvard all the way from Washington pretty regularly in order to visit the Lockheed factories in Los Angeles. Towards the end of my stay he invited me to accompany him and to put in my time in Hollywood while he took the Lockheed factories for a week's outing. To fly the whole breadth of the vast and variegated American continent and back in a single-engined two-seater at an average height of six thousand feet was an uncommon experience. Unhappily, my Colonel was by now bristling as never before in his state of sexual acridity. This made him extremely nervous and testy. When he first handed me the controls he immediately flew into a paroxysm and accused me of trying to crash him into a tract of country which, he alleged, was infested by rattlesnakes. But all ended well. The Colonel disappeared into the depths of the Lockheed factories and I had the satisfaction of spending my first and last week in Hollywood as a privileged visitor. I took the most artless pleasure in getting to know film stars whom I had hitherto admired only from a distance – Jean Arthur, Rosalind Russell, etc., particularly a remarkable character whom many will remember, Adolf Menjou. His hobby was to skim through every daily newspaper available first thing every morning and to retail every news item from all quarters and on every subject. During a lunchtime I enjoyed with him at Romanoff's I spent the whole meal listening to an unusually entertaining non-stop newsreader. An odd trait in a most affable Menjou.

Another lunchtime interview I have cause to remember was with Walt Disney, a distrait, rather gipsy-like man. I talked to him about Roald Dahl, whom he knew about already and subsequently adopted as a star writer. Dahl was at this time Assistant Air-Attaché at Washington and his friendship, along with that of Patrick Graham, now a high-court judge, and his family, Angus McDonnell, who was the British Ambassador's Public Relations Officer, a glorious jovial character, and several attractive English girls at the Embassy provided welcome relief from the Pentagon. Disney kindly sent me, under escort of one of his stooges, to inspect his studios. One department was a minor museum containing a vast number of gadgets designed to produce every conceivable sound effect. Here we were joined by a somewhat insignificant-looking little man who was, my escort told me, one of the most notable and popular artists the world over and one I would surely be glad to have myself get to know. Yes, sir – he was the voice of Donald Duck.

On our return flight we were grounded by mist for four days at Greensboro, North Carolina. Apart from manifesting the incomparable hospitality of the Deep South (almost the first words I heard on landing were 'Jasper, go get Mr Travers a bottle of that genuine ten-year-old corn liquor'). Greensboro interested me as being the birthplace of O. Henry. A building is devoted to his memory and displays many of his manuscripts, all in flawless copper-plate calligraphy which I have never seen matched except by law-scriveners, Robertson Hare and some of those monks. Anyone who still reads O. Henry may like to know that his stories, written in and out of gaol, and in and seldom out of the saloon, are as legible as on the printed page.

Back in England I took advantage of being entitled at my age to quit the service whenever I chose to. I chose to. My house at Burnham had long been used by the local authority for dumping evacuees and local war-workers. On my leave-visits I had been confronted by strange figures on my staircase and intimidating smells issued from temporary cooking-stoves in the bedrooms. My wife had borne all this with characteristic good humour which was now rewarded. She got the evacuees further evacuated to make way for our daughter; and my first grandchild, Andrew Morgan, was able to be born in a bedroom scoured clean of the last lingering hint of Woolton pie. By the time I got back there for good, home was itself again.

I got to work on – and completed quickly for once – a war-time farce called *She follows me about* ('She' being Misfortune). It was inspired by a notorious character, the Rector of Stiffkey, who had been constantly in the news at that time. He was mixed up in many scandals and ended his enterprising career in a lion's den, an ideal setting for Robertson Hare. But the person who actuated the tribulations of Bunny Hare (the vicar of Tufflock) was not Stiffkey or his lions but one of my naughtier nieces.

On the beach in Cornwall she and a girl friend had seen a small parson emerge from behind a rock in his bathing costume and deposit his camera on a ledge of the rock while he went for his swim. The girls stole from their cave, borrowed the camera, photographed each other in the nude, replaced the camera, hastily dressed and went their way. The sequel was never known. But it made a nice opening situation for a farce.

The farce suffered, like all plays at the time, from frequent interference from air-raids, but didn't do badly, being helped along by a truly wonderful comedy performance by Catherine Lacey (what an actress) as Bunny Hare's scatty wife. Hare himself, in the best acting part he has ever been given, remained an amusing automaton, but Basil Radford was a useful acquisition. What makes the production worth recording is that it provided the prime example I have ever known of the exasperatingly antiquated puerility of those appointed to enact censorship of plays on behalf of the Lord Chamberlain. (Always excepting Tim Nugent, the only unpretentious one of the lot.)

On being notified that the farce would not be licensed unless fourteen offensive lines were cut, Bill Linnit and I journeyed to Windsor Castle, where members of the Lord Chamberlain's staff were quartered, and after being conducted down long passages flanked by unoccupied sets of armour, we landed up in a large room and were confronted by a small man. He and his lieutenant in waiting were responsible for having chastised my filthy mind.

Two extracts from the long argument that took place will serve to illustrate the preposterous fatuities which plagued a playwright under the censorship and the type of individual involved. At one point I challenged the cock-sparrow of a censor rather heatedly. 'Well, dash it, do you want her to say straight out, "He slapped my bottom"?' 'Yes,' he replied readily. 'I pass bottom.' His eyes lit up and he added in a tone of confidential pride, 'I was the first censor to pass bottom.'

A little later – '*That* word,' he said. 'Oh, that must obviously be ruled out. It has an utterly unspeakable double meaning.'

'Really? Then I'm surprised I've never heard it. Have you, Bill?' Bill Linnit shook his head. Even the second inquisitor had to admit he hadn't heard it either.

'Come on then,' I said. 'What is it? What is this poor word's horrifying double meaning?'

The spokesman half raised himself in his chair and surveyed the room anxiously as if it might harbour some sneaking eavesdropper. His voice dropped to a cautious, confessional whisper – 'Cock,' he said.

My next farce, *Outrageous Fortune*, dealt with rationing and ration-cards which were the topical pains in the public neck. Though staged in the far-flung Winter Garden Theatre (now extinct) it was a great success. Ralph Lynn came back to rejoin Bunny Hare and it was during the run of this play that occurred an episode which showed Ralph at his most Ralphish, though it had nothing to do with the theatre.

I was visiting him at his house in Epsom. He said he was going to drive me over to see his daughter at Reigate, where her husband kept an hotel. It was my first experience of Ralph as chauffeur. I had known some hair-raising trips as a passenger (J. C. Squire once took me for one, after which he downed three quick whiskies and told me he had never driven a car before) but Ralph surpassed any rival in eccentricity. On our way he got terribly tangled up with an oncoming funeral procession and in a heated argument with a posse of mutes in top hats. It was a scene which came straight out of a René Clair film. When at length we pulled up at the daughter's husband's hotel we didn't pull up quite in time. The road was on a downward slope and at the foot of the slope was a stationary car of imposing size and aspect. Ralph forgot which of his feet were doing what and accelerated into the rear bumper of the stationary car. 'Don't say anything,' Ralph said. 'No,' I said. 'Except that it's just as well there's no-one in that car.' As I spoke a gigantic man in a startling check suit, looking like an outsize bookmaker, oozed himself from the driver's seat in front. He strode towards us, ejaculating as he came – 'What the fuckin' 'ell you think you're doin'?' Ralph looked up at him with a pitiable smile. '*I'm* sorry,' he said. 'It's my brakes.' Then with a quiver of pathos, 'Look at them. They've been like that for years.' The bookie's face swelled into a crimson balloon and burst into laughter. About the only time when I have known Ralph below his best was at the wheel.

Soon after the war we sold the house at Burnham and moved to a cottage at near-by Berrow – a genuine five-or-six-hundred-year-old cottage with walls a yard thick and made of mud or dung or something. It had rough-hewn beams and honeysuckle over the front porch and withy trees dotted about the little garden and a walnut tree and a woodpecker and a very old distorted apple tree that spread its gnarled branches in several directions, so that when it blossomed it looked like the soul of some old twisted martyr who had at last gained paradise and had been rather extravagantly garlanded by the angels.

It was an altogether blissful place until, only four years later, my wife was found to be suffering from cancer and, after a long and painful illness, she died in 1951. Disraeli said that time is the great physician and those who know me will agree with him in my case, but it really goes deeper than that. I didn't try to challenge sorrow or to ignore it. It is just that lasting affection gradually blends sorrow into being a gentle accepted part of happiness. Then one's memory turns to all those moments which were glad. Whenever I talk to my children now about their mother we always remember the things we all used to laugh about together. That's how it is with her and me and that's how it should be.

I stayed on in the cottage for another year or more, and fortunately Elizabeth Bradbeer, sister of all those golf pros, was able to come along on her bicycle and cater for me every morning (she had been with us for twenty-five years). Then, in the autumn of 1952, I began what became a regular routine for the next fifteen of our winters – I dodged the English winter by voyaging to some of the places farthest flung in the disintegrating empire. It all started because an ex-secretary of mine, Peggy Powell, had gone to Singapore to work for the BBC and had married a glorious American character, Dack, who was in the Firestone Rubber Company out there. Peggy brought him to England on leave and to Berrow to get acquainted with my forlorn self. They said, 'Come and spend next winter with us in Singapore.' I can't think of any invitation which gave me a greater kick or one which materialised more delightfully. I gave the Dacks no mercy. I was with them again next year and several times in the winters that followed and when Dack retired and left I planted myself with Murray Buttrose, who was the last surviving white judge in Singapore and who, with his wife Jean, was allotted a residence even more spacious and ornate than the Dack bungalow in Firestone Park. So I did myself very well and was done by. Perhaps avoiding those fifteen English winters may largely account for my having just reached my ninety-first birthday.

After the second year I thought, 'Damn it, I must give these kind Singapore people some respite,' so I went on my own to South Africa by merchant ship – much the pleasantest mode of voyaging at that time. Not so pleasant this time, as the ship caught fire in the hold in mid-Atlantic. The hold contained newsprint which developed spontaneous combustion, after the fashion of some acrimonious hay-stack. They steamed the hold to subdue the glowing newsprint but this created such heat that you couldn't put your hand on your cabin wall and I burned my foot on one of those metal bars which, for some reason, run between the cabin and the bathroom. So then they flooded the decks and cabins and I had two inches of water in mine. We were still on fire when we got to Cape Town where we were unceremoniously expelled. It was an intimidating experience, par-ticularly because the hold next to the newsprint contained a lavish supply of sulphate of ammonia. The reaction of the dozen passengers was interesting. The men indulged in intimate know-all forebodings ('Don't for God's sake tell any of the others, but I happen to have got it from the horse's mouth—'). The women chatted and knitted. Give me women.

One woman with whom I had always remained on affectionate terms throughout my married life was that convivial old girl, my mother-in-law. She outlived my wife for a year or two and died while I was still living alone in Berrow. Perhaps it's as well that she did, because she spent her last few years in a Burnham nursing home, in which she was going cheerfully dotty. She thought I was her brother. She used to enjoy trying to pluck imaginary butterflies from my shoulder. She gave me a book by Enid Blyton for a Christmas present. I was very fond of her.

On that almost forgotten former voyage, twenty-five years before, when I had come scooting back from Australia under orders from Tom Walls, one of my fellow passengers had been an Australian teenager named Peg Simpson. I was only reminded of this when she turned up at the M. of I., where she was also working during the war, and identified herself. I met her again when she decided to make a permanent home in London some years after the war and bought the lease of a house in Trevor Square. She wanted someone who would share the rent and upkeep and was wise enough not to settle for another woman. She asked me whether I would like to fill the bill and as, by now, I had become more and more bored and depressed by living alone in Berrow and wanted to go and live in London, I willingly fell for the prospect of comfortable quarters in one of the most desirable of all the house agent's eminently desirable residences. I shared the house with Peg Simpson for the next ten or twelve years and, with an occasional squall now and then, it was a very felicitous passage of time.

My home life, as it had been for the thirty-five years of my marriage, was a thing apart and could never be rediscovered. So perhaps it was just as well that my next long instalment of home life should be spent in so entirely different a setting and in company with a woman of so singular a nature that it and she call for a special little folio of reminiscence.

When I went with her to Trevor Square, Peg Simpson (Cynthia in her birth-certificate) was about forty-five. She had never been married; she had been let down by an Italian Count – oh, those Italian Counts, how often they crop up in rueful confidences. She was part-owner of a sheep-station in the North-Western slopes of New South Wales and had plenty of money. She possessed one outstanding quality – the sharpest and most retentive memory I have ever come across and, as she also took a never-ceasing and comprehensive interest in the arts and literature, she would have given any of the annually victorious Masterminds a very good run for their money. She was quick-witted – to get into an argument with her was to take a knock-out in the first round. She doesn't sound much fun as a house-mate does she? One of those prissy, superior intellectuals. But this is just what she wasn't. She had a great sense of humour and especially of the ridiculous and in all the books she read and the shows she saw, she enjoyed what she enjoyed with an almost childish enthusiasm. Friends like Emlyn Williams, Allen Lane, Tim Nugent, Peter O'Toole and many others delighted in her company and were devoted to her.

She was extravagant in her tastes and in kindness to people. She gave to charities in a spirit of a sort of reckless indignation at the misfortunes of others. She never passed a street beggar or one or more of the ex-service or non-ex-service performers on the cornet – or even the youths who play ghastly pop-music on guitars in pedestrian sub-ways – without stopping and delving into her handbag.

Apart from the Italian Count she had known some very unhappy experiences. One in particular might qualify as a Grand Guignol episode; when, sitting alone in a Sydney tea-shop, she had overheard a stranger at the next table, reading aloud the report of her fond father's death by his own hand. But her present, ever-present, trouble was her own health. She was never without aches and pains. After a short while I thought, 'Oh, my God. I have gone and saddled myself with a hypochondriac.' I learned later, to my shame, that it was all quite genuine.

She was very grateful to me for my companionship and never stopped saying so. I was for hers, and I look back on those seventeen years with great affection – seventeen years, because at the end of the ten or twelve in Trevor Square she went to spend a weekend with her friend, Pauline Baring, in Sussex and returned to tell me that she had been persuaded to leave London and to go and live in Rye. It was a surprising announcement, if only because the de-lightful Mrs Baring never finds it necessary to have to use persuasion. It was obviously Peg's own initiative. But the point was – did I want to move to Rye too? Well, by that time, I was in the eighties and didn't feel like having to start again and to try to get along on my own. So if I didn't altogether fall in with the proposal, I agreed to wade in. But London was by now my spiritual home and remained so for the five years I spent in Rye. It became that stage in the career of the aged, aged man when he temporarily forsook a-sitting on his gate to search the grassy knolls for wheels of hansom cabs.

Not that I could possibly have wanted better accommodation than I had at Rye. Throughout the whole of our association my comfort had always been Peg Simpson's first consideration and now I had the best top-floor bedroom suite in the best house with the best view of a long stretch of Channel coast, not only in Rye but anywhere in the South of England. Moreover, Olive came along every day to beatify the household. Any inhabitant of Rye will agree with me that in the hereafter Olive will be crowned patron saint of that blessed race, now practically extinct, who progress from being the flawless and frownless daily help to being a lifelong friend of oneself and one's family.

During the latter part of 1973 Peg's inherent ill-health took a final turn for the worse and she died in November of that year. The estate-duty people played a typically long and tedious innings against the sustained attack of Australian executors and nearly two years went by before the Rye house could become the property of Peg's cousin and only relative. It was sold in about five minutes and back I came to London.

I kept possession of the Berrow cottage and handed it over to my younger son who was and is working for Harvey's of Bristol. I, myself, don't say no to a vintage port but I can do without sherry thick or clear. If I were told that I could be allowed only three types of drink (bar water) for the rest of my life I would choose champagne, beer and coffee. Which three would you choose?

But, leaving drink for the moment (though I have a tankard of beer beside me as I write) I must return to the theatre. What did I get up to, as an author, during this seventeen-year period at Trevor Square and Rye? A year after my wife's death Bill Linnit promoted a farce of mine called *Wild Horses*, with Ralph Lynn and Robertson Hare. It was produced at the Aldwych but underwent the unusual process of being tried out for a preliminary month in various parts of West Germany, where the British Army was in occupation. On its first night it received a rapturous reception from the select audience of uninitiated and flattering officers and their wives. As the result of what we had seen Linnit and I spent the rest of that night until dawn, discussing what the hell we could do to knock the play into shape. With us was Charles Hickman, the director, who had already done an excellent job for us with *Outrageous Fortune*. I left the scene immediately and returned to England to rewrite practically the whole thing and enjoyed about two hours sleep per night for a fortnight. The revised version made a very good start at the Aldwych, so the last of my Aldwych farces was safely delivered, after a tough childbirth, in the old maternity home.

It hadn't been running long before Ralph Lynn slipped on a sheet of ice in his garden and dislocated his spine while he was playing with his dog or some such folly. I have become a stern and uncompromising anti-dog man. I think dogs should be licensed purely for utilitarian purposes, such as guiding policemen and the blind and conveying flasks of brandy to people who are big enough damned fools as to get stranded in Alpine avalanches.

This aversion has only developed in my tetchy old age. My wife loved dogs and our Burnham home was never without two or three of them and since they were part of her happiness they automatically became part of mine. And I still can be quite attracted by Pekinese but I think they are a separate species outside the dog world and are the result of Nature having had a freakish bit of fun out of school at some period in the past history of the mysterious East.

Ralph's accident did little good to *Wild Horses*, though David Stoll put up a creditable show in the part, and it only survived about six months. My next essay in play-writing didn't survive at all but is worth recording as providing a sidelight on the subtle character of the celebrated Binkie Beaumont, an eminent diplomatic impresario, genuinely charming in deportment, hard as nails at the core. He bore a remarkable physical likeness to one of those species of larger lizards from Brazil or some such place, which you see in travel documentaries on TV, even to the flickering tongue, which you felt Nature had been guilty of an oversight in not forking. When the play had flopped through the few weeks of its try-out provincial tour, I said to him, 'You don't intend to bring this thing to town, do you?' He replied, 'That's entirely up to you. I will if you say you want me to.' He knew there was only one answer to that, and tactfully retained my appreciation of his generous attitude by passing the buck.

From then until 1975 my various efforts to participate in providing entertainment were aberrant and desultory. I completed the funniest farce I have ever written for the Lynn–Hare combination about explorers in deepest Africa, which contained the excellent situation of Bunny Hare being rescued in the nick of time from being eaten by cannibals. But Robertson Hare objected to performing with the coloured community and, before we had succeeded in wheedling the obstinate little man, all this racial discrimination stuff had begun to become a national issue, so there it was.

Many years ago, I forget when, I was asked to supply the BBC with a television play. It was quite a good little comedy and went down well but I will never write another. My Aldwych farces have been produced on TV, some of them three or four times. A series, which had ideal actors for the Lynn–Walls parts – Richard Briers and Arthur Lowe – proved a disappointment to all concerned; principally because it was subjected to the exasperating ordeal of being performed in the presence of a slow-witted invited audience. (No dubbed laughter allowed in this case.) Television can provide marvellous entertainment when it sticks to actualities, all forms of sport and documentaries (*The World about Us*, etc.) but, for me, it is the wrong medium for adaptations of stage plays. I always argue that when you go to into a theatre your eyes belong to you. When you watch anything on a screen they are at the mercy of the director or editor or whatever. The live theatre is so irreplaceable that any attempt by television to rival it in some limited, abbreviated form is deficient and irksome. As in the case of films, there can be excellent entertainment in plays devised directly for television (Alan Ayckbourn wrote a beauty) but adaptations of stage plays seldom come off. *The Long Day's Journey into Night*, with Laurence Olivier, goes to prove that I am an opinionated old stick-in-the-mud, but I stick in it and admire and enjoy only the very few exceptions that come along.

There is another play which I first wrote about thirty years ago

138

and have written about seven or eight editions of. I am still writing another edition so it may sooner or later see the light. Jack Hylton bought one of the editions when I was still living in Berrow. He called for a conference to discuss the casting but I couldn't get to town for some reason and asked my then agent to represent me and express my views. My then agent had another great interest in life in addition to, or along with, being an agent, namely his great attachment to the bottle. This attachment was in full swing at the time appointed for the conference which he failed to attend. Jack Hylton very reasonably said, 'Oh, well, if Ben Travers can't be bothered' and that was the end of that. A good job perhaps – the latest edition is a great deal more promising than the rejects.

There was a revivial of *Thark*, which was put on at the Yvonne Arnaud Theatre, Guildford, with, I suppose, the hope of a transfer to the West End. The transfer did in fact take place and marked the début of Ray Cooney in management. He directed the show and made a very good job of it, but presumably the prospective backers only backed one way, namely out. Ray Cooney courageously went ahead on his own; the production was pitched headlong into the Garrick Theatre and deserved to have a successful run; for Alec McCowen was tremendously funny, playing the Ralph Lynn part on the requisitely straight comedy lines. Unfortunately he had previously been booked for another play and had to quit the cast after about ten weeks. The revival did not long survive this, but I look back on it as a very pleasant memory. For one thing I was delighted to have Kathleen Harrison back in a play of mine. She had partaken in my most outstanding flop, *O Mistress Mine*, a bright gleam in the general gloom. Like Mary Brough, she has, in her generation, monopolised a particular type of stage personality and I have envied Emlyn Williams and Terence Rattigan in supplying her with ideal Kathleen Harrison parts. She may be said to be one of those performers whose scope is limited by their own individuality. But thank goodness for the individuality.

Let me see, what else cropped up during that long Trevor Square period? Reps and Amateurs' regular patronage of some of the old Aldwych farces, *Rookery Nook* in particular, provided me with a moderate but sufficient income and I'm afraid I relapsed into a state of settled and rather unenterprising contentment. At one time another impresario, whose somewhat lugubrious nature had earned him in the trade the label of Jolly Jack Minster, undertook, with uncharacteristic optimism, the self-imposed experiment of producing *Rookery Nook* as an up-to-date, contemporary farce. Though nobody could have wanted a more efficient pair of would-be rescuers than Richard Briers and Moray Watson, it was laid to rest after a few weeks in the provinces. The same farce had a more regrettable failure when presented as the basis for a musical show a few years later with Daniel Massey and John Standing, neither of whom I had ever suspected of being expert in the song-and-dance business but who both turned out to be brilliantly so. So was Isla Blair in the leading girl part. I never felt much confidence in the thing but I was won over when I heard David Heneker's score. He has a gift for composing numbers with a sort of frisky delicacy of their own. The title song *Half-a-Sixpence* is one of my favourite musical-show numbers of all time; and a Massey–Standing duet in this show ran it close. But the latter production suffered a considerable amount of botchery in its try-out stages, being directed, apparently, at times by a number of people at once and at other times by nobody at all. I, as an occasional observer, contributed a few suggestions which were enthusiastically welcomed and completely ignored. The first night at the Globe was accorded the ultimatum which is so often described as 'a friendly reception'. The Press was lenient with the exception of the *Daily Express* which contributed the worst notice that any pitiless critic could be capable of thinking up. I thought it was an engaging little show and it was a shame that it was doomed to die so young.

As against these rather melancholy experiments I rejoiced in two revivals, limited to a month's run in each case. The Royal Court Theatre, of all places, produced *A Cuckoo in the Nest* with Anthony Page directing. He gathered a company which dismayed old Mr W. H. Darlington, who recalled and compared the original, but oh, delighted me. That Nicol Williamson should be cast for the Ralph Lynn part perplexed a good many people both in anticipation and result, but not me. It gave me a glow of self-satisfaction to prove to myself that, although Ralph was inimitable, there was material in his Aldwych parts for an actor of entirely different personality and method. Nicol Williamson portrayed some sort of bewildered, mother's son, Old Etonian. Arthur Lowe, recognised at that stage of his career as the uppermost of all up-and-uppers in the profession, played Tom Walls' part, and Beatrix Lehmann, Mary Brough's. Minor parts were played by Alan Bennett and Polly James, whom I had seen in her recent RADA days. Anthony Page informed me during the casting period that John Osborne had put in a request that he might join the ranks of the company. I was incredulous but, sure enough, there was John (the first time I had ever set eyes on him) at the first read-through. Dressing-room space at the Royal Court is restricted and John shared quarters with Arthur Lowe. The latter, as might have been anticipated, was singled out by the critics, and on the second night when I looked in to express my thanks to the company, John presented Arthur Lowe to me in the manner of a television compère. 'Here he is – better than Tom Walls – and cheaper.'

Plunder, revived at the Old Vic, Bristol, and also astutely directed, this time by Nat Brenner, gave me, especially in one particular way, as great an exhilaration as I have ever felt at one of my plays. Once again a Ralph Lynn character in the hands of a star actor of fifty years later – Peter O'Toole. I can't be blamed for keeping on being cocky at having written a part created by a great farce, but purely farce, actor in which one of the most eminent and versatile actors of our present day can glory and be glorified. Whether you like or dislike me, whether you like or dislike Peter O'Toole, I defy you not to have been entranced by this performance. One outstanding moment came at the end of the second act – when D'Arcy Tuck is left alone on the stage to contemplate the possibility of being found guilty of participation in wilful murder and condemned to being hanged by the neck. Peter O'Toole, an accomplished dancer in his day, stood staring into space. He rose involuntarily on his toes and as he rose, or appeared to rise, a few inches higher, Nat Brenner's beautifully timed curtain descended to meet him. It was the best 'curtain' I have ever seen on any stage and another vindication of my plea for the retention of the good old proscenium arch and of the curtain, as opposed to that dispassionate blackout.

It will be seen that during all this time I participated very little in the activities of the entertainment world. My befogged memory, my only informant, seems to think that I broadcast occasionally. I certainly took my turn in one of those Desert Island Discs programmes – I was pleased with myself for contrasting the mastery of two great modern pianists, Artur Rubinstein and Fats Waller, in the same section. When I am told by myself and others that I was much too lazy for too long, I have to take into consideration that I spent three months of every year in foreign parts. There you are – an ideal opportunity for writing some play for the first or fifth or sixth time but I was never in the mood or had the opportunity. Balls to that – sheer laziness – oh, very well, then, have it your way. But do you blame me?

Even if I could consult the diary which I never kept about my various and unadventurous voyages and travels I would not do so. A catalogue of my visits to Australia (on several occasions), to Singapore (for varying lengths of time almost every year), to Malacca (I seldom failed to put in a fortnight or so on my old stamping ground; the Pinero plays were still in the library and probably still are), to Hong Kong sometimes, North Borneo sometimes, Malaya sometimes (The Majestic Hotel, Kuala Lumpur, with the monkeys in the garden: the glorious West Coast with the turtle beaches), Delhi, Beirut, Jerusalem will amply suffice. Any attempt on my part to embark on a detailed travelogue would justifiably have caused even that long-suffering Victorian patron, the 'gentle reader', to startle the spouse by hurling the volume at the fireplace, missing it and smashing the mantelpiece clock.

I will mention one occasion though. It gives a good example of the historic vitality of the late and remarkable Sybil Thorndyke. She was touring in *The Chalk Garden* in Sydney. I chose, unwittingly, to go and see the play on the hottest night following the hottest day of the Sydney summer – how ever the audience endured the atmosphere I don't know, let alone the players. I paid the Dame a brief visit in her dressing-room after the show – the second performance that day. She was skipping around in her dressing-gown and told me that her morning had been spent in visiting a girls' school, speeding off to keep a date at a film studio, where she rehearsed and shot a scene in a picture in which she was playing one of those star-support parts, and getting through with it just in time to arrive at the theatre in time for the matinée. I cut short my visit to her dressing-room because she wanted to put in an early night's sleep in order to rise in good time to start on a climb to the top of a neighbouring hill. She would set out for this all the more readily if she awoke feeling as fresh and full of zest as she did at the moment.

The recollection of my visit to Jerusalem should also be singled out, because I went there on a personal mission of religious curiosity and to satisfy a spiritual obligation, rather like that which instigates a Moslem's pilgrimage to Mecca. At the time I went there Jerusalem was in two sections and once you had quitted the Jordanian section and set foot in the Israeli portion of the city there was no turning back. When you left Jordan a porter carried your baggage to the centre of a certain square and an Israeli porter emerged from the opposite side, took charge of the baggage and without a word or even a look at his opposite Jordanian number, conveyed it into Israel and that was that. Since so many of the Holy Places were in Jordan I chose to spend practically the whole of my time in the Jordanian Jerusalem and in visiting and contemplating the actual country and authentic scenes where the various incidents of Christ's life on earth took place. Jobs were so hard to come by in the city that one of the best and most remunerative was to qualify as an authorised guide to European and American tourists and I managed to get about the best of them, a scion of the most revered Jordanian families, and an intelligent and jocular chap, who spoke fluent English. (He was adopted by a rich and romantic elderly American lady in the year after my visit and I gave him lunch at the Café Royal on his way to New York.) We motored together to Bethlehem and through the miles of stony wilderness from Jerusalem to Jericho – a delightful town, from which we proceeded to the shores of the Dead Sea. I have never seen a more deserted and dilapidated spot than the allegedly inhabited township where we drew up. The occupants of one or two fishing boats appeared (when on land) to constitute the entire population. The various buildings were derelict. Only one of them appeared to claim any connection with the rest of the world at large. This building bore a length of banner running across the frontage above its broken-down doorway. The inscription read: The Dead Sea Night Club.

There has been one great interest in my life – I mean my out-of-home life – apart from languishing in foreign parts. Ever since 1931 to the present moment I have shared with successions of others the privilege of being a member of the Court of the Fishmongers' Company. I became Prime Warden by rotation in 1945, when, unfortunately, Fishmongers' Hall was still being reconstructed, following minor damage wrought by German fire-bombs on its roof and major damage wrought by the over-insistent enthusiasm of the gallant fire brigade. This, together with the limitations imposed still at that time by rationing, meant that my year of office had to be spent beneath the clouds of war which took so long a time to disperse.

Fishmongers' Hall stands on London Bridge overlooking the river, the most favoured site of all the City Livery Companies' stately homes and only a few yards from the fruit-brokers' office from which I used to emerge laden with sultanas and pessimism. I am now the senior member of the Court, on which my associates, past and present, would send the name-dropper to bed with a sore throat. Unlike nearly all the other City of London Livery Companies, the Fishmongers' is still actively involved in the running of its own trade and with the associations involved. When I was Prime Warden I had occasion to pay an early-morning visit to Billingsgate Market, an enticing opportunity to glean some of the authentic and traditional expressions of exasperation and abuse which have made the term 'Billingsgate' part of our language. I purposely took up my stance in the direct path of a fish-porter trundling a barrow laden with crates. He halted. I waited, with one hand on a pocketed notebook. He gave utterance. He said, 'I beg your pardon: do you mind?'

Annigoni's portrait of the Queen, approved and publicised beyond any portrait of recent times, was commissioned by the Fishmongers' Company but, strange to say, the original on view in the Hall, only got there after an unusually sticky debate. There was an exhibition of Annigoni's work in a Bond Street gallery in the year 1953. I went there with Peg Simpson and so did the Prime Warden of that year, Edward Chadwyck-Healey. He suggested, at the next Court meeting that Annigoni should be approached, with, of course, Her Majesty's consent, to furnish the walls of our Hall with his esoteric conception of her likeness. Several of the elderly members of the Court, steeped

143

in patriotic tradition, expressed their strong objections. Never mind the artist's esoteric qualities (whatever they might mean) the point was that, though it was highly desirable to have a portrait of the Queen in the Hall, it was unthinkable that this should be painted by some damn foreigner. It was agreed to defer any decision until the next meeting of the Court. Meanwhile I reported the preliminary goings-on in conversation with Peg Simpson, who immediately provided me with the right answer. 'If we were organising a gala concert for the entertainment of Her Majesty, undoubtedly our first and ideal course of action would be to engage Toscanini. But, alas, we couldn't do that, because he has the misfortune to be a damn foreigner.' This settled it. Annigoni was commissioned. It is, I think, worthy of record, that while Edward Chadwyck-Healey was primarily responsible for the Annigoni portrait being in existence at all, Peg Simpson played a pretty telling part in its inception.

Gresham's School was founded in the middle of the 1550s – before my time but nearer my time than the time of anybody else still associated with it. The endowment of the foundation is administered by the Fishmongers' Company and I was on the Board of Governors for a number of years; in fact I was deputy chairman for a while and had to take the utmost pains to conceal my abiding ignorance of anything to do with finance. Gresham's School has always shone as a training-ground for the Arts and Sciences. The Science experts progressed into another of the worlds beyond my ken and some of the Arts boys (Benjamin Britten, W. H. Auden) gained the highest summits. It was at Gresham's that I saw Michael Aldridge play Sir Toby Belch in the annual school Shakespeare play and to provide me with the most salient example of stealing a show in the whole of my experience.

Towards the latter end of 1975 I could be spending one of my last nights in that pleasant house in dull Rye – in a comfortable drawing-room chair with the open fire at my toes. And as I gazed into the fire I could have ruminated on the similarity it bore to one of my own life's past experiences over eighty-eight years and to that life's present condition. At one time it had been a flaring blaze which had gradually died down and now had shrunken into a steady uniform glow, still friendly as it neared its quiet eclipse. But, as is sometimes the way with fires, there would remain one little corner which still insisted on throwing up an intermittent flicker, now flashing, now vanishing above the steady dying glow. Two little bits of fuel had been chucked on the fire at a late moment without expectation that they would rekindle that sleepy line of smouldering affectionate farewell.

Suddenly, within a few moments, the whole fire was ablaze again, ablaze as it had never blazed before. A miracle? Yes, but the fire of my life had always been tended by that Hand sensed by Robert Browning, 'ever above my shoulder' – the hand that alone orders and creates the miraculous.

Since that visionary evening at Rye, I have been thrice in company with Michael Parkinson, responding to his infectious chuckle on that television programme of his. I picture myself with him again, or undergoing the more regulated probing of one of those many amicable press boys:

QUESTION – Do you really mean, Ben, that you believe in miracles?
ANSWER – I believe only in miracles.

10

One morning in the summer of 1975 the telephone in my bed-sitter at 29 Watchbell Street, Rye, roused me with a grunt of irritation from whatever I was or wasn't doing. Long-distance – London – 'Hello, yes? This is Ben Travers.'

The caller (do you remember the old 'trunks, please' days of those terse, eavesdropping female operators? 'Speak up, caller') was Robin Dalton. Robin is usually a man but in this case I am glad to say she is a woman and I have every reason to be grateful that this is so. She is not only a humorous, pull-no-punches friend and hostess but an agent of sudden inspirations and of an ability to extract stunning terms from managerial males by a blend of tenacity and charm. She has a very choice and individual taste in velvet gloves.

She informed me in the most matter-of-fact manner that my comedy *The Bed Before Yesterday* was to be produced later in the year at the Lyric Theatre with Lindsay Anderson as director and with Joan Plowright in the lead. I thanked her for these tidings, hung up the receiver and fell on my knees.

I had written this play some time during the previous year I suppose (past dates fly from my mind like startled sparrows) and had shown my own typescript to Anthony Page. After his direction of the *Cuckoo* revival at the Royal Court he was the one and only chap for me. I knew it was a good period (1930) comedy with an excellent part for a comedy actress but I rather funked the idea of getting it put on with my name as author for two reasons. Firstly, I was afraid it might shock some of my family and the more staid of my elderly friends; secondly, I anticipated that the critics might regard with a mixture of scorn and pity the efforts of a poor old farce-writer of bygone days competing with the bright young playwrights revelling in permissiveness.

I think I really started to write the play for my own enjoyment and self-satisfaction – to prove to myself – if to no-one else, that I could exploit this new-found freedom in subject and dialogue. I hit on the idea of a woman of young middle-age and ample means, who had been brought up in the aftermath of the Victorian age, uninitiated

146

in the secrets of sinful sex. In this state of ignorance she was to fall victim to a rotter (period term) outraged and agonised on her bridal night (exit the rotter) and thereafter avoiding and abhorring the very thought of sexual intercourse until she becomes lured into giving it one further try-out many years later; when, discovering and revelling in the delights of the orgasm, she is driven to the verge of nymphomania. There was obviously comedy to be found in this character and context, so long as I avoided any temptation to lug in what might be termed smut for smut's sake – a common pitfall at a time when stage characters had become free to do or say anything their authors cared to cook up for them. They could strip, copulate, rape to their hearts' content and 'fuck' had become as accepted a word in stage dialogue as 'bloody' had been a few years before ('and not too many bloodys, please' – the Censor). Some producers had naturally enough availed themselves enthusiastically of this wholesale licence. Shows featuring nudes as their primary attraction were already monopolising one or two of the West End theatres from this time forth for, apparently, evermore. All the more need for a straight comedy, however licentious, to be kept straight.

I must hasten, in parenthesis, to admit that I am the last person who could conscientiously object to the advent of those nudes. Had I been a good many years younger you would never have kept me away from them. Naked female bosoms have always had an irresistible fascination for me. To judge by the unceasing flow of photographs in the popular daily press and by the advertisements displayed alongside tube escalators (recently modified, at the request of the GLC or some sham-pi authority in a position to request modifications), Nature has long since discovered that a brace of breasts form the first appeal to man's sexual curiosity; so I am only one of a vast majority. But I think I must be pretty well placed in the queue. There can be nothing shameful in appreciating and extolling the most outstanding (but not for my taste too outstanding) of the most beautiful woman's physical attractions.

Anthony Page liked the play and ridiculed my reluctance to put my name to it. He was keen to direct it but he was just off to America on some television job. This proved such a success that America commandeered Anthony for a long time ahead. Meanwhile the script remained knocking about in the precincts of the Royal Court and Lindsay Anderson, who was still there at that time, read it and approved. And Anthony, on one of his fleeting visits to London, sent it to Helen Montagu of H. M. Tennent Ltd, or Helen had heard about it and had asked to read it or something. (In July 1977 Helen Montagu severed her connection, as the cliché goes, with H. M. Tennent and started out as a theatre impresario on her own – and good luck to her. Her first venture, *Filumena*, is one of the biggest current hits in London.)

There are multitudes of ideal wives and mothers nowadays who manage to do a strenuous and successful professional job at the same time but Helen Montagu must top the lot. She has a husband who ranks high in the psychoanalysis line and a son and three delicious daughters. And I'll bet she is as dedicated and efficient in the home as she is in the theatre world. It is not generally known that Helen Montagu is responsible above any individual in the country for having ridded us of the intolerable burden of the censorship of plays. She spent seven years at it, briefing parliamentarians and often writing their speeches for them. Then, in the London branch of H. M. Tennent, she managed all the business on hand there, in all its ramifications major and minor, answering a call from America, with another from Australia on another line, and carrying on snatches of debate with an anxious author on the side, always with outbursts of laughter punctuating the conversation and always with practical unflappiness in the face of opposition or adversity. She has a flair for casting; I love sitting with her at auditions when she will spot merits or fallibilities which only become obvious when her intimate, slightly lisping whisper tells you so.

Helen said that the first essential for *The Bed* was to get an absolutely top-ranking actress for the part of Alma and that we must wait in patience until we got one. I agreed to wait in patience and did so for what seemed a pretty long time. I paid occasional visits to London from Rye and one day Helen suggested that we found out what Anthony Page was up to and what the prospects were of his being able to come and direct a production over here. We had better go and see his agent, Robin Dalton. So I met Robin for the first time and in the course of some preliminary chit-chat heard that she hailed from Sydney (you would never have detected this from her accent). I asked her whether she had ever happened to come across Peg Simpson and Robin replied, 'She was my godmother.' This was a good start but, whoever had been her godmother, Robin's efficiency – telephoning America on the spot and finding out what we wanted to know – decided me there and then that she was to be my agent for *The Bed* and for anything else that came along.

The Bed itself came along without much further delay. Tennent's and Eddie Kulukundis formed a rep. company headed by Joan Plowright to appear in two plays running alternately, week-in, week-out, at the Lyric Theatre. Both plays were to be directed by Lindsay Anderson and one of them, Chekhov's *The Seagull*, had been proposed and accepted as an attractive opener. At some point or other Joan Plowright had been given *The Bed* to read and she thought it would make a nice contrast to *The Seagull* (which, by Thespis, it did) and also give her one of those good light-comedy parts in which she excels and which, I think, she enjoys playing now and then. ('Joan Plowright can be one of the funniest women on the stage' – Anthony Page in one of his letters to me.)

I was sorry, of course, at the time that Anthony had to be ruled out but he, characteristically, sent me an enthusiastic letter, telling me how pleased he was about it all and how lucky I was to get Joan and Lindsay.

Lindsay Anderson and I got on splendidly from the first and still do. He liked my play and knew that I relied on him to get the best he could out of it and Lindsay's best is the best anyone could look for. Lindsay Anderson is the most unusual individual I know. Occult is a gloomy adjective but occult he is. I and everybody who knows him may tell you their opinion of him, but I don't think that any of his associates in the theatre can tell you what they really *know* about him. I have the idea that this is mainly because he takes good care that they don't. Outwardly he is very practical, practical in the way in which he clothes himself to suit his own comfort and convenience, practical in his decisions and opinions. I take a special delight in his speaking voice, clear and cultured and assertive; the decisions and opinions are often expressed with remorseless candour, but there is a note of friendly inducement in his tone, like an April sunbeam appearing through a break in a thundercloud. Morevoer even his close friends in the theatre can never be quite certain when he is not giving the assertiveness a little time off in order to indulge his rather Puckish sense of humour – ('My God, do you know what Lindsay said to me on the phone this morning?' ... 'Oh, well; that's just Lindsay all over; you know what he's like'). But nobody does quite know. And I think he relishes this.

Never since the days of Tom Walls have I known anybody exercising greater authority in the theatre and Lindsay's brief smile clinches rather than diminishes the authority. And no-one could be a greater contrast to Tom Walls whose sole aim was self-interest, engaging character as he was. Lindsay's sole interest at any given time lies with the job on hand. There is another way in which he is practical: he knows that he is the best director of plays and films in the country. Others may disagree; he doesn't care whether they do or not, he knows it and they don't, that's all. This has nothing to do with vanity. His satisfaction in knowing it is that it gives him a warrant to go ahead and do things in his own way. (I had reason to esteem his own way before I ever knew him. I saw his film *If* at my local Rye cinema and went to its next showing to see it all through again.) It always crops up when I recall or discuss the favourite films of my lifetime – *Desire, Big Deal at Dodge City, Nothing Sacred, Rachel Rachel, The Best of Buster Keaton, The Seven-Year Itch* and *Jour de Fête*.

149

As a stage director Lindsay was shortly to provide me with a night of magic. I admire and enjoy him on-stage and off, this side idolatry.

Eddie Kulukundis is another remarkable individual; a big figure (in every sense) and one of great esteem in the theatre world. This is only to be expected, since he is the biggest backer in the business. I, like Damon Runyan's narrators, make it a rule to refrain from being inquisitive and all I know is that Eddie inherited and now runs one of those amplitudinous concerns in the world of shipping which seem to be profitably exploited by merchant venturers of his nationality. The Greeks have a gift for it.

But thank goodness Eddie spends a great deal of his time and money in his absorbing interest in the theatre. He seems to know pretty nearly everyone in the profession and anyone he doesn't know he knows about, and is a shrewd judge of his or her capabilities. A great deal of the immediate and future fun I have got out of life at this late stage has been due to his friendship and benevolence.

The Seagull came on at the end of October 1975 and was given a run on its own for a month while the same company rehearsed *The Bed*. I went to the first night of *The Seagull* and sat through it for three or four nights later on. There is one scene in it – when the mother binds a wound in her son's head and they engage in un-wonted endearments which quickly develop into a flaming row – which was so beautifully played by Joan Plowright and Frank Grimes that I used sometimes to sneak into the theatre and out again to see this one episode. I know I am a pitiable, unashamed Philistine, worthy to be lynched and to have my remnants thrown into the Thames or Volga, but I simply cannot abide the plays of Anton Chekhov. I saw Peter O'Toole, Edward Hardwicke and Sara Kestelman in *Uncle Vanya* and at odd times in the past I have seen *The Three Sisters* and things and now this *Seagull*. Many of the characters spend their time sitting with their chins in their waistcoats, deliberating at great length whether or not they will commit suicide. Anyone can tell them the right answer, but they ought to have arrived at it themselves before they came on.

On the very day that I arrived in London, bidding Rye a joyful farewell and to start out on by far the busiest and most exciting years of my lifetime, I was dated by Helen Montagu to go with her and have my photograph taken with some of *The Bed* company. This was while they were still rehearsing *The Seagull* and I had never met any of them except Royce Mills. Helen drove me to the most extraordinary-looking building (I think it was somewhere in Fulham) which looked like the relic of a Charles Addams' house (you half expected the shade of Boris Karloff to open the door to you). It was here that a photographic agency conducted their operations and hither members of the Lyric company obligingly came. Joan Plowright was early on the scene. I took her in my arms and said, 'I love you more than any woman I've never met' and she responded graciously. Later, as we patiently sat while the photographers fiddled about with their lenses and with those silly strips of white screens hung on poles, we briefly discussed *The Bed* and she said something which delighted me and which I have always treasured. She said, 'I love it because it is so genuine.' That is the one adjective which I have always striven to have justly applied to all the plays I have ever written, farces and all.

Helen Mirren was in the photo party too. She had just reached the stage of having become a notoriety, welcome to the theatre-gossip columns, which, while acknowledging her acting abilities, presented her as a good-time girl with a special and rather unpredictable good-time nature of her own. Where they went wrong was in presuming that the good time came first; she is above all a gifted and versatile and conscientious actress. I don't know much about her private affairs (well, I do know a bit because she and I used to exchange confidences sometimes during rehearsals) but it is her stage job that comes first with her and although her performances are liable to vary she is always the first to say so and to repent a lapse. I really only got her in a support part in *The Bed* because she was playing a leading part in *The Seagull*. As an enterprising young woman of the 1930s, she implored Lindsay to let her wear a platinum wig and Lindsay let her have her way. I didn't care for it and still don't, chiefly because females of the 1930 period always wore hats out of doors, but it suited the character. Lindsay said to me, 'You only want Helen to wear her own hair because you're in love with her like everybody else.' I said 'That's perfectly true.'

It may earn me a black mark as a biographer (no animadversions, no naughty back-stage giggly secrets) but I have nothing but affection for everybody connected with that first production of *The Bed* and for those who from time to time replaced them. None of them regarded me as a venerable old has-been to be polite to: I was the same age as any of them. I told Lindsay that I sometimes suspected myself of being a humbug. He said no, but that I was prone to overdo my outspoken admiration in some cases. This is true; people like me and I like them back a bit effusively on occasions but quite sincerely.

John Moffatt, in the male lead, was a good foil to Joan Plowright and did a lot towards keeping the comedy running smoothly during the various changes in the cast in the first year of the run. He takes a special interest, more or less a hobby, in the records and personalities of the theatre as it was in my younger days and possesses a remarkable collection of ancient phonograph and gramophone discs and records – I only wish I still had some of mine: four-to-six-inch discs with the preliminary announcement, 'Liberty Bell, played by

Sousa's Band, Columbia Record, London made', rotating on the wound-by-hand phonograph which was Edison's earliest product.

Others in the original cast besides John Moffatt and Helen Mirren were Patsy Rowlands, Frank Grimes, Royce Mills, Gabrielle Daye and Leonard Fenton, the latter a splendid character actor for whom I have a special regard. His one-scene appearance as a gentleman whose dual occupations were part-time stick-man at an illegal gambling-house and part-time pimp delighted me afresh every time I saw the show. The Duke of Devonshire's first comment to me about *The Bed* was, 'I loved that pimp.'

Never in the whole of my theatre experience have I had such an enjoyable and exhilarating time as during the four weeks' rehearsals of *The Bed*. Lindsay Anderson's supreme talent as a director lies in his appreciation or rather judgment, of values – the value of an in-flection, of a pause, of the movement or reaction of a character at the right moment; the value, too, of rephrasing of a line or of cutting it altogether (out, out, any line, laughter-line or no, which impedes the flow of action). He is tremendously punctilious; time is no object so long as he gets a scene set and played as he wants. I knew better than to interrupt him and didn't often have reason to, but when, at an appropriate break in the proceedings, I had a suggestion to make he would either accept it readily as a good idea, which it gener-ally was, or oppose it only after deep consideration. Carlyle's defini-tion of genius, 'transcendent capacity of taking trouble' has never been better illustrated.

Joan Plowright's approach to a part and characterisation of a part are naturally and purely constructive. Once she is on the job there is never for a moment the slightest suggestion of any sort of prima donna disdain ('Oh, I can't be asked to say a line like that'). If she is unhappy about a line it is because she doesn't feel that it is quite how the character would express herself. And it was never what Joan Plowright would rather say, it was what Alma would be more likely to say. After a ten-minute discussion (never an argument) between her and Lindsay about a line, or even an inflection, they'd agree about it and Joan Plowright would say 'Yes'. From that moment onwards there was never a variation. Joan Plowright's 'Yes' at rehearsals is the most decisive monosyllable I have ever heard spoken in a theatre.

Peter O'Toole was in London on the first night (9 December 1975) and gladdened my heart by insisting on calling for me and taking me along to the Lyric. We called on the way to see Judi Dench at the Globe (I wanted to thank her for a charming message of good wishes) then for a brief visit to a pub and eventually we arrived in time to participate in a preliminary champagne bout, optimistically organised by Helen Montagu. I hovered about during the show in a box with her husband and two daughters and was glad to hear it all going very well. Then, soon after the genuine and enthusiastic laughter at the opening of the second act, I sensed, mistakenly I'm glad to say, that dreaded sensation of chill which, at times on first nights, seems to emanate from where the orchestra pit used to be and to creep outward over the stalls audience. I knew of old the right deterrent for this. I sneaked unseen along to the gents' lavatory and spent a minute or two in fervent prayer, screwing my face up in intensity of appeal. I have often, in fact pretty nearly always, done this at some point or other on a first night with very satisfactory results.

There was one feature of Lindsay Anderson's direction which caused a good deal of preliminary head-shaking and muttered protest. Having given an exhilarating kick to the production by choosing some appropriate 1930 period records to be played during the brief intervals between the various scenes of the play (I loved Jack Buchanan at work on 'Everything stops for tea') Lindsay was inspired with the notion of repeating these numbers in a general song-and-dance act by the company to replace the conventional and static curtain-call routine. This idea met with strong opposition, not from the company but from others concerned, including myself. My own objection was that it seemed to involve a star of Joan Plowright's status in a proceeding beneath her dignity. But Lindsay was adamant and was proved to be completely justified – well, not completely until it was decided to drop the curtain on the play itself and immediately to raise it again for the revels to begin. My grandson, Andrew Morgan, suggested this to me and I passed it on. Lindsay's brassy innovation became a little independent smash hit on its own.

The critics were unanimously favourable, some of them enthusiastic. We waited anxiously for Harold Hobson's comments in *The Sunday Times*. His opening words were, '*The Bed Before Yesterday* calls not so much for a review as for a cry of ecstasy. Rabelais would have revelled in it. Wycherley would have been green with envy.' We were home.

Helen Mirren gave me an eighty-ninth birthday present at the bar-party organised by the management to celebrate this event. The present was a bright red pullover with green sleeves and a picture of a beatnik couple in a tango attitude on the chest. I wore it at every subsequent rehearsal and under my dinner-suit shirt on the first night. I appeared in it, displayed, at the first of my Michael Parkinson television interviews. All this because of my unshakable devotion to superstition, which I regard as a frequent and useful reminder that there's a Providence sits up aloft, to keep watch for the life of poor Jack. I watch the clock so as to make certain that my first word of any month is 'rabbits'. I grope my way out of doors with my eyes shut in order to avoid seeing a new moon through glass.

Ridiculous? All right then, I'm ridiculous; but I don't think so. Not so ridiculous as to kid oneself that one's motives and actions are not known to and judged by a higher power who, I am sure, smiles indulgently on one's funny little acknowledgements of belief. Superstition is God's approved and congenial clown.

On Joan Plowright's departure the part of Alma in *The Bed* was taken over by Sheila Hancock, who played it for about six months and was succeeded in her turn by Judy Cornwell. Each of these two actresses showed that the eccentric and exceptional Alma could be interpreted by ladies of entirely different appearance and personality and yet remain convincing and fascinating to feminine members of the audience, who may not have experienced Alma's sex problems themselves but know damn well that they were on the cards. I got the same sort of private self-esteem when I saw the parts that had been so brilliantly originated by Ralph Lynn in the Aldwych farces (fatuous-cum-eyeglass stuff) played equally brilliantly but on different lines by Peter O'Toole and Alec McCowen. Sheila Hancock's Alma was on broader lines than the others. She went for the laughs and got the loudest of the lot; she has a gift of using her long and agile physique in sudden moments of reaction or protest. Judy Cornwell emphasised Alma's outbursts of uncontrollable anger and subsequent contrition, which (I speak from experience, shared, I guess, by many of my sex) can scarcely be overplayed. Michael Aldridge joined the company at the same time as Judy Cornwell, in John Moffatt's part. This was an inspired bit of casting. Michael made the man exactly as described in a line from the play, 'Ah, a pipe-smoker. Yes, I thought he looked that sort. Tweedy-suity sort of chap ... He's nice, Alma. You made a good pick.' I was very lucky to have actors and actresses of such outstanding ability to play the two leads throughout the run of *The Bed*.

For her performance in *The Bed* Joan Plowright received, rather belatedly, first prize in her particular section from the Variety Club at its annual awards luncheon at the beginning of 1977. In the previous year I had been presented with a special award by the *Evening Standard*. This was really quite an exceptional honour as it was only the third of these special awards to be bestowed in all the years since the inception of this newspaper's enterprising annual prize-days (Peggy Ashcroft received the fourth in 1977). Rex Harrison was officiating as the hander-outer of the trophy – a very weighty lady of singular proportions, seated on a marble slab on which was a metal plate inscribed 'Special Award Ben Travers for services to the Theatre'.

My beneath-the-surface self-satisfaction was given another boost when I was elected a member of the Beefsteak Club I was proposed by Robert Speaight, a man of theatrical distinction if never of great public acclaim. He was in very ill-health at this time; I took him as my guest to a City dinner and he fainted during the third course, which wasn't the fault of the dinner. He died in the following year, young enough to be obviously beloved by the gods for his erudition.

A traditional feature of the Beefsteak Club seats its members at the same long table for their luncheons and dinners, in places allotted to them according to their time of arrival. A newly-joined member, especially a very aged one whose knowledge and recognition of his eminent contemporaries has become blurred, is liable to find himself sitting alongside gentlemen of obvious authority and distinction and seeking tactfully to discover who the hell they are. (An Ambassador on leave? An editor of note? One of those long-service Tory MPs?) While I myself have never failed to enjoy a most congenial and interesting meal, my next-door neighbours must have found the old boy beside them singularly reticent, groping and experimental in his efforts at conversation.

How different it is with women. You have only to encounter the right sort of lady for the first time to be in her arms in a matter of minutes and indeed, in this sophisticated age, it often starts that way. I recall a nice example of feminine conversational ice-breaking on an occasion demanding the strictest social reserve. It was in 1945, when I was invited to some posh luncheon given by the Lord Mayor at the Mansion House. I found myself seated next to Lady Lavery, whom I had never set eyes on before but whom I judged at first glance to be gifted with a confident sense of humour. Almost the first words we exchanged were:

LADY L. 'What do you think of Mrs Attlee's hat?'
I. 'I think it's a bugger.'
LADY L. 'I double bugger.'

If the Beefsteak Club tends to have a rather intimidating effect on my self-conscious and easily overawed nature, it at least retains all the best qualities of the stately past – the prestige and polish you seldom come across anywhere else nowadays. My other club, the Garrick, is an institution notable for its past rather than for its present. I have been a member for nearly fifty years, having been proposed, as an act of gratitude, during the run of *Plunder*, by Herbert Waring. He was a veteran actor of distinction who had been cast for a showy one-scene part in Act three. This delighted the old boy, as he was able to enjoy a good dinner at the club before proceeding along to his Aldwych Theatre dressing-room.

When I first joined, the place was true to its traditions and all the leading actors and playwrights were to be found there. Anyone proposed for membership had to have gained enough distinction in his profession or job to meet with the committee's approval. Some years before, some undistinguished Guardee officer had managed, by some oversight, to have slipped in. This gave rise to one of Henry Kemble's characteristic comments: 'That Captain Somebody has just entered the club and he has gone to tether his charger to the door of the WC.'

I was too timid to show my face in the club for some years. When at last I took the plunge I peered round the door of the coffee (dining) room at lunchtime and was encouraged to spot a vacant seat next to a man who was already a friend of mine, P. G. Wodehouse. On the other side of me sat an elderly character who was extremely genial and coversational and who I later discovered to be the Lord Chancellor, Lord Buckmaster. That was what the Garrick was like in those days. I had crept in, nervous and apprehensive, and left after spending a carefree hour with the Lord Chancellor and Plum Wodehouse. But the apprehension had been justified. Opposite me at the lunch table had been seated none other than the sinister Sir Horace Avory, Mr Justice Avory, notorious throughout the land and especially in criminal circles as 'the hanging judge'. He exhibited, according to all reports, a personal relish in pronouncing the death sentence and a trenchant unction in the pronouncement – 'You, too, shall die.'

All through that lunch he seemed to be keeping his eyes fixed on me. He wore an introspective and speculative smile. It was decidedly unnerving and it was only later that the reason dawned on me. Nature had omitted to provide me with a neck – my chin and my chest have barely enough room between them for an Adam's apple. What Mr Justice Avory found so intriguing was the problem I would set to the hangman.

I needn't have been in such a funk of the Garrick: its stage members were very friendly with one or two exceptions. Alan Aynesworth always displayed a somewhat chilly superiority; but he was self-important by nature. On one occasion near the end of his prolonged life he was conveyed to the club in order that he might be shown where his portrait had been hung in the bar. This, at the time, was at right angles to another portrait by the same artist, Codner, showing Seymour Hicks in the flamboyant character-part of *The Man in Dress Clothes*. Aynesworth compared the two portraits with an elaborate gesture of satisfaction, 'The Hicks portrait is less conspicuous than mine. And, by comparison, how unspeakably vulgar.'

The comparison didn't stop there. Seymour Hicks was the best company you could find in the Garrick or any other all-male community. He was the best raconteur I have ever met, a jubilantly witty character. The club still houses a gigantic and utterly inept landscape featuring six gigantic pillars, which is known by Hicks' nickname of 'Brighter Cricket'. He was as entertaining to have a meal with as he was capricious to work with. He wanted me to write for him and I had one or two shots at it but soon gave up. On one occasion, when I had a ready-made farce-comedy perfectly suited to his personality and method, my wife and I went all the way to Plymouth, where he was touring in something or other, in order to discuss the glowing prospects. A french-window and balcony apiece afforded easy communication between our hotel bedroom and his. At frequent intervals throughout the night until early dawn, Hicks kept popping to and fro, landing on my wife's bed and stroking her arm, while he elaborated his latest, substitutional and utterly ruinous brainwave. I returned to London next day and consigned the script to my old friend the wastepaper-basket. But I seldom have spent a more delectably fruitless night. My wife had characteristic-ally slept through most of it, the arm-stroking no doubt contributing to her blissful dreams.

Apart from its actors the Garrick Club has always housed some notable individuals, especially from the legal and literary professions. I was on the general committee when Malcolm Muggeridge created a storm-in-a-teacup but nationwide sensation by publishing his article criticising the royal family. Some dogmatic members of the committee made strenuous efforts to get him booted out of the club for conduct unbecoming to a gentleman. But they left it a bit late, as the next committee meeting didn't take place until a fortnight after publication, by which time, as I ventured to point out, several other impressive events had driven Mr Muggeridge from front pages into temporary obscurity. (A dog from Russia or America or some-where had been dispatched on a probationary trip round the moon and so on.) Why lug or propel our unbecoming fellow-member back into the limelight? So no action was taken except by Mr Muggeridge himself, who not long afterwards resigned on his own account.

Bernard Darwin was one of the exalted exhibits of the Garrick. I knew him from the days of the Halford Hewitt golf competitions at Deal. He used to stay with the Old Carthusians at their hotel, in order to avoid his own Old Etonians, though he played for them in the competition so long as he was capable. He always played with the same long-suffering foursomes partner, whose name was Jobson. I recall the latter driving some fifty yards from the first tee at Deal and an inflamed Darwin preparing to play the second shot – 'Fore – stand aside, will you – fore. Incredible as it may seem, this is my partner's drive.'

Of the many changes that have taken place in the Garrick Club, particularly in recent years, one has brought me great satisfaction. In the old days ladies were allowed the exceptional privilege of being invited as guests for luncheon (not lunch) on Sundays. Now they are made welcome at any meal at any day of the week; doubly welcome because their member host has to present the club with sums of money for their entertainment almost as prodigious as he would have to fork out at any of those overcrowded and dingy Italian restaurants. True, the food at some of the latter may be better, but in some circles, thank goodness, where you eat is still of greater concern than what you eat. The atmosphere of the Garrick Club as an historic theatrical institution still lingers from the days when Henry Irving and his crony, the comedian Toole, would meet there every night for supper after their respective shows – Irving accompanied by a young man in his company, Seymour Hicks, whose duty it was to listen in silence throughout the meal (imagine Hicks silently listening) and to convey his venerable charge home in his hansom cab in the small hours, making sure that he was landed safely at the correct address, if not always in the strictly correct condition.

I think that the old Garrick spirit is kept going to a great extent by its pictures. Lady guests, far more interested and appreciative of course than most of the men, are now given the opportunity of seeing all these pictures. That coffee (dining) room features Zoffany's 'Clandestine Marriage' and others of his works, and every other foot of available space in this room, and in the room above, the morning (pre-dinner drinks) room, and on the walls of the broad winding staircase is occupied by the portraits of stage celebrities of past centuries with, here and there, a depiction of some dramatic scene which provided full scope for the performers' fulminations and semaphore.

In the morning room I like to gaze on Mrs Bracegirdle, possessor of one of the most delicious names I have ever encountered or even invented. (I have habitually taken great trouble about finding the right names for my characters – see J. C. Trewin's Collected Works for an appreciation of Poppy Dickey, Tilly Winn, Queenie Deed, Mrs Gather, D'Arcy Tuck, Steeth, Mrs Orlock, etc.) Mrs Bracegirdle must have been an early pin-up girl in her girlehood (sorry I have been reading my Nabokov again). I would have signed on as Mr Bracegirdle for a short spell on almost any terms short of physical pain.

The artist has taken Mrs Bracegirdle's name too literally but this is fortunately compensated for by Nell Gwyn, who from the staircase landing challenges the incoming lady visitor with an exposure so piquant that it never fails to fill my ninety-year-old ears with the baying of the dogs that plague John Betjeman's *Senex*. On a slightly higher landing is the bust of William Terriss, an actor who, in my early boyhood days, had the singular experience of being shot dead at his stage-door by a lunatic. His daughter, Ellaline, became Lady Hicks, Seymour's wife. Unlike her ill-fated father, she enjoyed a very long life. I opened some function at the British Theatre Museum with her when she was ninety-seven and she duly went on to reach her century.

Nearly all the more modern Garrick Club portraits are exhibited in the bar, though our lady guests in the room assigned for their mid-week lunches, enjoy the company of a majestic young Gladys Cooper in *My Lady's Dress*, offering welcome relief from the ponderous nothingness of 'Brighter Cricket'. But the bar is the location, appropriately in some instances, for the comparative youngsters, though changes occur from time to time and Marie Tempest and H. B. Irving and their close contemporaries will no doubt be making way for less mature company. Alan Aynesworth was long since removed from his conspicuous position and bundled to the nether end of his line, to the accompaniment of a distant grumble of thunder.

I figure among the more recent of the bar exhibits. Edward Halliday, a friend of mine from many years back and a fellow-member of the Garrick for some of them, offered to paint my portrait gratuitously for the club. The committee said yes; and if the primary motive of some of its members was to secure a Halliday for the asking, the subject has during the past year or two justified his presence on the wall. It is a cheerful portrait of Puck's great-grandfather – I have been told that Ted Halliday caught me telling a dirty story. Remarkable how these master portrait-painters manage to divulge a victim's character along with his features.

In the Queen's Birthday Honours in 1976, I was given the CBE. I took my daughter-in-law and Olive to the Palace to see me given it. Her Majesty told me that I had two plays running in London and I mumbled my 'yes, Ma'am', confirmation of this. So this was a sort of official recognition that all this Press hoo-ha and so on about myself had been justified. I had, and still have, one curious little reaction to it all. I had always felt confident that I was a dab at my own particular line of business but I had always cherished the feeling that this was my own secret. Now the secret was out and although I was proud and pleased and all that, I felt a funny little wistful regret at having to part with it. Paradoxical self-esteem? Paradoxical modesty? I don't know which myself and after all it is only my own concern is it not?

Robin Dalton, with characteristic aplomb and extracting what appeared to me to be extortionate advance payments, sold the rights of *The Bed* to every European country this side of the Iron Curtain and also to some unlikely-sounding customers such as Mexico and Turkey. Productions had also been scheduled for South Africa and America and Helen Montagu and I paid a flying visit to Johannesburg to attend the launching of the play there with Jean Kent in the lead. Our six-day stay followed a period of native unrest in the neighbourhood – some of our friends in England had implored us not to go; but the only sinister incident we experienced had nothing to do with native unrest. Helen made a broadcast in which brief mention was made of her successful efforts in bringing about the abolition of the censorship and next morning she was assaulted in the street by a Dutch-Afrikaans woman, screaming broken-English abuse and swinging at her with a handbag.

It seemed rather strange to plunge, in this unfamiliar environment, into the same old publicity routine; only, in this case, twice as strenuous. In the space of four days I took part in two TV programmes, six or seven radio turns and about a dozen Press interviews. All this to say nothing of having to attend a dress-rehearsal, two previews and a first night at the theatre. On my second day I was giving Press interviews for eight hours on end before scooting off to the theatre and then having to get up early to do an hour's talk on the radio next morning. All very complimentary but a bit strenuous on the verge of ninety. And, of course, I enjoyed every minute of it.

Towards the end of the last century four of my mother's brothers had emigrated to Natal as missionaries. Being conscientious Church of England clerics they bred like consecrated rabbits. I possess an unspecified number of the offspring of first cousins in various parts of South Africa and, the female of the species having married white Afrikaaners, I am used to getting letters claiming relationship with people whose names sound like the whistle of an hotel doorman calling a cab. It is the South Africans whose origins and sympathies are British who subsidise and patronise the theatres producing British plays and the welcome they gave to me and Helen and our comedy was enthusiastic.

Helen and I snatched a few hours off from the otherwise non-stop jobs on hand and were driven to Pretoria, where I was fascinated to find that Paul Krüger's house is still preserved in its original state with the railway carriage (in which he toured around, supervising the conduct of Boer warfare) on show at the bottom of the garden. Few visitors can, as I do, recall the ups-and-downs (mostly downs) of that war and have survived to inspect the actual, austere, abode of Oom Paul, the Bible-smiting Beelzebub of my boyhood days. By way of contrast we visited the local lion-park. It has become a common experience for tourists to exchange nods with the king of beasts and his wives and progeny through the windows of cars ('Motor slowly but do not stop your car; the lions may bite your tyres' – public notice board) but a special and delectable prank was staged for our benefit. In an enclosure reserved for lions of various ages earmarked for export some fifty specimens strolled, lolled and occasionally, for no obvious reason, roared. One quite young lion felt (how natural at his age) the urgent claims of copulation. He was accommodated by a lioness a good deal older than himself but in an apathetic, oh-go-ahead-then-if-you-must, manner. A fully-grown lion standing by took strong exception to the literally cocky presumption of one so young, and approaching in sedate schoolmasterly style knocked the culprit headlong off his perch. Then, after a moment's deliberation, the schoolmaster himself mounted complaisant madam. She immediately responded with far greater alacrity to the more experienced suitor and finished up rolling on her back in gratification; while the thwarted youth stood roaring in protest from a safe distance. There is surely the germ of a comedy here. Some lions are very like schoolmasters and vice versa.

The tour of *The Bed* in South Africa (courageously including Rhodesia at the height of its disaccord) was successful enough. Its career in America was not.

Carol Channing, darling of the musical-comedy world, came and saw *The Bed* at the Lyric during Joan Plowright's innings and was delighted by the play and the part. She gave us a special boost in a TV interview and soon afterwards agreed to a tour of three months in the States in the winter of 1976 before opening on Broadway.

Another noteworthy (no, make that notorious) visitor from the theatre world of the USA spent some time in London in the summer of 1976 and made a round of inspection of several of the productions on offer. As dramatic critic of *The New York Times*, at this time, he exercised a sort of spectral ascendancy regarding the fortunes of any new show on Broadway. I have never met Clive Barnes but I have been told by some of his acquaintances that he is a very agreeable man and this I can well believe as I admire and enjoy his animated style, establishing a personal and at time wise-cracking contact with the reader, rather after the manner of our master of this idiom, Clive James. On his return to America he wrote a résumé of his opinion of our shows and while he stopped short of actually lambasting *The Bed* and acknowledged that it was well performed at Wyndham's Theatre (sic) by Sheila Hancock and John Moffat (sic) he clearly indicated that he disliked the play and would be awaiting it, dagger in hand, if ever it tried to poke its nose into Broadway.

In this same *New York Times* article he gave me an irresistible chance of debunking him as a reporter. Quote: 'I always thought Mr Travers rather overrated as a writer of farces – they were written most of them, for a semi-resident company at the Aldwych Theatre, and during the years of World War II, I saw revivals of a number of them, usually with the original, if slightly ageing casts, led by Tom Walls, Ralph Lynn and Robertson Hare.' In point of fact the last time these three appeared on the stage together was in 1932, over seven years before the outbreak of the war. No further comment is needed on Clive Barnes' reliability as a theatre chronologer. And as a critic he redeemed himself in my eyes by his appreciation of Alan Ayckbourn. Quote: 'Mr Ayckbourn can write rings around Mr Travers, with one hand in a splint and one leg tied behind his back.' (Fair enough, if a trifle barbed) .... 'The best and most extended of them (*Confusions*) is a hilarious sketch called *Gosforth's Fete*.' I fully agree. I think the sketch is the funniest and most ingenious playlet I have ever seen and *Table Manners* in *The Norman Conquests* one of the funniest comedies. I am ready to believe that Clive Barnes is personally the very nice chap that our mutual friends salute and no hard feelings. But I just had to put on record that clanger about the Aldwych stars.

Lindsay Anderson went over (at Carol Channing's request) to direct the American *Bed*. I have some treasured letters and post-cards describing his intractable job ('You must be prepared for anything' – the 'anything' underlined). Apparently, after her years and years of smash-hit success and experience as a musical comedy star, Carol Channing found it difficult to adapt herself to the straight part of the vacillating Alma. Lindsay never ceased to pay tribute to her resolution and to the amount of hard work she put in, but I can only conclude that the basic obstacle to her efforts was that here was a crucial example of miscasting – enthusiastic self-miscasting perhaps.

And, never mind whether she was right for the part or not, Carol Channing's immense popularity in the States guaranteed that hosts of the experienced, welcoming, advance-booking devotees she had won for herself would go and see the show wherever it went. Which they did; and despite the almost invariably dire Press notices of the play, they seem to have enjoyed it.

Robin Dalton and I had intended to go over to Boston and have a look at the show and had booked passages in the *QE2*, sailing on 25 November. Then along came Thames Television with a proposition that I should take part in a *This is Your Life* programme, the life being Sheila Hancock's and the show scheduled for that same night of the twenty-fifth. Naturally I consented, being very fond of Sheila and especially of her delightfully candid way of expressing herself, always accompanied by a laugh. Incidentally the TV show was very good publicity, for it took place in the Lyric Theatre itself; there was a full house and everybody stayed on. So Robin and I decided to travel by air two days later. Once more I was held up; this time by a cable from America suggesting that I should postpone my visit for a week or two. The *QE2* encountered about the worst Atlantic gale of her career and limped into Boston two days late – passengers have recounted the sheer terror of that voyage. The plane in which we had managed to engage and cancel last minute berths

162

was struck by lightning and had to make a forced landing in Ireland. I thanked Providence for a pretty straight tip to stay put in England and to give the American *Bed* a miss.

Fortunately there were no protests or recriminations. The play continued and completed its three months' tour, with, I believe, variations in the text from time to time, and though the popularity of Carol Channing brought in excellent returns, it was decided by mutual consent to fight shy of the hazards of Broadway. So that is the story of the only play of mine which has ever seen the light in the United States. (Dim that light.) But I am happy to hear that Miss Channing is once again delighting her Broadway fans in her true environment and yet another revival of *Hallo Dolly*. Everybody will be glad to see her back where she belongs.

The year 1976, during which I reached my ninetieth birthday, was by far the most eventful and rewarding of my lifetime, for two of my farces were revived and I found myself the rather bewildered old author of three simultaneous London successes. Eventually *The Bed* experienced the unusual ordeal of having to be taken off for a week for Judy Cornwell and Michael Aldridge to complete rehearsals before taking over as principals. I don't recall any other instance of a theatre being forced to remain dark for a week for this reason but it can't be calculated to boost the attraction and, although business soon perked up and I was still unable to find a seat in the house on a Saturday night, the week's lapse and the somewhat gradual recovery from the same and the general slump and all enabled the Lyric Theatre owners to serve notice.

Ah, well – we had enjoyed a run of, I am told, 499 performances, but I felt very saddened that a play which had been greeted by critics and public as a smash hit should have met with an abrupt finish. Perhaps my feelings at the time were aggravated by the fact that I had another good reason for being sore. In the fifth month of my ninety-first year I was compelled to undergo the ordeal of an operation for hernia. I paid sixty-five pounds a day to be lodged in the private ward of a London hospital, where the medical side of the job was efficient enough; but it is perhaps typical of the conditions prevailing in our hospitals today that the well-intentioned nurses of sundry oriental races could not make themselves understood in English and that a patient of ninety years old should be compelled to shave himself, in the hirsute and vulnerable parts associated with hernia, on the night before his early-morning operation. Moreover the meals offered and rejected might have been the subject of complaint to a prison governor. I am not one of 'the country's gone to the dogs' old grousers, but I do hope I may avoid having to end up in one of our London hospitals as they function today.

The National Theatre people had decided to produce *Plunder* a long time before all this *Bed* business started; in fact the National had to renew its one-year option on *Plunder* some time before it saw the light. I had been to see Michael Blakemore (who had been given the job of directing it) on 25 September 1974, almost a year to the day before I left Rye to come and live in London. The National Theatre's offices were then in a makeshift and dilapidated row of one-storey buildings in Aquinas Street, at an address which few taxi-drivers seemed to know and couldn't drive up to if they did. However temporary, it seemed rather a forbidding asylum for the executive quarters of a national institution, though it may be said that when the whole outfit was eventually transported to its monumental maze on the South Bank the description asylum remained pretty appropriate.

After several postponements (alterations in schedule, casting diffi-culties, Peter Hall having too much on his plate and all the rest of it) *Plunder* was produced at the Old Vic in January 1976. Michael Blakemore is now established as one of the fashionable directors in the West End and from the author's point of view (mine, anyhow) you couldn't wish for a more co-operative and compliant member of the species. He showed this at our first consultation, when I sug-gested that he should get in touch with Nat Brenner, on the strength of the latter's masterly handling of the play at the Bristol Old Vic. Michael readily agreed and I was glad to see Nat Brenner's name among the credits in the programme. Frank Finlay played Freddy Malone, Tom Walls' part in the original, and Dandy Nichols rolled on to the stage in the footprints of Mary Brough. Dandy was a natural for the part and I have always (and still do) regarded Frank Finlay as just about the most infallible and versatile character actor of the day. Then Polly Adams, a favourite of mine and of a lot of other people's, was cast for the Winifred Shotter part. But before all these glad tidings came along I had survived, as best I could, a really shattering disappointment.

I had been to see *The Gay Lord Quex* – well, of course I had; one of the plays by my patron saint Pinero with Judi Dench, Dan Massey and Seán Phillips (Mrs Peter O'Toole at the time) in the leading parts. I had an additional and personal motive: Peter O'Toole was in Mexico, rounding off a film, and I wanted to see Siân and find out how he was getting on. She told me and I gave vent to one of Harold Hobson's 'cries of ecstasy'. Peter had returned home that very morning and had agreed to play D'Arcy Tuck in the National Theatre production of *Plunder*. I rejoiced not only for myself; I rejoiced that the London public and Press should be given the oppor-tunity of seeing that superb performance. Then, a few weeks later, wallop. A pathetic letter from Peter. He had had a row with Peter Hall – I don't know to this day what about, but along with the pathos

Peter expressed his gall in terms which I must refrain from quoting.

The part of D'Arcy Tuck was then offered to and accepted by Dinsdale Landen. He played it on forthright farcical lines and made a big hit with the critics and audiences. When I saw the show at the dress-rehearsal and previews I felt that, here and there, he and the production in general were too pointedly 'funny' for my liking but the judicious Michael Blakemore toned it down and, after a rather sticky first act, the first night at the Old Vic got a reception which admonished me for being such a crotchety exacting old Blimp in my strictures about how farce should be produced and played – though I still stick to them. And, apart from the occasional lapses into extraneous funniness, which he duly modified, Michael Blakemore's direction was as vivid and comprehensive as I could desire. The bedroom scene was beautifully timed to give full value to its unpredictable vagaries and the Scotland Yard team were much more convincing than their original deceased predecessors. The best of the company, for my money, was Polly Adams – a beautifully straight and convincing performance to motivate Dinsdale's frantic enterprise on her behalf. The greatest departure from the Aldwych version was Frank Finlay's conception of Freddy Malone. Tom Walls had created him as what in his day was known as a heavy swell, vainglorious of his high-society status and treating the very idea of his being suspected and interrogated by the police with a dignified and cynical scorn. Frank, from the start, both in manner and appearance, was a pretty obvious but cheerful, confident crook with a brash, catch-me-if-you-can flippancy in his dealings with Scotland Yard. I am bound to say that I never envisaged the character Finlay-style, which was very effective in its way and enlivened the play. But I've no doubt that Tom Walls turned in his urn.

I was in the stalls on the first night and, after the normal curtain calls, my presence was announced by the stage butler; they threw a spotlight on to me and somebody from the wings brought me a glass of champagne. In the agitation of the moment I spilled some of it and, true to my superstitiousness, I decorated the gentleman sitting in front of me behind the ears. I discovered afterwards that he was Frank Marcus, the *Sunday Telegraph* critic and author of my favourite satirical comedy of all time, *The Killing of Sister George*. In spite of my having bedewed him with a damp forefinger he gave me a good notice, which shows him to be a very fair-minded critic.

When the Lyttleton Theatre was ready to open they decided to let the public in while they finished off the other two theatres on the same site. Some months later one of the newspapers put a tricky question in one of those quiz items, with the answers printed upside down at the foot of the page, which seem to be a feature of their reading matter nowadays. The question was 'Which was the first play to be produced at the National Theatre?' The right answer, as given, was *Plunder*. The official opening was with a performance of the National's current production of *Hamlet*. But the very first show available to the public was on the previous night, when *Plunder* was staged for a charity performance, the object of the charity being the National Theatre itself with stalls at ten pounds a time. So I (*I*, Clive Barnes, do you hear that?) was the author of the first play to be staged in the history of the National Theatre.

In one respect the auditorium of the Lyttleton has been well designed; you can see and hear what goes on from any seat in the house – that is if you are not as old, short-sighted and deaf as I am. But to have provided a complete block of stalls, row upon row with thirty or more stalls in each row, without a centre gangway, appears to me to argue either insistent gluttony on the part of the management or that the designer must have been a teetotaller. On one of my visits I was allotted a stall numbered 15. I felt in urgent need to jostle my way to the bar in the interval (I was seeing a play by Ibsen). What a hope. By the time I had got within sight of the bar the 'take-your-seats-please' bells were busily buzzing. Nor (as a member of the public I haven't the slightest claim to any knowledge of architecture) can I escape a feeling of antagonising bewilderment when plunged into the vast area of the front-of-the-house ground floor. The first floor is paradise in comparison; the antagonism dissolves as you mount the stairs (which stairs? there are so many flights and all alike) but that ground floor is rambling, raucous and rabblesome. And surely the ceiling's too low – thank God I don't suffer from claustrophobia. Moreover, the directions of where to go are displayed in barely legible typography against a coy, arty background of puce. On my first visit, in search for the gentlemen's lavatory, I finished up in the box-office.

I saw two or three of the other National Theatre plays on offer at the time and went sound asleep during the second act of *John Gabriel Borkman*, leaving Sir Ralph Richardson and Dame Peggy Ashcroft engaged in conversation on a settee, only to rediscover them sitting on the same settee and still engaged in the same conversation when I awoke twenty minutes later, or however long it really was. Ibsen is another of these chosen few honoured by the erudite as one of the greatest dramatists of all time, whom an impervious numskull like myself finds hard to take.

Much easier to take I found John Osborne's *Watch it Come Down*, an unblenching exhibit of a small cross-section of our social pandemonium, with a husband and wife at loggerheads (autobiographical?), played to perfection by Frank Finlay and Jill Bennett. But I found the play began to wilt towards its closing stages in comparison with its first act and when I went along to John's house at a party after the first night, I managed to get a few minutes alone with him. This wasn't easy, because the party quickly developed into the not unfamiliar post-first-night symposium which follows an ostensible mis-hit and anticipates some thankless notices. But I remained sober enough to put a theory of mine to John (also sober and completely nonchalant). This is that John's characters, being almost invariably haters, hating themselves, other people, the social conditions, the country in general, the world in general, the whole environment and course of the play is bound to be pessimistic. In *Watch it Come Down* the only benevolent character is a girl whose cordiality extends to a readiness to go to bed with friends of either sex, but this sole optimist finishes by throwing herself under a train. My contention to John was that a play disseminating pessimism runs a grave risk of becoming dull. John listened to this with sceptical tolerance; and when, being rather bumptious about this theory, I put it to Lindsay Anderson a few days later, Lindsay floored me in ten seconds. He said, 'What about *Inadmissible Evidence*?' This is perhaps John Osborne's best play and is about as cheerful and optimistic throughout as the wake of a Presbyterian sinner in the rain. My conclusion is that my theory is right in principle but it takes a John Osborne to confute it.

There is one particularly silly but, I think, common form of prejudice which bamboozles our weak natures. We assume a dislike for the actual personality of an author we don't even know by sight but whose books or plays antagonise us. ('He must be a terrible feller' – elderly, besotted Pall Mall club-member.) I dare say that this automatic hostility exists in the case of John Osborne, not that he would care a hoot. The surprising thing about John is his simplicity; simplicity first of all in his freedom from outside influence: he does what he wants to, he writes what he wants to. But simplicity too in his appreciation and enjoyment of merit as it appeals to the average man in the street. He abruptly left a party at Robin Dalton's to go to the next room where her TV set was showing that remarkable song-and-dance act of Angela Rippon's and came back rollicking with delight. At another of Robin's parties, a dinner-party this time, at which the Oliviers and I were in attendance, John inaugurated the lapse into after-dinner ribaldry by reciting some of the nearest-the-knuckle fragments from the repertoire of Max Miller. He is never self-assertive or argumentative except in print. Any disagreement with what you say is a smile which is far more disarming than any heated retort. He will never do anything or write anything that will impair my fondness and admiration.

I was able to convey this in a speech which I had to make as a member guest of honour at a Dramatists' Club dinner, at which John was for once present – he was a rare attendant. I said, as I truly believe, that he, like Robertson and Galsworthy-cum-Granville Barker, had established a landmark in the history of the British theatre; he was the begetter of what was to be its greatest influence of the latter part of this century. I went on to say that our gratitude for this, if any, should also go to the Lord Chamberlain, who, soon after John's arrival on the scene, had surrendered and been consigned into exile. This enabled John and his satellites to let their characters express themselves in the familiar terms of English as she is spoken in our time. My sympathy with them was demonstrated by the fact that their favourite monosyllable and my own favourite monosyllable differed in only the smallest detail The monosyllables in both cases began with f. The second letter in both cases was u. We all knew how they ended but I contented myself with but one more letter – f–u–n. I admitted that many people regarded both monosyllables to signify the same thing and indeed that, looking back over the years, I myself seemed to recall that I had shared this opinion.

With *Plunder* a sell-out, with *The Bed* going strong, with myself thoroughly reinstated in the theatre world, it was a good opportunity for someone to get a bright idea about what to do with me. There were some bumbling suggestions for a revival of *Rookery Nook* in the West End, but the National had secured an option on this old faithful. Robin Dalton is not a woman who contents herself with bright ideas, however. She only goes in for inspirations. Like some Biblical characters in one respect (if in only one) she is the recipient of beneficial visions. She had one now. She and I were dining with Eddie Kulukundis at the Mirabelle. I suppose we were discussing my old farces and the possibilities of revivals and that sort of thing and into Robin's imagination floated the apparition of Robert Morley replacing the correspondingly portly figure of Alfred Drayton in *Banana Ridge*. Eddie was interested in the idea, though he had never read *Banana Ridge* (who had?). I found an old published copy of the play from somewhere, but I sent it to Helen Montagu instead of to Eddie, which grieved Eddie; but I thought he and Helen were in partnership in the project. Anyhow, Helen sent it to Robert Morley, who declined it, changed his mind, accepted it and informed Ray Cooney, the lessee of the Savoy Theatre, that he would be agreeable to open at that theatre (Robert's old stamping-ground) in three months' time. Ray Cooney was likewise readily agreeable to stake a claim in the managerial side of the production.

Ray Cooney had, some years previously, done a very good job for me in the revival of *Thark* at the Garrick Theatre. Since then he had gone ahead and made a considerable impact as a West End impresario and I was glad to be associated with him again. But, opti mist as he is and brimful of enterprise, his unanticipated participation in the production resulted, naturally enough, in a certain amount of well-intentioned imbroglio. Happy as I was with the cast and direction, my own major regret was that Ray could not come to terms with Alan Tagg, the ace designer, who had provided such a delightful set for *The Bed*.

The sets and costumes on show during the month's try-out at the Yvonne Arnaud Theatre, Guildford, and intended for transfer to the Savoy, had to undergo a thorough overhaul at Helen's insistence. She had left it a bit late but neglected all her other business in a struggle against time. Joe Davis, the foremost lighting expert in the business did ditto. He was greatly handicapped by the fact that the hands who had been employed to do the lighting effects had apparently been recruited from some institute for what have become known as the retarded. He had to cope with this sort of thing:

Joe Davis: 'Blackout – God almighty – have you never heard of a blackout?'

Lighting operator: 'No.'

Thanks to Helen and Joe, the critics and audiences accepted what was offered them to behold with complete satisfaction. The casting was debated and determined by the whole committee concerned. Fortunately they got George Cole to accept the part of Willoughby Pink, in which he was to give a performance far more percipient than that of his predecessor, the popular automaton, Robertson Hare. Moreover, George Cole's adaptability and uncomplaining readiness to work in with the unending alterations and experiments during the rehearsals, the try-out month (in the most historic heat-wave of modern times) and indeed the run of the farce itself while he was with it, were quite astonishing. Sometimes in his dressing-room in the Guildford theatre he would be handed some new material comprising a number of lines and fresh business and wouldn't turn a hair but would just go on-stage and deliver the goods. He was far more involved with all the cuts and changes spontaneously thought up and tried out than anyone else in the company; with Vivienne Martin (Olga Lindo's successor and, again, an improvement on the original) also kept pretty busy in this respect. But why? Who promulgated all this experimental permutation?

I should have realised at the start, as I did after a couple of days' rehearsal, that Robert Morley is an unexampled figure in the contemporary British theatre both in personality and procedure. I should also have borne in mind that when Robert Morley is billed to star in a play, particularly a farce, it is Robert Morley that his king-size public come to see and that the play itself is of secondary importance. But if, as in the case of *Banana Ridge*, it gives him excellent scope, it encourages him to take delight in exploiting this boon to the full. Far from his having to make the best of a bad job, he revels in the non-stop pursuit of making the best of a good one.

The director was Val May, who had migrated from Bristol to take charge of the Yvonne Arnaud Theatre. He proved to be, as I had been told, a top expert at what I term the geography of a production – getting the characters into exactly the right place at the right moment and timing the entrances and exits to perfection. But I think he too realised that a Robert Morley show was a thing apart and that it all largely depended on Morley being allowed to cash in on his great popularity in his own way. Good nature is Robert Morley's prevailing characteristic. That is the reason why the production of *Banana Ridge* at Guildford and its run at the Savoy, despite all its ramifications and problems in the early stages, never lost its sense of enjoyment.

Of course a lot of credit for this must go to Val May and George Cole and the others, including myself, but it was really due to the influence of Robert. I suppose that, just as elephants go berserk or musk, or whatever elephants do at irrational moments, Robert may have had occasional lapses from this prevailing bonhomie, but not to my knowledge. The bonhomie is infectious too; although most of our conversations in his dressing-room and elsewhere were far from being solemn, his benignity did have a marked and lasting influence, even at my age, on my everlasting impetuosity and occasional irascibility. And, as with most charmers, he delights in the utterly ridiculous.

Sample: – on the subject of play-titles:

Robert: – They find very strange names for plays nowadays. I've heard of one called simply *And*. That must be one of yours. All your plays are entitled *And*.

I: – On the contrary, Robert. All my plays are entitled *But*.

The revival of *Banana Ridge* was not so genuine a farcical play as the original (though for the most part much better acted) but, produced on broader lines for the sole purpose of accommodating Robert Morley, it answered splendidly and (to hell with my playwright principles) it brought me a lot of fun and some useful royalties. To linger in Robert's dressing-room, especially in his moments of disarming self-vindication of his latest experiment, was a passing joy in itself. To have gained his friendship is a permanent one.

So here I was – an old author with three plays in London, one on top of another and all doing well. I could relax and put my feet up and count my blessings, couldn't I? Count my blessings I did, I spent considerable time thanking God and praying that my luck might continue. But relax? Put my feet up? Never in my life from the autumn of 1975 onwards have I had to cope with such never ceasing, daily-increasing obligations, oh, pleasant enough but overwhelming. I remember on one occasion writing seventy-five letters of thanks to well-meaning friends and well-wishers in a day. ('Why didn't the old fool engage a secretary?') I *did* engage a secretary to lend a hand with my correspondence from time to time but a regular secretary couldn't have helped because most of the stuff I had to deal with was personal. The Press found something freakish, 'a story' in what I had got up to at my time of life. Helen Montagu has a keen eye for publicity and would frequently call me up, 'Darling, don't unless you like, but if you'd give an interview to Sam Blinker of the Daily Blank it would be very useful to us', and of course I would comply without a murmur, a willing prey to that beguiling voice. I've no reckoning of how many of these Press interviews I gave ('My dear chap, I don't know what to talk about; I've said it all so many times already') but the chaps were always good company. And, after all, they were being very complimentary as well as generally a bit thirsty. It was, however, a non-drinker who contributed what was to me the high-spot of these conversations, which was a 3,000-word impression of myself in the Talk of the Town column of *The New Yorker*, the best thing of its kind I have ever read. I later learned that it had been suggested and advocated by Penelope Gilliat.

I was also roped in for about five or six radio talks and four (I think it was four) television appearances during this period, one of them with Peter Hall. To me the most important and enjoyable were my two participations in the Parkinson shows. I was in the opening Saturday night of his programmes two years running. My first went very well, so well in fact that I was invited to take part in the second. In this John Snow was my opposite number and the talk was largely about cricket; but I related my golf-lesson from the champion of the period ('stand to pee') and finished up by demonstrating my secret of keeping fit. For the past fifty years I have lain flat on my back every morning and raised my legs stiff-kneed over my head to toe the floor behind it. I performed this in the studio and challenged the others to do the same. John Snow had no difficulty but Michael Parkinson temporarily dislocated himself in his vain attempt and was in great discomfort for the rest of the show. I was first taught the exercise by Robert Hale, Binnie's father, in 1921 and have revered him as one of my guardian angels ever since. My stunt caused quite a ripple of temporary public interest. I was accosted in the street by total strangers. 'I got my old man to try it, coo, you should have seen his struggles.' 'I 'ad a go this mornin'. Struth; I'd rather die.' To which I could only reply 'Well then, I'm afraid that's what will happen.'

Apart from the blissful memories of my married life I have never

171

enjoyed such happiness as in that year of 1976. There were some tiresome duties, inescapable letter-writing, shopping and eating – how eating bores me nowadays; I sometimes avoid it as far as possible – but every day brought its new pleasurable interest and my nights one long sequence of excitation or serenity. Parties after the shows at one or other of the theatres took place whenever a reason could be found for one; Robert Morley frequently discovered his own reason and both Helen Montagu and Eddie Kulukundis were always on the look-out for an ante-show crush in the ample Lyric Theatre bar. Robin Dalton preferred to entertain her own little special congregations, craftily selected as the right mixture for the right time. I have never come across anybody who knows so many big-wigs in the theatre and literary world. She kindly roped me in (I didn't need much roping) for many of her junkets at her eminently desirable residence in St John's Wood and here I met or remet many of the pick of Robin's copious bunch. Here in a joyous moment I met Penelope Gilliat again after a dozen years or more. She was passing through from Paris on her way to perform her regular half-yearly job as film critic of *The New Yorker*. It is hard to reconcile the fact that one of the most naturally generous-hearted women to be found can occasionally show such acute admonishment as a critic. I have always treasured her description of one of the most ostentatiously unfunny of our comedians – 'begging for laughs like a dog watching you cook'. She was kinder to me; she had seen *The Bed* and told me I was Congreve. Curiously enough, James Bridie had said the same thing in the distant past. It is flattery no doubt but I wonder what gave rise to the comparison. I must read some of the plays of Congreve and find out.

At Robin's too I met, among many others, a lady novelist who won my heart within a couple of minutes. I like meeting extraordinary women and always get on well with them. This one was Edna O'Brien. Her honeying Irish voice and personality fascinated me and we immediately became friends. I hadn't read her novels but forthwith forsook Nabokov for the time being, wisely starting with *The Country Girls*. Re-read it, according to my wont when I find myself absolutely entranced by the writing. I have read some of the Nabokov's four times, five times; in the case of *Pale Fire* a number of times not yet determined. Edna O'Brien has to be re-read. Her *Mother Ireland*, non-fictional, is a revelation of the complex mosaic of her genius, the ability to express both intense terror and intense tenderness. Chesterton wrote that *Wuthering Heights* might have been written by an eagle. Edna's books might have been written by a nursing mother lioness. Whatever may be the general source of inspiration, Edna seems to enjoy a special inspiration which is hers alone: a loving influence, like that of the good fairy, watching over a birth in a fairytale.

Oh, and here's another of Robin's friends and now mine, bearing the blushing honours of her two Oscars as a film star still upon her, Luise Rainer. When many years ago I saw her in *The Good Earth* (all right, Luise, I won't say how many years) it was quite on the cards that I might have had the pleasure of her acquaintance, since I was still mixed up in the motion-picture business at that time; but I hardly expected that I would find myself sitting (pretty close) and exchanging recollections of old mutual friends and of this and that with Luise Rainer in the year 1976. She was gratified to the extent of writing me an adulatory letter to tell me what delight she had experienced from our meeting. I replied by sending her a preposterous Ballade, my favourite form of poem.

BALLADE ON RECEIPT OF A TREASURED LETTER

Accept this yell of youthful rapture, please:
Though ninety years have passed beyond recall,
Ah, but Love's warmth defies the blood to freeze:
And drowns Old Age's dreary warning drawl.
Unlike so many poor old blokes who crawl
From chair to bed and limp and pant and wheeze,
I dance and sing: my heart plays skittle-ball:
I have a letter from divine Luise.

Returns and cheques for playwright's luscious fees,
Found in my morning's mail-box in the hall,
And love-notes from my host of fond sweet-peas,
Compared with hers are vinegar and gall.
Farewell that furtive romp, that taxi maul,
Henceforth I serve endearing Charm's decrees:
Gone with the wind each past promiscuous fall:
I have a letter from divine Luise.

Pooh, champion jockey of triumphant gees:
Pooh, gangster felling coppers in a brawl:
Pooh, scholar with vast numbers of degrees:
Pooh, gaol-break expert leaping from his wall:
Pooh, truculent Goliath, ten feet tall:
Pooh, pop-star mobbed by frenzied devotees:
Pooh, Gentiles getting letters from St Paul:
I have a letter from divine Luise.

Envoi

Prince, you may boast the majesty of Saul,
Bejewelled houris swooning at your knees:
Gold, oil-fields, Concordes, cars – go, stuff them all:
I have a letter from divine Luise.

All the ballyhoo about my return to the theatrical land of the living marked me down as an interesting exhibit as guest of honour at the annual dinners of institutions connected with the stage – the Green Room Club, the First-Nighters – and how I enjoyed them. I love making speeches in the same way that I love appearing on television. At the First-Nighters I had the good luck to sit next to Avril Angers and Michael Crawford. Avril gave a turn in the entertainment which followed and finished with her special performance of 'If Love were all' from Noël Coward's *Bitter Sweet*. This was the most beautiful, sensitive rendering of any song I have ever heard and if I were given my choice of hearing a repeat of any song by any singer I would pick on this one without hesitation. I have a special admiration for Avril. She is very accomplished, very versatile, is modest and practical about it and is a delightful hobnobber.

With Michael Crawford I got talking, I don't know why, about my early days of flying. He evidently shared with me an appreciation of the humour which is based on tragedy. When I told him about the appalling fate of a First World War friend of mine who fell from two thousand feet from the top of a loop, leaving his passenger, an air-mechanic, who had never been in an aeroplane before, to face, with fatal results of course, the most nightmarish predicament conceivable, Michael Crawford simply collapsed with laughter. This ability to view in retrospect the funny side of a tragic event is surely part of a natural comedian's equipment.

At the Green Room Club dinner I was teamed up with Dorothy Tutin as the pair of guests of honour. It isn't easy to pay a tribute which hasn't been paid dozens of times before to a top-ranking actress but the treasured memory of a compliment paid by Peter Ustinov in a blurb for a Vladimir Nabokov novel proved effective: 'I am not worthy to kiss the hem of his mosquito net.' I quoted this and added that I would dearly love the opportunity of kissing the hem of Dorothy Tutin's mosquito net but I supposed that wasn't on.

Of all these functions – dinners, get-togethers in and out of the theatres, return-the-compliment evenings at the Garrick Club, oh, and those very enjoyable but wearing cocktail-parties (how hard on my troublesome old feet and spillsome to the waistcoat) one occasion shines forth like the moon amid the stars.

12 November 1976 was my ninetieth birthday. My three 'presenters', Helen Montagu, Eddie Kulukundis and Ray Cooney, decided that this called for a party. The party that resulted outshone any party of the theatrical world of that year or, so far as it concerned me, of any other year of any other world. It was well organised; I was given a free hand to invite my family and personal friends and Helen and Ray saw to it that all the stage people and others

who ought to be there were given the chance. But they will agree that what turned out to be a really glorious late-night, after-the-show occasion was due initially to Eddie. It was he who managed to pull the strings (purse-strings I guess) in order to secure the Drury Lane Theatre bar for the party – the only theatre bar in London that could have found space for the number of people who turned up as well as the long line of eats-and-drinks help-yourself tables and waitresses. Eddie's generosity went even to the extent of bringing his own special cook from Greece to prepare and supervise the service of a Greek dinner, as it was described on the invitation card, and which went to prove that the Greeks are as proficient at exotic cooking as they are when they get their noses into the shipping business. All the members of the Lyric and Savoy companies were there and some from the National and many of my past and present stars and starlets, the critics, the backroom boys and girls of the theatre. I am not emotional but I was, and still am, gladdened by the certainty that they came there for my sake and not just to participate in a beano. To recall a nice instance of this, Peter O'Toole and John Standing, who were in a play in Brighton, caught the train from there after their show on purpose to get to the party.

I had to make a speech of course, standing (or perilously wobbling) on a chair. Again I found help from outside – when apologising for too often trying to appear to myself and others that I was young for my years. I remarked that I did occasionally receive friendly reminders of my age. Irving Wardle, in a notice of one of my plays, had asserted that I am old enough to have sired Malcolm Muggeridge. I didn't think that Irving had meant to imply that I was actually responsible for this notable achievement, though what he had stated was in fact quite true. I also quoted my great-grandson, Nicholas Morgan, aged eight, who on listening to some of his schoolmates boasting of the attainments of their fathers and grandfathers, capped the lot with the lofty affirmation, 'My great-grandfather is a bit of a miracle.'

One of the birthday presents I was given, and there were plenty, has become my most valued possession, materially speaking. The Lyric Theatre cast gave me an ebony cane with a silver top on which was inscribed 'To Ben. 90. With love from his Bed Mates.' This gives it great additional sentimental value to me and I am careful to use it only on special occasions; though I always took it with me when I visited the Lyric from that time onward. (I also always wore Helen Mirren's pullover inside my shirt, a brown tie which John Moffatt had given me and a pair of socks which I had worn on the first night – I have already dealt with my kink about superstition.) My one reservation in my devotion to the silver-topped cane is my dread of losing it. I am a chronic mind-wandering leaver-abouter. In the solitude of my room I am constantly searching for my glasses (no, not that pair, my reading-ones), my magnifying glass, my watch, my slippers, my shoe-horn, my tobacco-pouch. That tie I wanted to wear, where the hell did I put it down? – oh, it's all right; I've got it on. Why do I find my spectacles in the fridge? I recently bought a new hat for about fifteen pounds and left the damn thing in the taxi on the way home. It isn't simply because I am so old and going gaga; I've been like it all my life. My dread of losing the silver-topped cane fills me with apprehension every time I take it along. I some-times wake in the middle of the night with a heart-stop of misgiving and have to turn on the light to check up that I've really brought it home safely.

Just at the time when *The Bed* ended its run in London, I was astonished almost beyond belief to receive an honour which is about the greatest that can be bestowed on anyone of any profession. The headmaster of Charterhouse, Brian Rees, wrote and told me that it had been decided to build a theatre at the school and asked for my consent for it to be known as the Ben Travers Theatre. I had always since the Aldwych days hoped that my name would occupy a modest place in the stage records, but that it should be exalted in this way for posterity by a long-established, permanent institution, now the best public school in the country, seemed almost inconceivable. Did I consent? But I was intimidated too, in a way – it was a distinction that I would have to be careful to try to live up to for the rest of my short time on earth. Dick Scott, a friend of mine from the later Halford Hewitt golf days, was to be the architect. As such he had inherited a famous name and worthily so. He had designed the Char-terhouse boarding houses which had been rebuilt (and about time too) and greatly acclaimed. At this moment of writing I hope he will design an equally acclaimed Ben Travers Theatre and that I may survive to participate in the acclamation on its opening night.

I am cautioned by my publisher that the time has come for me to discontinue and to let him get on with his invidious function in pro-ducing this thingum (as Vladimir Nabokov would describe it). This notice to quit comes at a very inconvenient time. The fire of my life is still burning busily – I have just been informed that the National Theatre is going to reinstate *Plunder* in its forthcoming programme for 1978 and perhaps beyond. A contract has been signed for staging my latest comedy; which has for its subject a reflection on the essence of human kindness and consequently for its title, *After You with the Milk*. My *Thark* has enjoyed a successful season, edging in on the Shaw Festival in Niagara Falls. A long-lost friend, *A Cup of Kindness*, is to be rediscovered in the forthcoming Pitlochrie season. Oh, and the continental productions of *The Bed Before Yesterday* (some have already been successfully staged). My only recently encountered but already beloved friend, Eduardo di Filippo, is adapting *The Bed* in its Italian version. Australia, after a lot of negotiations about getting the most talented leading lady available, has now made definite plans for *The Bed* to be produced.

All the while that second small piece of fuel which I cast on the dying fire in 1975 is still alight. On two or three of my winter visits to Malacca I enjoyed the hospitality of the district's most eminent resident, a massive sportsman whose figure insisted on his being known as 'Jumbo' Downs. He was manager of a large local rubber estate and his dwelling was in great contrast to the shacks on poles which I used to visit at the beginning of the century, a spacious solid stone building designed to cater for all the features, good and bad, of the tropics – a perfect setting for the comedy which I wrote four or five times and called *Malacca Linda*. The clap-trap bungalow of the *Banana Ridge* manager was an incomparably inferior residence to that of Jumbo Downs, but the *Banana Ridge* revival put paid to the production of another play by the same author set in the same out-of-the-way location for the time being. Helen Montagu still possesses the latest script of *Malacca Linda*, and, who knows, *Linda* may one day appear on the scene – perhaps as a post-mortem curio.

Before closing time I would like to report that I recently participated in my third Michael Parkinson show, a singular one because the three interviewees were all in their nineties – Elizabeth Craig, ninety-four – Lord Shinwell, ninety-three, and I, the youngster of the party, ninety-one. We had a bit of a disagreement; I seemed to rejoice in the benefits of very old age a good deal more than the other two did.

And why shouldn't I rejoice? Apart from my various jobs I am loved and cared for by my sons, my daughter, my fourteen grandchildren and three great-grandchildren and innumerable friends. I would like to mention them all but they know who they are without being told. Mark Hodson, the ex-Bishop of Hereford, for instance, and his wife, Susanna, all those Fishmongers' Company chaps, Jane Armitage, my hostess for my annual pilgrimage to Canterbury cricket week, and what about Jean Flynn? I cannot close what is alleged to be a record of my life without telling anybody who doesn't know already what her companionship has meant to me.

On the first Sunday of my return to London in 1975 I went to lunch with Beatrice Christie-Miller, the generous widow of an old and equally generous friend. My fellow-guest was, I discovered (I never cotton on to names on introduction) a Mrs Flynn – about the same age as my daughter, widowed, oh, two or three times – she is American by adoption. You know the way one spots a future star in the theatre when you first see him or her in a small, maybe a walk-on part, as I have in the past (Meggie Albanesi, Richard Burton). I think one spots a future star-friend in much the same way. When I am feeling whacked from overwork (and I am still working harder than ever) I make a bee-line for Jean's flat, where she provides an instant cure with a blend of humour and tranquillity – she also provides the best blend of gin and Cinzano bianco mixable. My now permanent or, should I say penultimate, home is a flat in the house belonging to my grandson, Andrew Morgan, where he and his unflappably and merrily efficient wife, Jacki, see to my well-being without, I hope, letting me be a responsibility. But my poor old excitable brain has to live there along with my not too troublesome body; so it is a pretty busy little flat and my soothing visits to Jean Flynn contribute a great deal to my being kept light-hearted when I sometimes feel the foreboding of becoming light-headed.

Should one trying to write about himself and his life homilise about his individual tastes – the plays and reading that have especially appealed to him? What about his religion and his odd likes and dislikes? These are really nobody's concern but his own. Perhaps the best course is for him to tell them to himself and if any others than himself have the slightest desire to listen in, by all means let them.

So here follows a take-it-or-leave-it soliloquy.

SOLILOQUY

I am talking to myself – people who begin to converse about the plays and books they like and dislike, however loudly and insistently they vociferate (and vociferate they do) are, in effect, talking only to themselves.

I can't tell myself much about the theatre of the present day, except that the general standard of acting is immeasurably better today than ever before. But I am afflicted by a troublesome form of deafness. I can hear actors' and actresses' voices clearly enough, but I seldom hear what they say. (In some instances I don't think this applies only to the deaf.) I am near-sighted too – well, what can I expect at my age? I always have to ask my gentle companion in the interval what I haven't been hearing and have only been dimly seeing. I have formed the idea that, while the players of today are on the whole much better than they used to be, the plays are not – but how can I judge?

In spite of all this, I still love the theatre and four quite recent London productions have given me the four most delightful nights in the whole of my lifetime. Even a commonplace middle-brow mentality, as I rate mine to be, is bound to regard Shakespeare as dwelling in a realm of his own, almost as distinct from the rest of the day-in, day-out entertainment world as the soul is from the body. For many years I prized Granville Barker's *Twelfth Night*, with Henry Ainley as Malvolio, as the supreme, never-to-be-surpassed joy of my life. Now, in the final furlong of my playgoing, it is overtaken and finishes only fifth.

My winner (no doubt many other people's winner) is Peter Brooks' production of *A Midsummer Night's Dream*. My runner-up is Trevor Nunn's musical adaptation of *A Comedy of Errors*. There is a dead-heat for third place between Franco Zeffirelli's *Much Ado About Nothing* and Jonathan Miller's *Merchant of Venice*. All four productions prove that the Bard is indeed immortal. Insight and true wit can give a Dogberry or a Shylock a new and greater vitality and value aloft Frank Finlay's bicycle or beneath Laurence Olivier's top hat.

On and off for over eighty-odd years I have been one of the average well-inclined pleasure-bent members of the audience of all manner of entertainment – I once sat behind a theatre-party when a wife leaned forward and exclaimed commandingly down her row of stalls, 'Bertram, enjoy yourself' – I am no Bertram – I have always taken myself with my approval and, in most cases, enthusiasm, to whatever sort of show I wanted to see, as the spirit moved me – melodramas (now extinct) dramas not so melo, comedies straight and non-straight thrillers, detective-plays, farces, Gilbert and Sullivan operas, light-opera and musical comedies, revues (full scale and 'intimate'), Pelissier's Follies, The Crazy Gang – (I am still keeping Shakespeare sacrosanct). And music-halls, of course, when there were a dozen within a hansom-cab or a shilling taxi-drive of each other – I wish there were one or two now.

Which of all of these flash across my mind as having given me special enjoyment? I should now proceed to the Garrick Club library and give my erratic old memory an overhaul, but I find it more fun to linger in my room and smoke my pipe (I have been an interminable pipe-smoker since I was eighteen), and serve the soliloquy with the deep-rooted this and the suddenly-remembered but indispensable that – very short listed: only the absolute tops – and, oh how venerable, or at any rate well on in years, anybody who overhears me will have to be to join in my appreciations.

PLAYS

(apart from Shakespeare)
The Admirable Crichton (original production)
His House in Order ditto
Trelawny of the Wells (Dion Boucicault's revival)
Justice
Loyalties
The Little Damozel
Potash and Perlmutter
Journey's End
Tobias and the Angel
Spring Meeting

MUSICALS

Princess Ida and *Trial by Jury*
Guys and Dolls
No, no, Nanette
To-Night's the Night

REVUES

The Bing Boys
Up and Doing

PASTICHE

The Follies
The Crazy Gang

Some Favourite British performers (male and deceased)

Henry Ainley, H. B. Irving, Charles Hawtrey, Gerald du Maurier, Dennis Eadie, A. E. Matthews, Arthur Wontner, Frederick Ross, C. V. France, Arthur Playfair, Eric Lewis, Ralph Lynn, Weedon Grossmith
Martyn Green (Gilbert and Sullivan)
Leslie Henson, George Graves, Cyril Ritchard (musicals)
Lewis Sydney (The Follies)
Harry Tate, George Robey, Max Miller, Billy Bennett (music-hall)

Female deceased

Yvonne Arnaud, Edyth Goodall, Irene Vanbrugh, Ellis Jeffreys, Edith Evans, Henrietta Watson, Mabel Russell, Evelyn Weedon.
Jessie Rose (Gilbert and Sullivan)
Denise Orme and Gracie Leigh (musicals)

I have not forgotten all the other great planets which shine and many of the stars which twinkle from all those miles away – Tree, Wyndham, Alexander, Maude, Waller, Fred Terry, Bourchier, Robert Loraine, Tom Walls, Laurence Irving, Jack Buchanan, Ellen Terry, Mrs Patrick Campbell, Gertrude Lawrence, Gertie Millar, Lily Elsie – several more planets, dozens more twinklers – but the first-listed are those which seem to come foremost into my line of vision.

I have generally seen any sort of stage show which specially pleased me for a second or third or even fourth time – I saw four generations of the Gilbert and Sullivan operas and every new production of The Follies. I went to *Guys and Dolls* eight times.

When it comes to reading I realise that I have carried this encore sort of self-indulgence to such an extent that I have neglected many of the masterpieces of literature, ancient and modern. I pretend to other people that I have read them, whereas I have had only a peep at some of them – I wonder whether there are other people who have this addiction. Robert Browning is to me (as Shakespeare is) a spirit existing on a special little plane in Paradise, set apart from the comfortable quarters occupied by many of the others as an acknowledgement of their contributions to the world's literature and the pleasure they have given. I tell myself I have been rather immodest in flaunting this worship of Browning – The Browning Society has fallen for me and has elected me a Vice-President and a year or two ago I was appointed to perform the ceremony of laying the wreath and spouting a noble passage from the Pope's monologue in *The Ring and the Book* at the annual Browning memorial service at Poets' Corner. But the obsession is quite genuine – I have read *The Ring and the Book* at least fifteen times from cover to cover and many of

Browning's other poems over and over again – with a particular affection for *The Flight of the Duchess* and *Fra Lippo Lippi*. My first eager motive on a week's visit to Rome was to search out the actual sites of *The Ring and the Book* locations and I spent a day in Arezzo on the same quest.

Good fortune has granted me a special privilege in my zest. The only European city which I have visited often and for weeks on end has been Florence. In Bellosguardo is the villa and estate of Patricia Volterra, hostess of so many of the illustrious that I enjoy a rather snobbish feeling of gratitude in the knowledge that she is one of the dearer friends of my old age. Just across the road from her villa is that which Browning was wont to visit in the summer months, when the Casa Guidi may have become a bit stuffy. So I have been able to explore this occasional residence of his. I pinched two or three bay-leaves from the garden as souvenirs, but they no longer exist. Back in England an idolatrous cook found them and used them to flavour the soup.

Apart from this Browning fanaticism, I suppose I am what is known as the general reader – or rather non-general, because I have read comparatively so few books so many times. The one writer of the last half-century who has driven me to paroxysms of delight and incessant re-reading is Vladimir Nabokov. Even those devotees who share my enthusiasm have, apparently, failed to appreciate the blend of imagination, satire and actual composition of *Pale Fire*, my favourite work of fiction, which I have read, re-read and will never tire of reading. I am glad I am able to discuss and appreciate Nabokov's intense but rather concealed sense of humour which is really the secret of his inspiration – never more so than in *Lolita*, erotic, yes, but far more exotic than erotic and one of the most beautiful love-stories conceivable.

On and off I have taken my place in the general-reader queue – one of the eager hundreds of well-rewarded thousands of fiction readers of the years gone by – I could at one time have passed a pretty stiff examination in Sherlock Holmes. I have always had and still have a special yearning for Raymond Chandler. Among the old masterpieces *Vanity Fair* and *Bleak House* are still for me the outstandingly best novels written by their respective prolific authors. The same goes for *The Old Wives' Tale*.

I like authors who without giving any impression of challenge or defiance, launch out in a style of their own, disregarding what is generally accepted as admissible. Perhaps this is why I turn time and time again to Carlyle's *French Revolution* – prolific with long passages of repetitive exuberance, though with many of incident related with a dramatic fervour which sweeps you into the actual scene. It is the style, egotistically, insistently individual which I find irresistible. I was greatly attracted by Maurice Hewlett (I must read *The Queen's Quair* again once more) as was Graham Greene, my best living novelist (especially *The Quiet American* and *The Comedians*). There was a novelist, Ernest Bramah, who discovered a new form of originality. I recommended him to Allen Lane, with the result that Bramah made a big hit as a Penguin seller.

Although my eternal re-reading weakness completely disqualifies me from discussing literature as a subject even for soliloquy, it amuses me to call to mind the authors and their works which have most greatly encouraged this wilful habit of mine.

Browning, Nabokov, Chandler, Carlyle (*French Revolution* only), Thackeray (*Vanity Fair* only), Dickens (*Bleak House* only), Damon Runyan (the funniest ever of the funnies), Stephen Leacock, G. K. Chesterton, O. Henry, Marquand, Bennett (*Old Wives' Tale* only), H. H. Munro, Conan Doyle (*Sherlock Holmes* only), Somerset Maugham (short stories only, and submitting to the inescapable feeling of being patronised as a reader, but, dash it, he could tell a story in an unputdownable way), a forgotten but delicious book of short stories by Eden Phillpotts called *The Human Boy*, an ignored but glorious mock-historical novel called *Fortune* by J. C. Snaith. There are also two poems which I especially hold dear, the universally familiar *Lucifer by Starlight* by Meredith and *Winter Nightfall* by J. C. Squire. I re-read and re-re-read many living authors too, of course – the poems of John Betjeman, the novels of Graham Greene, the short stories of Roald Dahl come among the first to hand.

My Religion

Anything I have had to say in public on this subject has been overheard by several millions of people, because I said it in a Michael Parkinson television show. Michael asked me (an impromptu question, off the cuff, if he wears cuffs), 'Are you afraid of death?' I said, 'Like everybody, I'm afraid of the actual process of death but I'm not afraid of what comes next. There's only one thing we know about what comes next and the one thing we know is that we don't know. But I have faith, and faith is stronger than knowledge.'

A newspaper interviewer asked me what I would like to have engraved on my tombstone. I told him I didn't desire or expect to have a tombstone but that I would like my last words to be, 'This is where the real fun begins.'

From this it will appear that my religious thoughts concern my soul rather than my temporary earthly existence – but apart from an overheard declaration that I am a confirmed believer in the Christian faith, this is where the soliloquist becomes inaudible. Inaudible but busier than ever. If his contemplations and beatitudes and yes, prayers were words, what a self-assured, ridiculous old chatterbox he would appear. Self-assured, yes, though he tries to be humble about it – ridiculous, no.

Some likes and dislikes hitherto unmentioned

Some likes	Some dislikes
Women	Airports
Young children	Anything to do with Post Offices (Position Closed)
Irish stew	
Cats	Parsnips
Paintings by Rubens	Patronising or facetious radio announcers
Isolation in railway carriages (no longer possible in these new-fangled free-for-alls)	Changing a typewriter ribbon
	Present-day poetry
Dressed crab	Any form of breakfast cereals
Hot-water bottles (in my bed all the year round)	The noise made by church organs or any organs except barrel-organs
Gin-rummy (the American 'Knock' version)	Cellophane
Cox's Orange Pippins	All 'innards' as edibles
Barrel-organs (when there were any)	The more poppish type of pop-music and pop-singers
Monkeys	Dim lighting and background music in restaurants
	Dim lighting
	Background music
	Most restaurants

So, if the itinerant wayfarer comes across the aged, aged man, a-sitting and rocking to and fro on his gate at the age of ninety-one, and pauses to inquire who he is and how is it he lives, the answer is contained in the miscellany which has trickled through the indulgent listener's head like water through a sieve.

In the course of the trickle the old babbler has disclosed that he has been by profession a writer of farces and a couple of comedies: by constraint a participant in those two wars; a cricket-lover; a dedicated auxiliary of the Fishmongers' Company and an excursionist. He is blissfully contented because he is not yet out of a job and is made contented by the appreciation of the public (the old boy thinks that the public has always shown very good taste in the matter). He is also blissfully happy because he is made happy by the love and help showered upon him, not only by his family and friends but now, in his senility, by strangers (crooks very likely) who hand him into buses and by pretty, probably immoral, girls who offer him their seats in tube-trains.

A final wave of his walking-stick and the wayfarer passes on. The

184

aged, still rocking to and fro, rambles on for a brief while in soliloquy, but the trickle soon drips its last. The rocking to and fro slows down into a dead pendulum in reverse. The curtain of night falls on an immobile figure, becalmed on his gate and smiling in his sleep.

INDEX

Rees, Brian 176
Referee, The 67
religion 6, 7, 178, 183
Reynolds, Tom 80
Richardson, Sir Ralph 166
Richardson, Vic 118
Ring, The 15
Ring and the Book, The 181, 182
Rippon, Angela 167
Roberts, John 10
Robertson, Forbes 31
Robertson, T. W. 20
Robertson-Glasgow, Raymond 126
Robinson, Heath 124
Rogers, J. Innes 25
Rookery Nook 15, 77, 84, 85, 94–8, 100, 102–4, 109–11, 124, 139, 168
Ross, Adrian 35
Rowlands, Patsy 152
Royal Court Theatre (London) 32, 140
Royal Flying Corps 52
Royal Naval Air Service 47–55
Rubinstein, Artur 141
Russell, Rosalind 130
Rye, Sussex 136, 137, 144–6, 149, 150

Sacks, J. L. 79–83
St James Theatre 31, 121
St Margaret's Bay 11, 21
'Saki' (H. H. Munro) 15, 46, 74
Salome 40
Sanders, George 121
Sandow 10
San Toy 36
Savoy Hotel 44, 60
Scheidemantel, Karl 16
School 20
Scotland Yard 104
Scott, Dick 176
Scott, Margaretta 113, 122
Scott, Mrs (Ben Travers' daily help) 111
Seagull, The 148, 150, 151
Seaman, Owen 67
Second in Command, The 74
Second Mrs Tanqueray, The 63
Selous, F. C. 35

sex 7, 8, 9, 14, 29, 147
Shaftesbury Theatre 88
Shakespeare, 2, 179, 181
Shanghai 24
Shaw, George Bernard 70
She Follows me about 131
Sherlock Holmes 18, 20
Shinwell, Lord 177
Shore, W. Teignmouth 34, 47
Shotter, Winifred 96, 97, 108, 110, 112
'*Shropshire Lad, A*' 10
Siege of Sidney Street 35
Silver Box, The 32
Simpson, Peg 135, 136, 143, 144, 148
Sims, George R. 35
Singapore 8, 23, 26–8, 30, 57, 134
Sin of David, The 42
Sitwell, Commander 53
Smith, F. E. 35
Smith, Thorne 77
Smith-Bingham, Mr 52
Snaith, J. C. 183
Snow, John 171
Somerset and Dorset Railway 68
Sopwith, T. O. M. 57
Sopwith gun-bus 49–51
Sousa's Band 35
South Africa 134, 159–61
South Pacific 76
Southsea, Hants 104, 105
Sowers, The 35
Speaight, Robert 155
Spectator, The 42
speed 9, 36
Spotted Dick 123, 124
Spurgeon, C. H. 35
Squire, J. C. 132
Stacey (Ben Travers' gardener at Burnham) 101
Standing, John 140, 175
Stapleforth 25, 26
Star, The 67
Stoll, David 137
Straker, Squire car 47
Strand Theatre 123, 124
Strife 32
Stuart, Leslie 15

195